The Academic Job Search Handbook

Fourth Edition

The Academic Job Search Handbook

Fourth Edition

Julia Miller Vick and Jennifer S. Furlong

PENN

University of Pennsylvania Press

Philadelphia

Published by
University of Pennsylvania Press
Philadelphia, Pennsylvania 19104-4112

Printed in the United States of America on acid-free paper

10 9 8 7 6 5 4 3 2

A Cataloging-in-Publication Record is available from the Library of Congress

ISBN 978-0-8122-2016-2

Contents

V. After You Take the Job

VI. Additional Considerations

Appendices

Acknowledgments

This fourth edition of the *Academic Job Search Handbook* rests on the contributions of all those who have been mentioned in the Acknowledgments of the first three editions. This edition builds on the previous work of the late Mary Morris Heiberger and adds the voice of new coauthor Jennifer S. Furlong.

Thanks go to all past contributors—doctoral students, alumni, postdoctoral fellows, faculty, and administrators—who provided insight and ideas, a reading of the manuscript, or actual job hunting materials. For years faculty members from the University of Pennsylvania and many local colleges and universities have generously shared their insight and experience at programs we have organized for graduate students and postdocs. It is impossible to thank all the speakers here individually, but we are well aware that but for them this book could not exist. Graduate students, postdocs, graduate alumni, and junior faculty members have discussed their own job searches with us; they have broadened our awareness of the range of what may happen and increased our ability to predict what is likely to happen.

Our colleagues at Career Services at the University of Pennsylvania have been consistently encouraging and tolerant of the disruption writing a book imposes on a busy student services office. We feel fortunate that its director, Patricia Rose, has been uniformly enthusiastic about and supportive of this project since its inception in the early 1990s.

Our colleagues at peer institutions, who use this book in their daily work advising Ph.D. students, graduates, and postdocs on career issues, provided ideas and direction for this edition.

Our editor at the University of Pennsylvania Press, Jo Joslyn, has provided valuable guidance. We are grateful to Theresa Mawn for updating the appendix of scholarly associations and Lori Strauss for updating the bibliography.

We are particularly grateful to the graduate students, alumni, and postdocs from the University of Pennsylvania and other institutions who shared their sample job-hunting materials with us. Because we promised them anonymity, we cannot thank them here by name. However, their generosity has provided what many will find to be the most useful part of this book.

Mary Morris Heiberger's dedication to and love for excellent career advising for Ph.D.s lives on in these pages. Mary was an outstanding inspiration for all of us who have the privilege of working with the talented men and women who pursue careers in research and teaching. In working with the third edition, it was a pleasure to regularly come upon a particular turn of phrase that was most decidedly Mary's. For twenty-seven years, she worked at University of Pennsylvania in Career Services, coordinating and providing career services to master's, doctoral, and postdoctoral students for nine of Penn's schools. Mary loved working on this book and was very proud of the third edition, which came out in 2001, just two years before her death from cancer. She knew there would be a fourth edition because there's always more to say about doctoral students, postdocs, junior faculty, and their careers.

This book is dedicated to the memory of Mary Morris Heiberger, Ed.D., Associate Director, Career Services, University of Pennsylvania.

Introduction to the Fourth Edition

The *Academic Job Search Handbook* is designed to be a comprehensive guide to what is sometimes a needlessly bewildering process. It is written to help recent Ph.D.s, as well as junior faculty members who are changing positions, benefit from the experience of those who have successfully navigated the academic market. Our guidance is geared toward those conducting a job search in the United States. Candidates looking for jobs in other countries may find our advice to be of use; however, it is beyond the scope of this book to comment on the nuances of the job search in other countries or regions of the world.

Since the *Handbook* was first published in 1992, and even since the third edition in 2001, the ways candidates look for jobs have not substantially changed, so much of the original advice remains the same. However, we have added some new materials.

We have enhanced the sections on interviewing, negotiating job offers, starting the first job, and expanded career opportunities for Ph.D.s. The sample job hunting materials have been updated and expanded to provide job candidates with an array of possibilities in terms of content, arrangement, and format. We have added a sample teaching portfolio, a sample interview schedule, and a sample letter of offer.

The book begins with an overview of academic careers and institutional structures. It then takes you step by step through the application process, from establishing relationships with advisors years before going on the market to making the most of a new position. Steps discussed include positioning yourself in the market, learning about job listings, preparing vitas, cover letters, and other application materials related to teaching and research, discussing plans with those who will recommend you, participating in conferences, and negotiating offers. The final chapter reflects the reality that many people, while having an academic career as their first choice, are also considering other options as they pursue their academic search. Sample written materials, a timetable for your search, an appendix of scholarly and professional associations, and an appendix of resources are included.

Because so many of the students and postdocs we work with are concerned with balancing family and a demanding career in research and teaching, we've expanded the section on dual career couples and included some first person narratives from members of academic couples. Similarly we have included the stories of candidates who've been pregnant or nursing when on the job market as well as suggestions concerning the "right time" to have children. It is our hope that these stories can provide job candidates with practical strategies for negotiating these situations. Increasingly universities are evaluating their family leave policies in an attempt to retain academics, particularly women, for whom family is a priority. We feel this is a positive trend and are optimistic that these policies will continue to become more widespread.

Though each discipline has its own customs we have found that there are fundamental similarities in effective searches, whether one is a scientist, a social scientist, a humanist, or an academic in a professional field. However, what is "right" is frequently what is done in one's own field. Thus, this guide should never replace the specific conventions of your discipline. You may find useful advice on job hunting from your national professional association. Faculty members in your own field will usually be able to give the best perspective on your search. In job hunting, as in anything else, unanimity is rare. When expert advice conflicts, we hope that the handbook will have given you a perspective from which to form your own judgment.

Even if you are particularly interested in a few specific topics, we suggest that you read the book in its entirety. If you do, you will begin to see how advice on one topic is related to advice on another. If you understand the logic of the approach suggested in the situations we do discuss, you will be able to improvise effectively when you encounter a new situation.

We hope that this revised volume is helpful. Academic careers offer the opportunity for intensely satisfying and productive work. For many years we have worked with doctoral students and postdoctoral fellows at our own institution and corresponded with Ph.D.s nationally who read our online column for *The Chronicle of Higher Education.* We have also spoken with faculty and administrators across disciplines about all aspects of the academic job search, as well as with graduate career advisors at other institutions. We hope that by clarifying some of the processes by which positions are obtained, we can reduce some of the anxiety and uncertainty of job hunting so that candidates can get on with their chosen teaching and research.

Part I
What You Should Know
Before You Start

Chapter 1
The Structure of Academic Careers

You will be entering the job market at a time when higher education is subject to intense financial constraints, self-scrutiny, external assessment, the whims of the national ranking systems, competition, and accelerating technological change. Higher education has shifted to a more consumer-oriented model, both with the development of for-profit institutions and with the increasing demands placed on institutions by employers, legislators, parents, and students themselves, given the skyrocketing tuition at both public and private institutions. Institutions of higher education are also coming under increased political scrutiny. The pressure to compete for research grants has intensified, and the amount of research required to achieve tenure has increased. One of the safest statements that can be made about your academic career, which may well extend over the next forty years, is that it will probably be unlike those of your predecessors. Nevertheless, you are entering the market as it exists now, so it is important to understand how academic jobs have traditionally been organized.

The system of higher education in the United States is bewildering in its variety and complexity. Unlike many countries, the United States has no national, in the sense of federally funded, universities. Its major universities, both private and state-funded, house faculties of arts and sciences and major professional schools. There are also small publicly funded institutions, and that peculiarly American institution, the four-year college, which is usually, but not always, private. Privately funded institutions are mostly secular. Those funded by religious institutions have a religious influence on campus that varies from nonexistent to omnipresent. Two-year community colleges constitute an increasingly important segment of higher education. Universities run as for-profit businesses are growing rapidly, and students at these institutions have been given the right to receive some types of federal loans.

Both colleges and universities (or campuses of major universities) may enjoy either regional or national reputations. As a general rule, universities of national reputation place the most emphasis upon research as the crite-rion of success for faculty members. Teaching is most likely to be emphasized at less prestigious universities and at four-year colleges, although four-year colleges of national reputation also require substantial research of their faculty members.

Both student and faculty life are affected by conditions of faculty employment. At some institutions, nearly all faculty are full-time. Others use many part-time instructors. Faculty and other staff members at some institutions are unionized. Where unions exist, membership may be high across the board, or it may vary widely from school to school and department to department.

The Structure of Academic Positions

Given the variety of institutions, the similarity of their promotional structures is surprising. The structure of academic hiring has been dominated by the tenure system, with a fairly orderly ladder that at most institutions leads from assistant professor to associate professor (with tenure) to full professor. This "tenure track" route leads to status as a standing member of the faculty with full rights of participation in institutional decision making, and what is close to a lifetime guarantee of a job, barring economic upheaval or conviction for criminal activity. Tenure is under increasing scrutiny by state legislatures and boards of trustees, and a few institutions have dismantled their tenure systems. For now, however, achieving it is still the goal of almost everyone who first accepts a faculty position.

Tenure-track positions have been supplanted in many institutions by a variety of positions conceived of as temporary: instructorships, lectureships, visiting and research assistant/associate professorships. These have always existed for a variety of institutional reasons: to cover heavy teaching loads for introductory courses in a department that does not have enough, or any, graduate students to meet the demand; to replace a faculty member who is on sabbatical; to enable individuals able to secure research funds to be associated with a university. In a professional school, such as a school of nursing or a school of architecture, there may be a preponderance of part-time clinical professors or professors of practice. These faculty members are professionals who supplement their main employment with teaching and provide students with hands-on experience.

These positions are primarily created as institutional attempts to save the costs of tenure-track positions. In addition to struggling with government cutbacks in funding for higher education, colleges and universities have to deal with the effects of the "uncapping" of a mandatory retirement age. By federal law, institutions no longer can require faculty members to retire merely because they have reached a certain age. Many tenured faculty members of traditional retirement age (who also tend to be the highest-salaried members of their departments) are choosing to continue teaching, thus adding greatly to schools' personnel costs and providing fewer entry opportunities for new Ph.D.s. Not uncommonly, when a faculty member does retire, his or her expensive tenure-track position is converted by the institution into a non-tenure-track position.

Even though these positions may be held by the same individual and renewed over a period of several years, they are best thought of by job candidates as temporary, because they are outside the school's structure of permanent employment. In many cases holding such a position does not offer an inside track for permanent employment with the department, because if a tenure-track position becomes available a national search will be conducted. Most candidates holding these temporary positions continue to compete for tenure-track positions, so that many assistant professor slots will draw applications from experienced Ph.D.s, as well as new ones.

Hiring and promotion have tended to become less "genteel" and more market-driven in the recent decade, with no sign that the trend will be reversed. It is very rare that candidates will obtain positions through a few phone calls made by an advisor, more likely that jobs will be nationally advertised, and more likely that institutions will compete for candidates in "hot" fields using salaries, reduced teaching loads, and special research facilities to attract candidates.

Paths to Academic Administration

Educational institutions, even small ones, are also complex organizations with managerial structures. They have physical plants, staff, investments, and budgets in at least the millions of dollars. Therefore they need the same sorts of managers as are found in the business world. Many of these individuals do not have academic backgrounds.

The management of academic programs, on the other hand, is a responsibility usually held by those who have followed an academic career path. A faculty member who is interested in academic administration typically begins by taking on a greater than ordinary share of administrative and committee tasks within his or her department and institution. A frequent path might lead from department chair to dean to provost, usually the title for an institution's chief academic officer. Some institutions choose their president from those who have followed this route. Others do not, looking for a president with substantial experience in a profession, business, or government, or on the business side of managing a university.

The climb to academic administration generally begins after at least obtaining tenure, and, more likely, after becoming a full professor. Individuals who are strongly drawn to administrative activity can certainly find entry-level positions with good possibilities for promotion. It is likely, however, that they will have a lower ceiling on career advancement than those who have begun as faculty members.

Movement Between Institutions During a Career

In some fields, particularly science and engineering, up to several years of postdoctoral fellowships and/or research appointments are required in order to build a candidate's record of research to a competitive level so as to obtain a tenure-track slot at a major research institution. People in those fields almost inevitably will change institutions early in their careers. In the past this type of research experience previous to obtaining a tenure-track position was necessary only for those pursuing a career in high-level research. Now it is difficult for candidates in certain fields without this experience to get tenure-track positions, even at institutions without a national reputation.

Despite tenure's presumption of lifetime employment, faculty members in all fields increasingly move between institutions in the course of a career. Typical occasions of moves may include not getting tenure at one institution; being "lured away" at a higher salary or rank by another that is trying to build its department; and responding to a job opportunity for a spouse or partner.

To some extent, there is a national hierarchy of colleges and universities, roughly correlated with the research reputations of their faculty members and their selectivity in admitting students. In addition, there is something of a national hierarchy of departments, based on approximately the same standards. For example, an institution of generally average quality may sometimes house one of the premier departments in a given discipline.

It is generally easier to move from an institution of higher status to one of lower status than to move in the other direction. To some extent, this is a function of "name recognition." In addition, the most prominent institutions generally provide the best facilities for research on the part of their faculty members, in terms of both equipment and libraries and reduced teaching loads. People at these institutions generally have more opportunities for the kind of research that will lead to additional opportunities. Therefore, candidates usually aim as high as possible in the choice of a first academic position.

Does this mean that a candidate who does not begin an academic career at a major research institution may never have a chance to be on the faculty of one? Of course not. Particularly in the tight job market of recent years, candidates have taken the best positions they were offered, continued to do research, and moved to other institutions within a few years. They have been able to make these moves through visibility generated from research, publication, and participation in national professional or scholarly organizations. It is the case, however, that if an individual does not move to an institution or department of national reputation within the first few years of a career, whatever the form of appointment, he or she becomes increasingly less likely to do so.

Some movement is also possible between academic and nonacademic employers. This is particularly likely to be the case in professional schools, in which candidates may join the faculty at a senior level after achieving a distinguished record of accomplishment in the profession. Scientific and technical areas have also seen increasing movement between academic and industrial research settings.

However, transferability of credentials between academic and nonacademic settings varies greatly from field to field. It is a good idea to seek advice from senior individuals on both "sides" so that you do not make a major career move without being aware of its probable implications. You may need, for example, to learn how long scholars in your field can refrain from pursuing active research before they risk being unable to resume it with any credibility.

Academic Lives

The kind of position one gets, and at what institution, will have important ramifications for one's life. Research universities may demand research conducted at practically nonstop intensity, and careers may be tied to continuously obtaining new grants. Four-year colleges may expect faculty members to spend lots of time with individual students outside of class, perhaps even opening one's home to them. Short-term contracts may require frequent relocation, perhaps nationally. The period between obtaining a tenure-track position and obtaining tenure requires constant juggling of priorities as it presents so many demands. Despite their heavy workloads, academics have more freedom to structure their own time than practically anyone else in the economy. For some people, this is the great advantage of the career path; for others, it is a source of stress.

Academics, like other people, establish long-term relationships, have children, buy houses, care for elderly parents, try to make time for hobbies and community service, and hope to have some retirement income. Since academics are particularly likely to bring work home, boundaries between work and the rest of life are often blurred. When you plan your academic career, inevitably you're planning the rest of your life as well.

Chapter 2
Hiring from the Institution's Point of View

Just as your vita presents the public face of your qualifications in a simple, organized form, without revealing the full complexity of your individual life, an advertised position is the public presentation of an outcome of complex negotiations within a department and possibly within an institution.

It will generally be impossible for you, as a job candidate, to have a full understanding of what goes on behind the scenes. Even if you are fortunate enough to have an inside contact who can give you additional perspective, it is still extremely unlikely that you will know everything about the hiring decision. Thus, throughout the job search process, you will need to present yourself in the strongest fashion possible without tying yourself into knots trying to second guess the institution that has advertised the position.

However, here are some of the considerations that might be at work.

Defining and Advertising a Position

It may be fairly easy for a department to obtain approval and funding for a renewable lectureship or sabbatical replacement position. When a tenure-track position is listed, however, it reflects efforts by a department to maintain or strengthen its hiring position vis-à-vis other departments in the school. In today's financially stringent climate, approval to fill a position that has been vacated is not granted routinely. The department that has lost a faculty member must defend to its dean the necessity of replacing the position. Meanwhile other departments are lobbying to expand their faculty. If the hiring department has been given a new position, that very fact may reflect even more intense departmental lobbying.

The definition of the position more frequently reflects discussion internal to the department. In some cases the definition is obvious: the department absolutely must replace a faculty member who has a particular expertise. Perhaps, too, the department has a long-range plan that calls for increasing areas of strength or adding new areas of expertise. At other times, there may be dissension within the department about how the new position should be defined. Some want the department to move in one direction, some in another. The debate is resolved to the point necessary to define and advertise a position, but it does not necessarily mean that everyone has been convinced.

Further complicating the situation is the tendency of departments to advertise positions simultaneously at the assistant and associate professor levels, leaving the area of specialization entirely open. In that case, the department has clearly chosen to "see who's out there," planning to make an offer to whoever in its view is the best candidate. New Ph.D.s are often unnecessarily frightened by an ad that mentions positions at both levels. The hiring department will not compare a new Ph.D. to a senior faculty member. The new Ph.D. will be compared to other new Ph.D.s, the more senior faculty member to other more senior faculty members, and an offer will be made to the individual who both is the best candidate relative to his or her peer group and can best fit the needs of the department.

Implications for Candidates

A department that has gone to considerable trouble to get approval to hire for a position will not take kindly to applicants who seem to view it as a second-best alternative to be abandoned as soon as something better comes along. Therefore, it is important that you as a candidate convey a serious interest in the position throughout the search process. Don't get bogged down in self-comparisons to imagined other candidates. Concentrate on communicating what you have to offer. The position may be even more appropriate and desirable than you realize.

Screening Candidates

In a small department, all faculty members may be involved in hiring, whereas in a larger one the logistics of managing the search, and a good deal of decision making, may be delegated to a search committee. In some cases the committee may include a student representative who could be either a graduate student or an undergraduate, depending on the focus of the institution. In most hiring bodies, there will be some members of the group who are intensely interested in who is ultimately hired and who take the process very seriously; others who take participation seriously, but view it as an obligation that interferes with things they would rather be doing; and, possibly, an individual who wishes he or she were elsewhere and who participates without giving the process full attention.

The hiring group will read through the materials submitted in response to the advertisement. At this stage, candidates get the least careful screening because it simply is not possible to do an in-depth evaluation of what may be up to several hundred sets of materials sent in response to an advertisement. Individuals in the hiring group are probably not yet wedded to the candidates they prefer, because most of these are still abstractions, presented on paper.

Therefore, if someone asks the group to pay special attention to a candidate at this stage, the request is likely to be honored. The request may take the form of a phone call from a dean who says, "X is the spouse of Y, who is department Z's top choice. We'll lose her unless we can make an offer to him. See what you think." It may take the form of a phone call from a department member's former dissertation advisor who says, "Dr. L. is the best student the department has had in the last five years and she is seriously interested in this job. Can you be sure to look at her application carefully?"

In some cases, those who are to be interviewed at a convention or who are to be directly invited to campus for an interview will be chosen from the materials sent initially. However, as the money available to bring candidates for campus interviews tightens, departments are often trying to narrow the pool of candidates to a smaller group, who will be asked to provide additional materials such as dissertation chapters or articles and/or to have initial screening interviews by phone.

Implications for Candidates

As will be discussed in detail in later chapters, make all the materials used in your application clear and accessible, even to someone who is not a specialist in your area. Don't be afraid to be slightly redundant. For example, if your cover letter repeats some of the material in your vita, someone who does not pay full attention to one may pick up key points from the other.

Consider asking a senior faculty member from your Ph.D.-granting institution whether he or she knows anyone at the school to which you are applying, and then ask for a phone call on your behalf. This call can draw attention to your candidacy and help keep your application in the group of those chosen for further examination.

Once you apply for a position, be prepared to submit additional supporting materials promptly and/or to be interviewed by phone on very short notice.

Interviewing

In some fields, departments interview many candidates at a national convention and then invite a smaller group for second interviews on campus. In other fields, the campus interview is the first and only one. Once the interviewing process begins, issues of personality, style, and the department's own history begin to come into play, in unpredictable fashion. Most departments have their own histories of hiring "successes" and "mistakes." Naturally they will attempt to repeat one and avoid the other. Therefore, statements made by a candidate during an interview may have resonances unknown to the candidate. For example, if your remarks closely parallel those of a candidate hired two years ago, they will probably be heard differently depending on the current consensus as to whether hiring that candidate was a coup or a mistake.

As a candidate, you are unlikely to have a full understanding of power and influence within the department. Obviously, you must be chosen by the hiring committee and approved by the chairperson. In addition, however, there may exist individuals of sufficient influence that the department may be reluctant to hire anyone to whom they strongly object. In some institutions, particularly community colleges, nondepartmental faculty members and administrators are significantly involved in hiring.

Implications for Candidates

When your interview is scheduled, find out with whom you'll meet during the course of your visit. Get all the firsthand information about the department and institution that you can possibly gather. However, you should recognize that you are likely to gain, at best, only a partial understanding of the departmental dynamics. Therefore, don't try to second guess your interviewers. Again, concentrate on the clear communication of what you have to say.

Decision Making

After a small number of candidates have been invited to campus for an interview, the department must decide to whom to offer the position. Sometimes the choice is simple; sometimes it is agonizing. Faced with the real people who have interviewed for the position, rather than the "ideal" represented by the ad, the department may need to make very concrete trade-offs. What if the candidate who is ideal in terms of the qualities described in the ad has charmed half of the department and totally alienated the other? What if no one really fits the job that was envisioned, but one candidate seems outstanding in every other respect?

The department must make its decisions, knowing that job offers and acceptances will occur over the space of a few months. It knows the highest salary that it can pay, and it knows that it must give its first-choice candidate at least a week or two to decide whether to accept the offer. It may believe that the first-choice candidate is extremely unlikely to accept the position, and that the second-choice candidate, also very good, is likely to accept, but only if the position is offered within the next few weeks. Finally, if none of the candidates seem entirely satisfactory, the department must decide whether to leave the position vacant for a year and risk losing it to some kind of budgetary constraint, in the hope of reopening the search the following year.

Usually the department comes to a decision that balances competing priorities. Depending upon the department's style, a job may be offered to the candidate who has not alienated anyone, to the candidate who is most strongly backed by a few influential department members, to the candidate who appears most neutral in terms of some controversy that has split the department, or to a candidate chosen in a close vote. Depending on the institution, the department's decision will be endorsed by the administration or must be vigorously defended to it.

Implications for Candidates

Do your best to accept the fact that hiring is usually a matter not of choosing the "best" candidate by some set of abstract criteria, but of making a reasonable choice among valid, if competing, priorities, an inherently political process. Do your best, therefore, not to dismiss the process as somehow unethical. If each member of a hiring committee honestly thinks a different candidate is the best choice for the department, a decision must be made somehow. Unless it is to be settled by a duel or a flip of a coin, it must be decided through a negotiated process that acknowledges several factors not necessarily known to the candidates.

If you insist on thinking either that there is an obviously "best" candidate for every job and that every time that person has not been chosen an immoral decision has been made, or that hiring is a random process amounting to no more than the luck of the draw, you will diminish your own ability to understand the difference between what is and is not in your control. Worse, you risk becoming angry, bitter, or cynical and therefore approaching potential employers with a visible presumption that they will be unfair.

Approach a department as if you expect it to behave in a fair and reasonable fashion. Make it easy for those who would like to hire you to lobby for you, by being well prepared, by communicating an attitude of respect for everyone you meet during the course of a day, and by making all your written application materials as clear and strong as you can. Let your enthusiasm for the position be obvious.

Keep a record of the people with whom you speak during each application. Even if you do go elsewhere, you can keep in touch with them, send papers to them, and cultivate a relationship with them over the years. They may invite you back after you establish a reputation elsewhere.

Negotiation and Acceptance

Once a position is offered, there will likely be a period of negotiation about salary, terms of employment (for example, research facilities, or how many classes are to be taught in the first year), and time given the candidate to make a decision. Sometimes there will be delays, as the department must receive approval from a higher level before making a specific offer. Usually other finalists will be notified of a decision only after a candidate has definitely accepted a position.

Implications for Candidates

Understand that delays may be inevitable. However, if your own situation changes (for example, if you get another offer), do not hesitate to let the department know immediately. If you are turned down, it's natural to wonder why. Except in the event that you have a friend in the department, you're unlikely to find out. However, you may wish to ask for constructive feedback. If you do ask, concentrate your questions on what you might have done to strengthen your presentation, rather than on how the decision was made.

Hiring and "Inside Candidates"

Sometimes, at the conclusion of a search, it is widely perceived that the advertised position was not truly open. There was a high probability at the outset that an offer would be made to someone who was already within the department; to someone whom the department had been wooing for the last few years; to a member of a group whose underrepresentation among faculty members was viewed as an intolerable situation; to a clone of those already in the department; and so on.

Implications for Candidates

Compete for every job you want as if you have a genuine chance of being offered it, whatever you guess or have been told. That way you best position yourself to take advantage of the uncertainty inherent in every hiring situation. Maybe the department does have a strong front-runner, but he or she will not accept the position in the end. Maybe you are very unlikely to get this job, but the campus interview you are offered will help you polish your interviewing skills so that you will do better at the next interview.

Remember that, even if you are not successful in getting a particular job, you have left behind an impression of abilities, talents, and personality. Frequently, faculty members will talk with colleagues at other schools about good candidates whom they interviewed but were not able to hire. Even if your interview at a particular school is unsuccessful, it can serve as good advertising, depending upon how you deal with the interview situation and, particularly, with any rejection.

When you are hired, there may well be disappointed candidates who think that you had some kind of unfair advantage, so try to be generous in your assessment of the decisions made by what are, by and large, well-intentioned people.

Part II
Planning and Timing Your Search

Chapter 3
Becoming a Job Candidate: The Timetable for Your Search

It is important to begin to prepare for your job search well before you expect to finish your dissertation or your postdoctoral research. In many fields it is also important to time the search to coincide with the completion of your dissertation. Many scientists are competitive on the tenure-track market only after a few years of postdoctoral research. Think about your job search, your participation in scholarly organizations, and the completion of your dissertation or postdoctoral research as a unified whole.

Most faculty members will advise you not to take a tenure-track position before your dissertation is completed. Similarly, postdocs should fulfill all their obligations to their current lab before leaving. A strong logic informs that view. In a tight job market, candidates who have completed their degrees are likely to be chosen over those who have not. A postdoc will want to start his or her own research program and not have to worry about finishing research done for someone else. Once you have accepted a position, you will gain tenure as a result of research done as a junior faculty member. If you are late beginning your new research agenda, you will already be late by the tenure clock, and in the position of a student with several incompletes, who can never catch up with current work.

Funding considerations may force you to look for paid employment before beginning your new position. If this is the case, choose the employment most conducive to finishing your research.

Use the timetable below to plan your job search while completing your dissertation or postdoctoral research and participating in scholarly activities. Each suggested step is discussed in detail elsewhere in this book. If, by chance, you read it thinking, "I wish I had done some of these things last year," don't despair! Fill in the gaps as best you can. Certainly many people obtain positions without having conducted the "perfect" job search. However, if you see gaps in your preparation and do not do as well as you hope in the job market this year, you may find much more success if you go on the market again next year after better preparation.

Timetable for Applying for Jobs That Begin in September

Two Years Before the Position Would Begin

- Make sure all members of your dissertation committee are selected. Consider getting a December degree, which enables you to apply with "degree in hand." (International scholars, however, should consider the visa implications of this timing.)
- Learn about conference dates and locations. Plan to attend and, if feasible, to give a presentation. Learn deadlines for submitting papers.
- Learn about all the important sources of job listings in your field. In some disciplines the job listings of one scholarly association cover almost everything. In other fields there may be multiple sources.
- Explore Internet resources and bookmark useful sites. There are many excellent resources, such as *The Chronicle of Higher Education, Tomorrow's Professor,* and *Preparing Future Faculty.*
- Give thought to your long-range goals and consider the kinds of jobs you will wish to apply for. If your plans will have an impact on a spouse or partner, begin to talk with that person about geographic locations you will both consider acceptable.
- If you have the opportunity to do so, start to sit in on the talks of job candidates in your department. Think about what they do that does and doesn't work well. If your department allows students to review candidates' application materials, take advantage of this opportunity to see a large collection of them.
- If you think a Web site would enhance a candidacy in your field, start to develop one.
- Consider submitting an article or articles to reputable journals in your field.
- Identify any relevant postdocs for which you may want to apply and learn their deadlines.
- If you are already in a postdoctoral position, you will want to seek a tenure-track position when you feel your research record is strong enough. Once you've decided you're ready to put yourself on the market, see "Fall, Twelve Months Before" below.
- Think about developing a backup plan. If it includes seeking nonacademic positions, start to educate yourself about the options. Two excellent resources are *So What Are You Going to Do with That?: Finding Careers Outside Academia* by Susan Basalla May and Maggie Debelius and *Nontraditional Careers in Science* by Karen Young Kreeger.

Summer, Fifteen Months Before

- Make sure your dissertation will be finished no later than the summer before the job begins, and preferably earlier. In many cases, hiring departments will not consider a candidate without a Ph.D. in hand.

- If you are a postdoc, you should be adding to your list of publications and planning to finish your research approximately twelve months from now.
- Discuss your plans with your advisor or postdoctoral supervisor and any others in the department who may be interested. If they don't think you will be ready to go on the market until the following year, consider their point of view very seriously. If you begin a new position and have not yet completed your dissertation, you will start off behind schedule in terms of the "tenure clock."
- Renew contacts with faculty members whom you may know at other institutions, letting them know of your progress and that you will be on the market soon.
- If you are a graduate student, find out how faculty in your department provide letters of recommendation. If those in your department use a credentials service provided by your campus career center, set up a file. Get letters of recommendation now from those with whom you will have no further significant contact.
- Collect all the materials you have that you might want to use or refer to as part of an application and make sure you can find them. Your collection could include reprints, copies of letters of commendation, newspaper articles about something you have done, syllabi you have prepared, and notes about things you want to remember to stress in a cover letter.
- Prepare your vita.
- Begin to prepare the additional written materials you will need in your search. You may be asked to provide an employer with an abstract or the first chapter of your dissertation, a research paper or article, a brief statement of your research plans or teaching philosophy, "evidence of successful teaching," and sample syllabi.
- You may also be asked for a copy of your transcript. Be sure you know how to order it and how long it takes to fill a request.
- Some conferences are held in the late summer or early fall. It is important to attend them and take advantage of the opportunity they provide for the formal and informal exchange of information.
- If you will be applying for individual postdoctoral funding, obtain and begin to prepare postdoc applications. If you will be applying to work on someone's research grant, start to network with potential principal investigators.
- Think about what resources you will need to do your research as a faculty member. Begin to look into ways of funding your research. You may be asked about this in an interview.
- If you are also considering non-academic options, be aware that timetables for non-academic employment are different from academic ones, and usually more flexible. If an academic position is your first choice, concentrate on that search at this time.

Fall, Twelve Months Before

- Finalize your vita. (You may need to update it a few times during the year.) Complete additional supporting written materials.
- Arrange for letters of recommendation to be written by everyone who will support your search. Your advisor will probably update his or her letter as your dissertation progresses through its final stages.
- Find out whether jobs in your field typically require "teaching portfolios." Most fields don't, but if yours does, begin to prepare one. Don't forget to include samples of your students' work.
- Keep working on your dissertation or research.
- If you're in an art or design field, prepare the slides and portfolios you'll be asked to submit with applications.
- Attend any programs on the academic job search that may be offered on campus or at conferences.
- Watch carefully for job listings and apply for everything that interests you. The first cover letters you write may take longer to compose than subsequent ones.
- Continue to keep in close touch with your advisor and other recommenders.
- Consider making a few direct inquiries at departments that particularly interest you (what you are most likely to discover in this way are non-tenure-track positions), if you can define reasonable criteria for selecting the departments.
- Review the literature in your field and subfield in preparation for interviews.
- Check to see that letters of application have been received by the departments to which you apply.
- Continue to apply for postdocs.
- Investigate sources of funding for your research so that you can discuss your plans with hiring institutions.
- Plan ways to maintain your perspective and sense of humor during what can be a trying time. Consider exercise, having fun, seeking out campus resources, supporting others who are going through the same thing, and nurturing your own support network.

Eight Months Before

- Interviewers will ask you about your long-range research plans. Even if you are so immersed in your research that you can't see beyond it at the moment, take time to give some thought to where your work will lead.
- Many conferences are held now that include first-round interviews for faculty positions. If this is true for your discipline, you should plan to attend whether or not you have interviews scheduled.

- Prepare carefully for each interview, whether it is a phone interview, a conference interview, or a campus interview. Remember to send thank you notes after each interview.
- Campus interviews take place during this period. If you give a presentation as part of an interview day on campus, practice it in advance.
- Continue to look, apply, and interview for positions.
- This may well be a stressful time. Plan to take some breaks for activities or events that you consider relaxing and renewing.

Six Months Before

- Continue to apply and interview for positions, although most openings will have been announced by now.
- You may begin to get offers. If you feel you need more time to make a decision about an offer, don't hesitate to ask for it. You will, however, have to abide by whatever time frame you and the employer agree on for your decision. You don't need to be totally open with everyone at this stage, but you must be completely honest. When you do accept a position, consider your acceptance a binding commitment.
- If the offers you want are not coming in, don't think that you must take absolutely any job that is offered to you, whether you want it or not. The job market will come around again next year. Talk with your advisor and others about the best way to position yourself for next year's market, if necessary. You can also keep watching for one-year appointments, which are often announced later than tenure-track positions.
- After you have accepted a job, take time to thank everyone who has been helpful to you in the process.

Chapter 4
Deciding Where and When to Apply

Before you begin a job search, think about what kind of job you want and whether you are currently prepared to compete successfully for it. Study position announcements to see what different types of institutions seem to require and use the information to help plan your next steps. If, realistically, you don't yet seem qualified to compete successfully for the jobs you really want, consider whether a postdoctoral position or fellowship, additional teaching experience, or anything else will position you for a successful search.

It's important to think about both your priorities and your realistic chances of achieving your goals. Even in a tight market where you feel options are limited, it's still useful to keep your sights on what you really want. The more articulate you can be about your plans and goals, the easier it will be for you to communicate with your advisor and others who will assist you in your job search, to prepare for interviewing, and to assess job offers.

Understanding the Market

You must know something about the job market before you begin your search. The more informed you are the better your search will be. The experience of graduate students a few years ahead of you in your department or postdocs who finished a few years earlier provides a very limited knowledge base. You need to do additional research to be conversant with the following:

- What is the hiring outlook in your discipline?
- What is the hiring outlook in your field of research?
- How broad is the market in your field? Opportunities may exist outside traditional departmental definitions. For example, although your degree is from an arts and sciences department, might you seek a position in a professional school (such as business, government, communi-

cations, education)? Would a short-term experience, such as a postdoctoral appointment, increase your long-term options? Are you in a field, such as biomedical science, where a postdoc is required?

- How great is the competition for positions in your field at prestigious institutions? What is realistically required should you choose to compete for them? For example, would several publications in major journals be required?

- If you are in a highly specialized field, when and where are openings anticipated?

There are several ways you can obtain this information. Read articles in *The Chronicle of Higher Education.* Contact your scholarly association (see Appendix 1) for reports it may have produced about the market. Check to see whether your university career center or graduate dean's office has records of the jobs taken by new Ph.D.s from your school. Talk with students in your department who are on the market or recent graduates who have new faculty positions. Even if you are not on the market yet, take a close look at the job postings for your field to get a sense of what is asked of job candidates. Above all, talk regularly with your department chair, mentor, and other faculty members about the job market in your field.

Should You Apply for a Postdoctoral Position?

A postdoctoral position can run the gamut from a long-standing, well-defined opportunity, to an endeavor that is funded on an ad hoc basis, to a job of undetermined time and structure that is improvised as the project develops. In the biomedical sciences it is difficult if not impossible to obtain a tenure-track position without postdoctoral experience. This is sometimes true in other fields of science and engineering, depending on the discipline. Increasingly, job candidates in the social sciences and humanities are doing postdocs as a way to move their research forward without the heavy teaching responsibilities associated with being a visiting assistant professor. It can also be a way to build your credentials if you don't obtain the desired tenure-track position on your first or second time on the job market. Conversely, job candidates in the sciences who have a well-developed research profile are taking on "teaching postdocs" to gain the teaching experience they may need to obtain tenure-track positions in teaching-focused institutions. As you near the end of your graduate work it is wise to have a sense of whether a postdoc is the natural next step for people in your discipline. Regardless of your discipline, it is likely that there will be many ways to learn about postdoctoral opportunities through your department and scholarly association.

Questions to Ask When Applying for a Postdoc

- Why are you planning to do a postdoc? Is your field one where postdoc experience is usually required?
- Do you want to use your postdoctoral experience to increase your expertise in your dissertation area or to broaden your skill set?
- Should you do your postdoc in a large, top research institution or in a smaller school?
- What qualities do you plan to look for in the supervisor who will serve as your mentor? How do you plan to assess those qualities?
- What type of facilities and other resources are required for the type of research you want to do?
- Will this postdoctoral position help you move your research forward in a way that will provide a strong basis for an independent scholarly career?

Deciding Where to Apply

Institutional Characteristics

Are you willing or eager to consider jobs at:

- A public or private institution?
- A large university or a small four-year teaching college or community college?
- A school with a distinctive institutional personality, such as a women's college, an institution with a strong religious affiliation, or a school offering an "innovative curriculum"?
- An institution that emphasizes research over teaching or one that emphasizes teaching over research? A competitive job market has enabled institutions that formerly emphasized only one of these things to require both; however, "teaching" and "research" institutions still may be distinguished from each other.
- A place that demands or offers heavy involvement in the life of the school (usually a teaching college) or one in which your major identification will be with your department?
- A highly selective institution or one that prides itself on offering educational opportunities to a broad section of the community?
- An institution where the faculty is unionized or one where individual salaries are market-driven?
- An institution that compensates new faculty members with salary or one that compensates them with prestige?
- A U.S. institution or one in another country?
- A for-profit university?

Departmental Characteristics

Do you prefer:

- Many colleagues in your field of research or an opportunity to be the in-house expert in your field?
- The opportunity to and expectation that you will socialize with others in the department or an atmosphere that encourages solely professional involvement?
- An emphasis on graduate or on undergraduate teaching?
- A department in which you would be the first person of your social background ever hired, or one in which you feel most people are like you?
- A department with a specific orientation ("traditional," "radical," "applied") or one whose faculty members take a variety of approaches?
- A department where teaching occurs mainly in seminars or one where classes are primarily large lectures?
- A department that emphasizes research or one that emphasizes teaching? Think about what kind of facilities you need to carry out your own research plans.
- A department with a hierarchical structure or one that emphasizes participatory decision making?

Geographic Considerations

- Is it important to you to be in a rural, small city, suburban, or urban environment?
- Does your research require resources that are available in limited geographic locations?
- Can you work and live comfortably in any region of the country?
- Will you need to limit the geographic range of your search, or find an institution near an airport, because of personal considerations, such as the career plans of a partner, a child's education, or the need to be near a relative who is ill?
- Will you look only in the United States or will you expand your search to other countries? Are you able to teach in a language other than English?

How Competitive Are You?

Be realistic in evaluating the type of institution where you will be able and willing to do what is necessary to attain tenure.

- In some fields, it is very important to be able to obtain funding for your own research. Do you feel willing and able to do this?
- Are you able to resist pressure from your own departmental culture to apply only to certain kinds of institutions?

- What balance do you want to strike between career-related features and nonprofessional aspects of a job? For example, would you take a position at a highly prestigious institution at which you would need to work nearly all your waking hours in order to have a reasonable chance of obtaining tenure?
- Do you see a discrepancy between your ability and willingness to perform in your first job and your ability to obtain it? For example, are you highly productive in research and publication and very awkward in oral presentations and conversations? In that case, work to improve your job hunting skills instead of letting them limit your job search, because your job hunting ability can always improve if you are willing to give it practice and attention. On the other hand, if you interview extremely well but seriously doubt your ability or willingness to perform the level of research required to get tenure, don't talk yourself into a job whose demands you may not want or be able to meet. The tenure clock usually starts the minute you accept a tenure-track position. If you feel you will be unable to do what will be required to achieve tenure, you will surely face another, possibly more difficult, job search down the road.

Additional Personal Considerations

Additional idiosyncratic personal considerations may be important in your job search. Even if you are the only candidate in the world who will choose one position over another because it will give you the most opportunity and time to use your pilot's license, take this preference into consideration if it is important to you.

When to Look

Because most jobs are advertised about a year before they are to begin, you will probably start your job search while you are still finishing your dissertation or postdoctoral research. Be realistic about when you will finish. For Ph.D. students it is crucial that you discuss with your advisor when to begin the search, because he or she will be knowledgeable about the advisability of being a candidate with an unfinished dissertation as opposed to one with the degree in hand. That is the most important factor in determining when to start looking.

On the other hand, if you are in a field with very few annual openings, and a good job is announced before you are entirely ready to apply, you and your advisor may decide that it is a good idea for you to accelerate your search. If you are in the first year of a postdoc with a two-year commitment and the perfect job opportunity comes along, you're in a difficult situation. You probably must discuss it with your supervisor, at least by the time you're invited for an interview, at which point the person will almost certainly find out about your application.

If it looks as if you will finish in a year in which very few openings are available, plan to search for good interim opportunities while you conduct the academic job search. Many postdoctoral and other fellowship opportunities, like academic positions, have very early deadlines for application. Don't wait until you find you have no job offers before you apply. Some faculty positions will continue to be listed throughout the academic year, so, while you must begin your search early, it may continue over several months.

If you are an international student, you should find out if there are visa considerations that might affect the timing of your search and the date when you might prefer to have your degree awarded. Start working on this task early to avoid problems or delays that might prevent an institution from offering you a job later on, or that might compromise your ability to remain long-term in the United States if that is your desire. If you are on a campus that has an office that offers good visa and immigration advising, use it. If not, consult a reputable immigration attorney.

Interdisciplinary Areas

If you have an interdisciplinary degree, you have the advantage of being able to apply for jobs in more than one kind of department. On the other hand, when you read job announcements, you may notice with dismay that they frequently occur within the confines of departments defined by traditional disciplinary distinctions. At times you may face the problem of seeming "neither fish nor fowl" to a search committee.

If you are looking outside your field, learn the language of that field and use that language in your vita, cover letter, and interview. Disciplines have their own strong identities, and search committees in a related discipline won't consider you if they think you can't talk to them in their language. If at all possible, try to have a letter of recommendation from someone in each discipline in which you are applying.

There appears to be an increase in joint appointments. Applying for such a position will affect how you frame your written materials, as the search committee will be made up of people from different departments with different priorities. If you accept a joint position, be sure you clarify responsibilities and expectations before you begin your new position.

In addition to those in your own discipline, join other scholarly associations so that you are current academically, as well as aware of job openings. Attend their conferences. To make sure you are aware of all possible openings, ask faculty and recent graduates in the disciplines that interest you for suggestions of places to look for job notices. For example, those whose work is best defined as American Studies may see appropriate jobs listed under English or History in *The Chronicle of Higher Education,* or in the Modern Language Association or American Historical Association job listings.

Discussing Your Plans with Others

Sharing your thoughts with your advisor, department placement chair, and others who will work with you in your search can help these individuals act effectively on your behalf. Conversation with them can help you clarify your own thinking as it evolves. Honest faculty feedback about how realistic your choices are can be enormously helpful to you. The best way for you to elicit it is to ask for candor, assuring those you ask that your feelings will not be hurt by what you hear. Needless to say, respond in a way that does not cause someone to regret his or her candor.

In talking to others, whether faculty members or peers, keep your own priorities clearly in mind, and use your own judgment. Consider, for instance, your feelings about raising research funds. In many fields in the sciences and engineering, you must do so successfully and repeatedly to achieve tenure at a major research institution. If you have a realistic chance of obtaining a position at a major research institution, but privately feel that meeting the research demands necessary to get tenure there will consign you to years of prolonged misery, then it may be wise for you to look at another type of institution.

Perhaps your research has only recently begun to take off because you were meeting personal obligations that you are convinced will now be lighter. In that case you may want to try for jobs that your advisor feels are beyond your reach, even if you need to take a postdoctoral position in the interim to strengthen your credentials. If you are a natural risk-taker convinced that a small but growing department may be the source of some of the most exciting work in your field, you may choose to ignore the cautions of more conservative friends who say, "Yes, but who's ever heard of it?"

Following your own instincts as to what you will find satisfying is easy if your goals are similar to those of the people around you. It is often more difficult if you want to follow a path that seems foreign to your advisor and most of the students in your department. In that case, use their skepticism as a prod to make sure that you get as much information as possible so that you make informed decisions. If you want to do something nontraditional, be able to explain your decision to others so they can support your search.

Balance this skepticism, however, with the enthusiasm of people who are doing what you would like to do, even if they are at other institutions and you have to seek them out. In the end, it is your career and your life, and you are most likely to be satisfied with both if you shape them according to your own priorities and values.

Chapter 5
The Importance of Advisors and Professional Networks

A job search may feel like a lonely enterprise, but it is always conducted within the context of a web of social relationships. You work within a discipline with its own language, conventions, and structure of communication. Your own research has undoubtedly been strengthened by communication with other people; in some fields it has been conducted as part of a team. You are leaving a department with one social structure and culture to enter another. You will be explicitly recommended by several people, and those who are considering your candidacy may hear about you from others.

Whether you find these facts reassuring or alarming, by taking account of them as early as possible in your graduate career, you can strengthen your prospects in the job market. If you have not paid sufficient attention to them until now, it is not too late to focus on them. Networking is crucial, not only to get a job, but also to succeed at it and at your research. Some candidates are put off by the potentially exploitative aspect of networking, as well they should be. The goal is not to use people in a one-way exchange, but to engage in a mutually beneficial relationship.

During graduate study it's critical that you change your self-concept from that of a "student" who primarily learns from others to that of a "colleague" who is actively engaged in his or her chosen discipline. If you view yourself merely as a job-hunting student, you will see networking as a petitionary activity, be hesitant to contact people, and perhaps run the risk of being bothersome. If you view yourself as an active member of your discipline, you will view networking more appropriately as an exchange of information, contact people confidently, and usually make them happy that they got to know you.

Advisors and Mentors

It is difficult to overemphasize the importance of an advisor in an academic career. When you enter the job market, and perhaps for years, you will often be viewed as "X's student" or "Y's protégé." In some fields, the post-doctoral supervisor is extremely important. If your advisor or supervisor is well known in the market you want to enter, thinks highly of you, spends time with you, is savvy about the employment market, and is enthusiastically supportive of your job search, you will be likely to think highly of the importance of the advisor's role. Your first job search may well go more smoothly because you will be able to discuss your goals with your advisor, who will in turn perhaps make phone calls that will pave the way to interviews.

While such a situation is generally enviable, you may also need to make a particular effort to distinguish between your own goals and your mentor's goals for you, if you feel they differ. Making choices that are disappointing to the advisor will be particularly difficult. You also may rely too heavily on your advisor's intervention and fail to master job-hunting skills as thoroughly as does someone who gets less assistance. If you are blessed with such an advisor, make a particular effort to learn from that person how best to make efforts on your own behalf. If you are doing postdoctoral research, your current supervisor can play a role in your search similar to that of an advisor. However, in addition to supporting your career development, a postdoctoral supervisor is also often dependent on your work to complete research. It may not be realistic to expect that person to enthusiastically support you for a position which would take you away before you completed the time you'd committed to the postdoctoral position.

You may have a less than ideal advising relationship. Perhaps your advisor is not particularly well known, brilliant but unskilled at interacting with other people, so formal and distant that you are honestly unsure what he or she thinks about your work, or, in fact, disappointed in your work and not hesitant to tell you so. Whatever the characteristics of this real human being, you can probably improve the relationship, profit from the individual's greatest strengths, and, if necessary, find additional mentors.

If things are not going well between you and your advisor, your natural tendency may be to avoid talking with him or her. Resist this temptation! It is only through interaction that you can identify problems and attempt to address them. Arrange regular meetings to discuss your work, come well prepared for them, ask for as much feedback as you can get, take your advisor's suggestions, and make sure he or she sees that you have done so.

If you sense that your advisor is not happy with what you are doing, but is not telling you why, ask more directly for feedback. You may learn that in fact there is no problem, or you may identify an issue you can address. View the immediate problem as an opportunity to learn more about how to manage conflict successfully, since you will encounter it again and again throughout your career.

Even though advisors have considerable power, it is not unlimited. Most will respect you more if you think independently, respectfully express disagreement when it exists, present your ideas persuasively, and generally act as if you accept responsibility for your own career.

Most advisors act responsibly; a few abuse their power. The latter are most likely to victimize those who are unwilling to challenge inappropriate treatment. If you honestly believe you are being treated unfairly or inappropriately, begin by learning what the norms for acceptable behavior are. For example, your advisor may be crediting your work appropriately according to standards in your field while you may feel it is being "stolen." You can ask questions of other faculty members, graduate students, and postdocs; see whether your institution has formal policies and guidelines governing the relationship between advisors and students; consult publications of your professional association; and use library and Internet resources to understand how your experience fits into the general scheme of things. If you determine that you truly are being treated unfairly, it is usually better, although not risk-free, to seek fairer treatment, preferably with extreme deliberation and the guidance and support of a senior person who understands your department well.

Whatever your relationship with your advisor, it is helpful to have as many senior people as possible interested in your success. Take advantage of every opportunity to talk to and get to know other faculty members in your department. Ask them for opinions, perspective, and feedback in areas where you genuinely value their expertise. It is not necessary or desirable to think of this interaction in terms of flattery. Research enterprises flourish on the exchange of ideas. Don't hesitate to develop mentors at other institutions as well.

Your peers in the department offer another valuable source of perspective and lifelong contacts. Be realistic about the extent to which you will be competing with them in the job market; many candidates overestimate it. By and large, you have different strengths and interests. You will be far more successful if you exchange information and ideas with others than if you avoid interaction for fear of somehow giving them a competitive edge. Beware, however, of becoming too involved in exchanging job-hunt horror stories. Every department has its share; some are apocryphal, and overindulgence in listening to and recounting them blurs your perspective.

The farther along you are in your academic career, the more important it is that you have established an independent network of colleagues and peers. If you are going on the market again several years after earning your final degree, some of your most important recommendations may come from outside your degree-granting department. However, if you've lost touch with faculty members there, before you begin a search is a good time to reconnect.

Professional Associations

Ideally, even in the early years of graduate study, you have begun to develop membership in professional networks that extend beyond your department and university. Whatever your field, there is at least one, if not several, scholarly or professional associations devoted to the exchange of ideas. Conferences, electronic discussion lists and blogs, publications, and local and regional meetings are the most common means of exchange. Because of the importance of these organizations, they will be referred to again and again throughout this handbook. If you don't know those that are important in your field, ask faculty members in your department.

Calls for papers are probably posted in your department, announced through print and electronic vehicles of your scholarly association, and listed in additional scholarly resources on the Internet. You can also consult the "Deadlines" section of the print version of *The Chronicle of Higher Education* or "Events and Deadlines" in the "Gazette" section of the online *Chronicle* for such notices. If you feel that publications in major journals or presentations at national conventions are slightly beyond your reach at this point, look for regional or local meetings of national organizations and respectable but less prestigious journals. Attend as many presentations as you can. In addition to learning and gaining ideas from the material presented, you can see how others present their work and form your own conclusions about the most effective way to communicate ideas.

Individual Contacts

If you are interested in the work of someone at another institution, whether you learn of it through a conference, a publication, or word of mouth, it is appropriate to approach that person, by phone, mail, or e-mail, for a further exchange of ideas. Share your comments; send a copy of a related paper or a reprint of an article you wrote. Ask questions. Suggest a meeting at a conference you both will be attending. It goes without saying that your comments and questions should be sincere and intelligent. Given that, however, by taking the initiative you greatly expand the range of intellectual resources upon which you can draw and develop a broad network of professional contacts with whom you can remain in touch throughout your career.

In between meetings, many listservs and discussion forums function as ongoing professional forums with conversation similar to what may be found in the breaks between presentations at conferences. Your thoughtful participation in relevant groups gives you an opportunity to cause a large number of people to recognize your name in a positive way, not a bad thing when you consider that yours may be one of hundreds in a pile of applications.

Just as reputations have been made by work people publish, so can they be made or destroyed by communications posted to the Internet. The Internet is faster. Journal referees will prevent you from publishing anything that is libelous, outrageous, or just plain stupid. The Internet offers no such protection. When you communicate on the Net, consider that your potential audience is literally worldwide, that you reach it instantly, and that your communication is probably archived. Look yourself up on a powerful search engine to see what potential employers may already know about you. You may also have concern for not precipitously putting out work that you plan to publish later, given how easy it is to appropriate material from the Web. Include a copyright statement on all documents you post.

Observers of people's responses to electronic communication have frequently noted that it tends to flow across normal hierarchical boundaries. If you find even very senior individuals who actively contribute to electronic newsgroups or who are avid users of electronic mail, you may find this a comfortable way to communicate with them, particularly after you have taken the time to become familiar with their work.

You impoverish your own work if you do not take advantage of the multiplicity of forums for the exchange of ideas and of the personal give and take that turns a good piece of work into an excellent one. While you should not do so for this reason alone, as you establish your own network of communication, you also expand the range of people who are interested in your success in the job market.

Chapter 6
Conference Presentations and Networking

Conferences and conventions are a major means of scholarly communication. They also provide an opportunity to meet people who can hire you or refer you to others who can. By the time you are an advanced graduate student, if not before, you should begin to participate in these meetings, which are an important means of communication in your discipline. As you near the end of your graduate work and enter the job market, conferences begin to play a more formal role in your job search. They may offer a job placement service or give you an opportunity to gain favorable exposure through presenting a paper, and they always give you a way to network informally with others.

You should almost certainly plan to attend the national meeting of the major association in your field in the year you are on the job market. If you can arrange to give a paper or participate in a poster session, try to do so.

Presentations

Each field has its own style for the delivery of presentations. If you are delivering a conference paper for the first time, ask your department what to expect and how to be prepared for it. In addition, check with your professional association to see whether it provides guidelines that help you answer the following questions.

Mode of Delivery

- Do you sit or stand?
- Do you speak from notes or read a paper?
- Do you answer questions at a "poster session"?
- How formally are papers presented? Is any form of humor ever appropriate?

- How long will you have to speak?
- Will there be questions from the audience? Will there be a moderator?

Presentation Aids

- Should you prepare handouts?
- Should you use slides or PowerPoint?
- How large should a poster be?
- Will you be able to project images from a computer? If so, will it have Internet access?

Practice your presentation before you offer it. If you can give a departmental seminar, so much the better, but, in any case, deliver the talk to an audience that will give you feedback. If you will use materials in your presentation, include them in your practice session so that you are thoroughly comfortable handling them. Ask your colleagues to question the vulnerable points in your thesis so that you can practice challenges to them. As you practice, make sure to speak loudly enough to be heard, look at your audience, and speak rapidly enough to hold your audience's attention but slowly enough that they can understand you.

Your materials should look as professional as you can make them. Design them with plenty of white space and keep content away from the outer edges so that they are easy to read. Don't cram too much information onto one slide. For text, use a font that is easy to see and make sure it is large enough for emeritus faculty in the back of the room to read. Check to make sure that materials when projected are clear from a distance. Your campus almost certainly has individuals who are expert in graphic presentation. Seek them out and use their help.

On the other hand, don't let graphics overtake your message. Visual and oral presentations should reinforce each other. The point of both is to communicate clearly and well, while maintaining the interest of the audience. Your presentation style, oral or on the screen, should never get in the way of the information. If you choose to use handouts, know their content very well. For example, if you use citations in a handout your audience might ask you in-depth questions about them. Also, know that some people might spend the entire presentation time reading over the handouts and not focusing on what you have to say. Consider carefully whether or not handouts will enhance your presentation.

Networking

Conferences vary in size according to your field, but they always offer you an opportunity to meet more people in your discipline in one place than you can ever encounter elsewhere. Even if they are not hiring, they are a source of potential information about their institutions, their departments, and their research. They may share information or remember you when you later apply to their departments; they may be people you can later contact for information.

But how do you meet them? Here are some suggestions.

- Determine some goals for the conference in advance to help you plan your time. For instance, perhaps you wish to meet particular people, attend specific presentations or discussions, and seek feedback on a topic connected with your research.
- Find out which faculty members from your department will attend. If there is anyone to whom you would particularly like to be introduced, see if they can help you.
- Find out whether your department will host a reception at the conference. If it will, be sure to attend. If not, see whether you can interest the department in arranging one.
- Give a presentation or poster session.
- Wear your nametag, and don't be shy about introducing yourself. Don't assume people will remember you.
- Attend sessions that interest you and talk with the speakers afterward, using your interest in their presentations as an icebreaker.
- Participate in smaller interest groups which may have meetings apart from presentations. Some organizations, for example, have active women's groups.
- If possible, take part in informal social gatherings attended by members of your department and faculty from other institutions.
- Much information gets exchanged at receptions and informal social gatherings. If you are comfortable joining a group you don't know and introducing yourself, by all means do so.
- Arrange brief meetings with someone whose work particularly interests you in advance of the conference, independent of a hiring context. Most fields are fairly small worlds, and having people know you is helpful, even if not immediately so.
- If there is a choice of hotels, stay in whichever is the main site for the conference. The central location will justify any extra expense because it will make it easier to meet people.
- Introduce people to each other when you have a chance.

It is appropriate to walk up even to well-established faculty or researchers and introduce yourself. Few people consider this an imposition. In fact, both established and less well-known faculty find it very flattering when less-experienced people in their field introduce themselves and say, "I've looked forward to meeting you" and state why.

If you are shy, you may prefer to meet people in structured situations.

Rather than letting yourself become nervous about meeting people, think about the links between your work and that of those you'd like to meet. If it helps, think of meeting new ideas, rather than new personalities. If you are very outgoing, it may be easier to introduce yourself to strangers. In either case, remember that networking works only if you make a good impression. When you meet new people, your interest in their work, your work, and the field should dominate your conversation.

If you are seeking information, elicit it naturally in the course of conversation. If people feel that your main interest is to pump them for job information, you would be better off not speaking with them in the first place. Avoid being overly pushy with or fawning over established researchers. Courtesy and consideration are good guidelines. People who are considering a candidate for a faculty position are looking not only for someone who is creative and smart and has a great future, but also for someone who is going to be a good colleague, that is, pleasant to have around and work with.

Serendipity can play a large part in your career path, and being prepared lets you make the most of chance encounters. You may ride an elevator with or find yourself seated next to a luminary in your field, someone whose work you've always admired. Introduce yourself and state your interest in or connection to this individual and don't shy away from having a little conversation. You never know, but this person may remember you sometime down the road while serving on a search committee, a review board, or in another professional context.

A conference mixes social and professional events and behaviors. As a job candidate, keep the professional aspect of the gathering foremost in your mind. There is the possibility that someone you approach may assume that your interest is social or romantic rather than professional. This is still more likely to be a problem for women, but occasionally is problematic for men as well. Make sure that your manner and attire convey a professional interest. If you are in doubt whether this is clear to the other person, stick to public settings (meetings and restaurants rather than suites or rooms), be extra cautious about your own alcohol consumption, and disengage yourself from anyone who drinks too much.

Participating in a professional network is a valuable activity that will help you, not only in your search for your first position, but throughout your career as well. From it come possibilities for collaborative efforts, invitations to submit papers, and professional stimulation. So it's worthwhile to begin the process, whether it comes easily or with difficulty.

Chapter 7
Letters of Recommendation

At some point in the screening process for nearly every job, and frequently as part of your initial application, you will be asked to ensure that letters supporting your candidacy reach the hiring department. The number requested varies, but three is typical. Since letters require the cooperation of others, allow yourself plenty of time to obtain them.

Choosing Your Recommenders and Asking for Letters

The choice of recommenders is important and merits careful thought. Your dissertation advisor, of course, and anyone else with whom you have worked closely will be your first and second letter writers. In choosing additional recommenders find someone who can talk about your teaching as well as a senior researcher in your field. Most of your letters will probably be from your own department, but it is also acceptable to ask for letters from scholars outside your institution, if they are very familiar with your work.

Of course it is helpful to have a letter from someone who is widely known in your field, but do not ask people to write on your behalf unless they really know your work. If you are applying for postdocs or for positions at top research institutions, letters will speak primarily to your strength as a researcher.

If you are applying for jobs that emphasize teaching, you will probably see some ads that require "evidence of excellence in teaching." Faculty generally agree that letters from students you have taught are not convincing on their own. One way to respond to this type of request is to ask the recommender who knows your teaching best to write a letter addressing your teaching. Give this person copies of student evaluations of your teaching, if you have them. He or she can incorporate overall numeric standings (perhaps giving a context for them, such as the departmental and school average scores), quotes from students' comments, and his or her own assessment based on first-hand observation.

In some professional fields, such as business and architecture, a letter from a former employer or consulting client may be helpful, especially for a school that values interaction with practitioners.

Ask for letters as much in advance as possible. Faculty members receive many requests for them. Phrase your request in such a way that if someone does not feel comfortable writing for you, he or she can gracefully decline. A tactful approach might be, "I'd appreciate a recommendation from you if you feel you know my work well enough to recommend me." If there is someone who must serve as a recommender, such as an advisor, about whose opinion of your work you are in doubt, you may want to ask that person to discuss with you frankly the types of institutions for which he or she can enthusiastically support your candidacy.

While you should never take for granted that someone will recommend you with enthusiasm, don't feel you are imposing on faculty by asking them to be recommenders. The success of its students in the job market is one of the ways by which a graduate department is evaluated, and advisors with highly successful students enhance their own reputations. Therefore, when someone can honestly write a strong recommendation for you, it's in that person's interest to do so.

Discuss your plans with those who agree to write for you. Recommendations are most effective when they describe you as well suited to a particular goal. If appropriate, remind the person who will recommend you of your work and experience. Provide him or her with your vita, a copy of a paper you wrote, a dissertation chapter, a statement of your research goals, or anything else that would be helpful.

Phone Calls

Sometimes a search committee, seeking what they feel will be a more candid evaluation, will call one or more of your recommenders. This is particularly likely to be the case when the recommender is known to someone at the hiring institution. Since letters of recommendation are almost uniformly positive, a spontaneous enthusiastic response to a potential employer's phone call is very helpful to you.

On the other hand, if the person who is called is totally surprised that you are applying to the institution that is calling, the call probably does not help your case. Thus, it is very important to keep recommenders apprised of every step of your job search. You can ask them to reassure those who call about any aspects of your candidacy that you believe schools may find problematic. For example, if you are married to someone who is genuinely willing to move to the location where you take a job, your recommender can reinforce your statement that this is true if an employer raises the subject. (While such inquiries on the part of an employer are not legal, they certainly can occur.)

Also be aware that people whose names you have not given as recommenders may be called or e-mailed "off the record" by someone on a
search committee. This is particularly likely to be the case if you've obviously worked closely with someone well known to a person in the hiring
department. So if there's someone with whom you've worked closely whose
name you are not giving as a reference, pay as much attention to that relationship as you do to those with your official recommenders.

Handling Negative Evaluations

Unfortunately, sometimes the difficult situation arises in which someone
who would normally be expected to be supportive of your job search, such
as an advisor, is not. Perhaps he or she is disappointed by the goals you
have set, or believes they are unrealistic. Perhaps he or she genuinely does
not believe you are as strong as other advisees in the past and does not want
to compromise a reputation by giving you a recommendation stronger
than he or she believes you deserve. Perhaps the person is retaliating for
your resistance to some form of harassment. Perhaps you are merely the
victim of hostility generated in another area of the person's life.

Whatever the cause, this situation is always difficult. Most likely you hear
of it from someone else who reports to you what has been said in a letter
or conversation. Perhaps you feel (rightly or wrongly) that, where you
might expect to find support, you are encountering an obstacle. Several
approaches are available to you, none totally risk-free, but all, on balance,
more likely to be productive than is suffering in silence.

Direct Conversation

If you are dealing with a reasonable person who honestly does not think
highly of your abilities, at least in relation to the arena in which you have
chosen to compete, direct conversation may be productive. For example,
you might begin by saying, "I know that you think I'm overreaching in
some of my applications. Could you give me examples of institutions for
which you could honestly be supportive of my candidacy?" It is helpful for
you to remind yourself that no one has an obligation to recommend a candidate against his or her better judgment. Even if the person's assessment
of you is incorrect, he or she does have the right to an opinion.

Advice

If you can find a knowledgeable person of whom to ask advice, it can be
very helpful. In choosing someone in whom to confide, consider that person's judgment, experience, and willingness to keep your communication
confidential. Individuals outside your department may be particularly help-

ful in the latter regard. Counselors in university counseling offices and career centers have a professional obligation to keep conversations confidential. So do campus ombudsmen, affirmative action officers, and staff members of other organizations, such as women's centers, chartered to protect the interests of members of a particular group. However, only personal counselors are legally able to hold reports of sexual harassment in confidence.

While such professionals may make a good sounding board, they are unlikely to know enough about the personalities of people in your department to be able to give you very specific advice. Another faculty member in the department is in the best position to suggest how you may strengthen your position with whoever is obstructing your search or, on occasion, to intervene tactfully. Also consider your dean's office. Frequently, it is structured so that an associate dean is responsible for graduate education. A good associate dean is a great place to start when a student has a real problem with an advisor. He or she will know the personalities of the people in the department and the standards and dynamics of the school, and may be helpful if he or she also has a reputation for keeping conversations in confidence.

Intervention

The best antidote to a negative or lukewarm evaluation is a positive one. Those who strongly support your candidacy can write particularly enthusiastic letters or make phone calls on your behalf. Conceivably they can, if willing, suggest to hiring institutions that one of your key recommenders is misjudging you. However, be extremely careful about an offer to do this on your behalf. Often any attempt to contradict criticism merely strengthens the hiring committee's impression that there must be something behind the controversy.

It is usually safer for your advocates merely to express enthusiasm for your candidacy, leaving employers free to form their own conclusions. Recommendations from those outside your department who know your work can be particularly helpful in this regard, as they obviously represent a different perspective.

University Credentials Services

Your university career center may offer you the valuable opportunity to keep a file of letters of recommendation which you can update easily and which are always immediately available. If it is the policy of your department to write new letters for each job a student applies for, you may want to have at least a backup file with the credentials service. Faculty go on sabbatical, get sick, or become extra busy and are not available to write customized letters for every job.

If you maintain a file of letters of recommendation, federal law gives you the option of maintaining nonconfidential letters to which you may have access. Generally these letters are not considered as credible as confidential ones.

Choosing the Recommendations to Send with an Application

Whatever you place on file, strengthen your presentation for a job by sending recommendations selectively. Even if your file contains many recommendations, don't send them all. Three or four strong letters are usually all you need. You may choose different subsets of recommendations depending upon the job's requirements.

Applicants often wonder if it is wrong to send more letters of recommendation than asked for in a job announcement. Generally speaking, it is advisable to respond only with the materials asked for in the job announcement. However, if you have four letters that you believe give a nuanced portrait of you as a candidate and the job announcement only asked for three, you might send your four letters, nonetheless.

Chapter 8
Learning About Openings

Once you have decided what kinds of jobs to pursue, there are several resources you can use to ensure that you learn about all the opportunities that might interest you.

Scholarly Associations

Every discipline has a scholarly association that serves its members in many ways. The association functions as the recorder and critic of scholarship in the discipline by producing one or more scholarly journals of refereed articles. It normally also holds a conference, usually on an annual basis, where the most recent research in the field is presented. There are many forms of conference presentations. Individual scholars, seasoned Ph.D.s and advanced graduate students, present papers they have prepared for the conference; groups of scholars participate in panel discussions; and individuals or research teams participate in poster sessions or other small group discussions of their work. Such conferences or conventions provide an opportunity for formal and informal communication on research and are crucial for keeping the discipline dynamic.

If you do not know which association is appropriate for your field, ask your advisor and other faculty in your department, check the subject index of the Scholarly Societies Project, www.scholarly-societies.org, or check Appendix 1 of this handbook for selected listings.

Scholarly associations sometimes provide job-related services that may include the following.

Job Listings

Sometimes as part of a journal, but more often as a separate bulletin and on a Web site, most scholarly associations regularly publish a listing of post-doctoral and tenure-track academic job openings. When an academic department has an opening, it is customary to advertise the position in an association job bank, in print or online. The institution pays the association a fee to place the advertisement.

In many cases, the job listings are available to members only. However, most associations offer membership to students at a reduced rate. Sometimes it is possible to subscribe to the job listings separately.

Your department probably receives job listings from the corresponding association and possibly listings from related associations as well. Find out which job opening publications your department subscribes to, and how to access them. Better still, get your own subscription. Also find out whether the listings are available electronically. When there are active electronic discussion lists in a field, jobs are often posted to them as well.

Job Placement

Many scholarly associations provide some kind of job placement program at their annual conventions. This can range from simply making interview rooms available to maintaining files of recent job openings to running formalized placement operations with scheduled interviews for employers and candidates. Check with your association to see what kind of placement program it has. Of course, individual institutions also conduct interviews in their rooms or suites during conventions (see Chapter 15, "Off-Site Interviews: Conference/Convention and Telephone Interviews").

Resources for Job Hunting

Some associations produce job hunting guides for their members. These can range from a single sheet of interviewing techniques to a well-developed Web page to a published book covering all aspects of the job search in that field. Such guides often cover nonacademic careers as well as academic employment.

Regional Associations

In addition to a regional chapter of your national association, you may find additional relevant local and regional associations. These usually have an annual meeting on a smaller scale and often offer some sort of job placement. Check with your advisor about these.

National and Local Publications

The Chronicle of Higher Education, the national newspaper of higher education, lists faculty openings at all types of institutions across the United States as well as some international ones. Most college and university libraries and campus career centers link to it and some receive it. Its job listings are searchable on the *Chronicle* Web site at www.chronicle.com/jobs at no cost to readers. In the print version, job openings are listed in two ways: an alphabetical listing by job title; and display listings, indexed by subject at the beginning of the section.

The bimonthly *Diverse Issues in Higher Education*, www.diverseeducation .com, is a newsmagazine dedicated exclusively to minority issues in higher education. It has an extensive job listing section in both the print and the online editions.

Never to be used as the sole source of job listings, but useful to those seeking part-time teaching jobs or positions in small two-year colleges, is the local newspaper employment section. Positions in higher education are usually listed under "Education," and mixed in with educational adminis-tration and elementary and secondary teaching. Job seekers looking for community college positions can also go to individual state government Web sites, which often list those positions among other state jobs.

Institutional Web Sites

Increasingly, institutions are posting faculty openings on their own Web sites. While it isn't practical to search every institution in the country regu-larly, if you have a geographic preference or constraint, it may be practical to bookmark every institution in a given radius that posts its faculty open-ings to its Web site and to check these locations regularly. A quick way to find the employment menus of college and university Web sites is to go to *Jobs in Higher Education* at www.academic360.com. The site has links to lists of international institutions and community colleges, as well.

In larger institutions, position announcements are often posted on departmental Web sites. When this occurs, it is usually the case that the position has also been posted elsewhere, such as in a national journal.

Your Network

Faculty in your department receive announcements from colleagues at other schools where there are openings. Keep a high profile in your depart-ment so that they will think of you when they hear about jobs. Know where your department posts jobs and check there regularly.

For temporary non-tenure-track jobs you may make direct inquiries of departments that interest you. This approach works best when you can give department chairs a rationale for your call or e-mail message, such as an interest in a particular kind of school or in schools in a clearly defined geo-graphic area.

Additionally, keep in touch with everyone you know who might hear about openings: for example, former fellow graduate students or former fellow postdocs who have already found jobs, former professors at other institutions, and people you have met at conferences. Let them know when you are beginning your job search and nearing the end of your dissertation. Be sure to thank anyone who notifies you of a job opening even if it doesn't work out or is not a good fit for you.

Part III
Written Materials for the Search: Suggestions and Samples

Chapter 9
Responding to Position Announcements

When you apply for any college or university teaching position, you will be asked to submit a "curriculum vitae," a "vita," or a "c.v." All these terms apply to the same document, which is a summary of your education, experience, publications, and other relevant data. In addition you may be asked for any or all of these: a research statement, a statement of your teaching philosophy, a writing sample which could be a chapter of your dissertation or an entire published research paper, "evidence of successful teaching," and a dissertation abstract. Members of the hiring committee may check your Web site, but a site is not generally required as part of an application. Some community colleges and state universities require that a completed application form accompany your other materials. Check to see whether a standard application is needed.

What is required varies from field to field. Check with your department to make sure that what you are sending is within the conventions of your field. Sometimes you may find that job announcements ask that you "send credentials" or "send dossier." These terms do not have a standard meaning. You can usually assume that what is meant is a cover letter, a vita, and letters of recommendation. Sometimes a list of coursework or an official transcript is also required. Be guided by your department's advice about what is usual in your field. Probably the only way to be absolutely certain about what is desired by a given department that has used a vague phrase in its ad is to call and ask.

Sometimes application is a two-stage process, in which applicants initially send minimal information and some are further selected to send more detailed materials, such as a dissertation chapter or letters of recommendation. Use discretion in sending supporting materials that have not been requested. If you do, explain in your cover letter why you have done so.

Chapter 10
Vitas

Whether or not it is accompanied by letters of recommendation, your vita is always the first thing you will send to a hiring institution, whether it is called a "vita," a "c.v.," a "curriculum vitae," or, occasionally, a "resume." In preparing it, your goal is to create enough interest in your candidacy that you will be granted a personal interview. Design your vita so that your strongest qualifications stand out if an employer skims it for only a few seconds, and with enough supporting detail so that it will stand up to scrutiny during a thorough reading.

Getting Started

Before beginning to write your vita, review your educational and professional history. Using the categories suggested below, list everything you imagine could possibly be included. Eventually you will decide what to include or exclude, but begin by ensuring that you are not overlooking anything relevant. Write a draft, experiment with the format, eliminate irrelevant information, have the vita critiqued, and make at least one more draft before you send it to any institution. Your vita will continue to evolve both as you target different types of institutions and as you move forward in your career and add credentials.

Organization and Content

A vita always includes your name and contact information and information about your education, professional experience, publications, presentations, and honors. It may also include professional, extracurricular, and community activities; professional memberships; foreign languages; research interests; teaching competencies; grants; and selected personal data. Your name and information about how to contact you should appear at the top of the first page. If you are completing a Ph.D., the first section will be "Education." If you are applying from a postdoc or current faculty position, you may put your experience first. Follow with categories in decreasing order of importance. One exception is publications; if you have a long list, convention usually places it at the end of your vita. Within each category, give information in reverse chronological order, from most recent backward. Be concise; use phrases rather than complete sentences.

Name

On the first page, list your full name at the top, separate from other information. Consider putting your name in a slightly larger font. After the first page, list your last name and a page number at the top or bottom of every page. If your name has recently changed and you have scholarly accomplishments in your older name, the clearest way to acknowledge this is to include your previous name on the vita: for example, Jane E. (Doe) Smith.

Contact Information

Include both home and office addresses, e-mail, phone and fax numbers, and URL, if you have one. Use only phone numbers at which you are sure that messages will be delivered reliably. If you will be available at a number or address before or after a specific date, say so.

Objective

A vita for a faculty or postdoctoral position, in contrast to a resume for a nonacademic position, typically does not include an "Objective," or statement of the type of position you want. A possible exception is the unusual situation in which your goals are very different from what most employers would imagine from your vita.

Education

Discuss your graduate and undergraduate work in detail. List each institution, degree, field of concentration, and date at which a degree was received. Search committees want to know when your dissertation will be finished, so indicate the anticipated date of completion. If you are just beginning your dissertation and are preparing a vita for a fellowship or part-time position, you may want to include a date for the latest formal stage of graduate work you have completed ("Coursework completed, May 2007"; "Passed examinations with distinction, May 2008"; or whatever formal marker of progress your program may have).

Always include the title of your dissertation and the name of your advisor. You may include the names of committee members if you think their inclusion will be helpful to you. You may also list additional research projects or additional areas of concentration. You may include activities related to your graduate training, for example, "President, Graduate Chemistry Society." If you have been very active in graduate student government, you may wish to create a separate section entitled "Committees" or "University Service," which would appear after listings of more relevant academic detail. You may include relevant undergraduate activities but do not go into detail about them. Omit high school. If you want to include it in case alumni will recognize it, mention it briefly in a personal section at the end.

Honors

Whether you make this a separate section or a category under "Education" depends on how important honors are in your qualifications. If you have received several prestigious and highly competitive awards, for example, you may highlight them in a separate section. On the other hand, if you have few honors, you probably do not want to call attention to that fact by creating a category with only one unimpressive entry.

If you are applying for jobs in the United States, commonly known academic honors such as Phi Beta Kappa need no explanation. International scholars applying in the U.S. may want to stress the degree to which an unfamiliar award was competitive (for example, "one of three selected from among 2,000 graduating chemists nationally"). Likewise, those trained at American institutions who are applying to institutions abroad should briefly explain the honors they have earned. For example, Phi Beta Kappa may sound like a social fraternity to academics outside the U.S. who are unfamiliar with the idea of fraternities as intellectual organizations.

Experience

In this section, include all the experience that you now view as relevant to your professional objectives. For each position you have held, include the name of the institution with which you were associated, your responsibilities and accomplishments, dates, and, in most cases, your position title. Pick a format that you plan to use consistently. List positions or employers first in each entry depending on which format, on balance, shows you to best advantage. Sometimes a general heading of "Experience" will be appropriate, but frequently you will want to subdivide the section. A common division is "Teaching Experience" and "Research Experience."

Describe each item to give the reader an overview of what you did, together with details about the most interesting or impressive aspects of your position. Stress what you accomplished and uniquely contributed. Use verb phrases and make every word count. Thus, "Responsibilities included developing various new course materials and instructional aids" becomes "Developed syllabus and diagnostic exam later adopted by department."

If you are describing a research project, give a brief introductory statement indicating what you set out to accomplish and what results you obtained. This is not, however, the place for a complete dissertation abstract.

Professional Experience

If you are applying for a position in a professional school and have experience working in that profession, describe it in some detail. If your professional experience is not related to your current scholarly pursuits, include it, but condense it drastically.

Licensure/Registration/Certification

List these credentials for positions in professional schools in fields where they are required, for example, nursing, education, architecture.

Publications/Presentations

Although these are of extreme importance for an academic position, convention usually places them last once they have grown beyond a few entries. They are listed in standard bibliographic form for your field. If you have a very long list, they may be subcategorized by topic or by publication format. Subcategorizing by topic is a good way to call attention to areas of expertise which may not be readily apparent. While it is acceptable to list articles as "submitted," or "in preparation," too many citations of this form not balanced by articles that are either published or in press can strike a pathetic note.

Be aware of prestige hierarchies, and don't dilute the credibility of presentations at established scholarly societies or articles in refereed journals by including term papers or publications in popular journals or newspapers. Separate refereed articles from everything else. Dissertations are not usually considered publications unless they are subsequently published in a journal or as a book by a recognized publisher. Don't pad your publications list, and don't include in it anything you would not want a hiring committee to read.

Grants

If you have received funding, list the funding agency and the project(s) for which it was awarded. Candidates frequently list dollar amounts for major funded research projects. Usually you would list fellowship or dissertation support with "Honors." Occasionally a grant will appear in two sections of the vita. It may be listed briefly in this section and the work it supported discussed in detail under "Experience."

Scholarly and Professional Memberships/Leadership

List memberships or committee work in scholarly or professional organizations. If you have been very active in university committee work, you might also include it here, or perhaps create a separate section to cover it. If you have organized or moderated conference sessions, this would be an appropriate place to say so.

Research Interests

This optional category gives a brief answer to the question: "What are your future research plans?" Interests listed here should be described at a level specific enough to be credible and general enough to indicate the direction your research might take over the next several years. You may also be asked to submit a brief (one or two page) discussion of your future research plans as a separate part of your application. Be prepared to discuss in detail anything that you put in this section.

Teaching Competencies

You may use this optional category if you feel that the areas you are qualified to teach are not entirely obvious from the rest of the entries in your vita. Its listings are more general than "Research Interests." Be careful not to list such a wide range of competencies that your list lacks credibility. If you list a subject as a teaching competency, some other part of the vita should reinforce your qualifications to teach it. Be prepared to discuss your ideas about a syllabus/text for any course you list in this section.

Additional Information

Sometimes called "Personal," this optional section may encompass miscellaneous information that does not fit elsewhere. You may include knowledge of foreign languages (if they are not very important to your research; if they are, you might give them their own section), extensive travel, and interests that you feel are important. If you worked prior to attending graduate school at jobs you now consider irrelevant, you may summarize them with a statement such as "Employment 2002–2004 included office and restaurant work." You need not include date of birth or a statement about your health. We recommend you do not include marital status unless you are sure it will work to your advantage to do so.

If anything in your vita may make an employer question whether you have United States work permission (for example, an undergraduate degree from another country), list U.S. citizenship or permanent residency if you have it. If you do not, either make the most positive statement you can about work eligibility, for example, "Visa status allows 18 months United States work permission," or omit any mention of citizenship.

References

List the names of the people who write letters of recommendation for you, with their titles and institutions. Providing their telephone numbers and e-mail addresses is an added convenience to employers, if your recommenders are prepared for informal inquiries. Complete mailing addresses are not really necessary on the vita, because when written recommendations are required it is almost always your responsibility to see that they arrive. For this reason, the names of references are sometimes omitted on the vita.

Tailoring Your Vita to Its Audience

Your vita should always include basic information, and the information you present should always be true. However, if you are applying for two distinct types of positions, or positions in different types of institutions or departments, you may wish to develop more than one version of your vita. Variations could include choosing headings to emphasize information of particular relevance to a situation (for example, including "Administrative Experience" for positions that involve both teaching and administrative components); giving details about additional areas of concentration more relevant to one field than another; and using different subsets of individuals to recommend you for different types of positions. Differences between versions of your vita are usually subtle, but can be effective nonetheless. Consider different versions if you are in an interdisciplinary field and will apply to more than one type of department.

If you plan to apply for nonacademic positions that are not research based, you will need an entirely different version of your vita, which will be called a "resume." In Chapter 23 we have included a few examples of resumes prepared by Ph.D.s pursuing nonacademic positions. For more discussion and examples, see the excellent *"So What Are You Going to Do with That?": Finding Careers Outside Academia*, by Susan Basalla May and Maggie Debelius. For scientists, *Put Your Science to Work: The Take-Charge Guide for Scientists*, by Peter S. Fiske, is a good additional source. *The Chronicle of Higher Education*, www.chronicle.com, and *Science*Careers, www.scienceca reers.org both have excellent content about nonacademic careers.

Experienced Candidates

If you are several years past your first academic position, your vita will be longer than that of a new Ph.D. Its general appearance and construction, however, will be similar. Generally you will omit details about earlier experience, while retaining mention of the experience itself. For example, your first vita may have given detail about what you did as a teaching assistant. Now you may merely list the position, without discussion of responsibilities. Your education will probably remain on the first page, although the amount of detail you provide about it may diminish.

If entries in some of the categories in your vita are growing numerous, you may begin to introduce subdivisions. For example, publications may be divided among books, papers, and reviews. Your listings of professional associations may begin to include discussions of conference sessions that you moderated or organized.

Length

How long a vita may be varies from field to field. Check with your department. In any case, be as concise as possible. Some graduate students will be able to manage with not more than two pages, including publications. Naturally, the vitas of more experienced candidates will be longer.

Layout and Reproduction

Remember that you are designing your vita to capture your readers' attention at a first glance. Therefore pay attention to where you put information and how you format it. Organize the first page so that it contains the information about your greatest assets. That way the reader will be motivated to turn the page! Longer entries will call more attention to themselves than will shorter ones. Material near the top of the page will stand out more than that at the bottom. The left-hand column usually gets the greatest visual emphasis, so don't waste it on dates. Put dates on the right-hand margin, and use the left-hand margin for content items, such as names of institutions. Bullets can be useful for organizing descriptive information within entries. However, because this is a formatting technique often used in resumes you should be judicious in your use of bullets.

Take advantage of bold type for emphasis and establish a consistent graphic hierarchy so that typeface for equivalent categories of information is the same. An example of one typical hierarchy appears below.

HEADING (for example, **EXPERIENCE**)
Important Item (for example, **University of Excellence**)
Less Important Item (for example, *Teaching Assistant*)

Use one, or, at the most, two conservative fonts. Fonts smaller than 10 point are very difficult to read. Given the availability of bold and italic type, there's no need to clutter the page with underlining. Avoid the graphic dizziness caused by introducing too many kinds of type or indentations.

Proofread your vita again and again. Typographical or spelling errors can cause you to be dropped from consideration. To be doubly sure, ask a friend who is a good proofreader to read the draft also. Print it on office-quality paper (and, of course, single-sided). Generate multiple copies on a high-quality printer or have copies made by a printing service. Paper may be white, cream, or any other very conservative tint. Do not staple pages together, and make sure your name and a page number appear on each page.

Although electronic submission is the norm in most work domains, the preference in academe seems to be for paper materials. If you are asked to submit your job hunting materials electronically, you should send them to yourself or a friend to make sure that your formatting stays in place. To maintain your formatting, avoid tables and templates, and use headers and/or footers for name and page numbers. If you're asked to cut and paste parts of your vita into an online application form, avoid using tabs and bullet points. With all job descriptions, it's important to submit your materials in the manner requested.

Help

Because a vita is often the first thing an employer sees of you, it is too important a document not to be thoroughly critiqued and revised. Show it to your advisor and others in your department. See whether your university career office has counselors who work with graduate students or postdocs and who are able to provide critiques and help you get your first draft together. To give your vita a good final test, show it briefly to someone who has not seen it and ask that person what he or she notices and remembers. If the most important items stand out, you're in good shape. Otherwise, more revision is in order.

A Note About the Sample Vitas That Follow

The following examples, generously volunteered by real candidates, are provided to give you an idea of what such materials look like. The names of job candidates, their advisors, committee members, and coauthors have been changed. Some dates have also been changed. The name of a candidate's most recent institution has been changed to something like University of X, University of State, X University, or some similar name. Other than that we have tried to alter these vitas as little as possible. In order to save space, some of the lists of presentations, publications, honors and awards, activities, and so on, have been truncated. If a section has been shortened there will be a note in brackets e.g., [Two additional presentations follow.]. The examples are arranged by broad field: humanities, social sciences, science, engineering, and professional disciplines. Professional disciplines include fields where professional practice as well as research and teaching are an intrinsic part. If the applicant has accepted a position, brief information about the type of institution is also provided.

These examples should be regarded as excellent, but not necessarily perfect. They are not all in the same format, and they do not all subscribe to the same stylistic conventions, so you can see there are many ways to construct a good vita. The custom in your own field, or an unusual combination of strengths in your background, might well dictate that your vita should be quite different in style, language, or appearance. Don't attempt to copy any single example. Rather, look at all of them to see which forms of presentation might suit your own taste or situation.

Sample Humanities Vita
Accepted position at a mid-sized private university

Anita Scholar

Department of Spanish
University of X
City, State, Zip code
Department phone
Fax
Email

Home Address
City, State, Zip code
Home phone
Cell phone

Education

Ph.D. in Hispanic Studies, University of X
August 2005 (expected)

Thesis: "Affect and the Critique of Market Culture in Latin American Literature and Film"

Advisor: Name

Representations of individual subjectivity in Latin American literature and film from the past decade correlate the progressive erosion of the traditional thinking self with an increasingly global capitalist market culture. Novels and films by César Aira (Argentina), Fernando Pérez (Cuba), Diamela Eltit (Chile), Alejandro González Iñárritu (Mexico), and Rodrigo Bellott (Bolivia) share a common insistence on emotion, affect, and sensory perception (rather than on an autonomy of intellect) as the defining element of human subjectivity. Set against the backdrop of market culture, these works emphasize the experience of a predominantly affective self as their primary narrative vehicle, and suggest that the native capacity for emotion is the human subject's last line of defense against the encroachment of dehumanizing market forces.

Ph.D. coursework, Y University
September 1998-May 2000

B.A. in Spanish Language and Literature, *magna cum laude*, Columbia University
February 1996

Honors and Fellowships

American Association of University Women Educational Foundation American Dissertation Fellowship, 2004-2005
Humanities Forum Dissertation Fellow, 2003-2004
 • participation in weekly Mellon Research Seminar on "Belief"
 • coordination of Graduate Humanities Forum seminar series and conference
 • design and direction of pilot graduate-undergraduate mentorship program
Dean's Scholar, School of Arts and Sciences, University of X, 2003
Department of Spanish Summer Travel Grant, 2003 (Cuba)
High honors, Ph.D. Comprehensive Examination, University of X, 2002
Benjamin Franklin Fellowship, University of X, 2000-2003
Phi Beta Kappa

Articles

"*Lumpérica*: el *ars teorica* de Diamela Eltit." *Revista Iberoamericana* 71 (April-June 2005).

Translations	Arrufat, Antón. "Learning to Sleep." Forthcoming in *New Laurel Review*.
	Bartra, Roger. "Allegories of Creativity and Territory." *PMLA* 118.1 (January 2003): 114-9.
Papers Delivered	"Deconstructing Castro." (20th-Century Latin American Literature Division Panel: "Cuba in the Postmillenial Imagination.") Modern Language Association Convention, December 2004. [Two additional papers follow.]
Other Professional Experience	Graduate commentator: Fernando Coronil, "Colonial or Imperial Studies? Rethinking Imperialism from the Americas," Ethnohistory Workshop, University of X, November 2003.
	Assistant Director, University of X Hispanic Studies Summer Graduate Program, Havana, Cuba, June-July 2004.
Teaching Experience	University of X

Course Coordination

- Spanish 219: "Contextos de la civilización hispánica," Fall 2002
  Seventh-semester bridge course on the cultural history of Spain and Latin America. Coordinated 11 sections of the course (10 instructors; 114 students) during its second semester of implementation: prepared instructor manuals; directed instructors through weekly meetings; developed and maintained course materials; prepared all examination materials.

Course Instruction in Spanish (full responsibility for courses taught)

- Spanish 219: " Contextos de la civilización hispánica," Spring 2002
  Taught this course during its pilot semester; developed course materials with a team of instructors (3 faculty, 3 lecturers, 3 graduate students)--wrote historical summaries and selected accompanying primary source readings for two of thirteen study units; performed intensive evaluation of students' writing (twelve short papers and a final 8-10 page research paper) with the aim of developing their critical reading and writing skills in Spanish.

- Spanish 140: Intermediate II, Spring 2001
- Spanish 130: Intermediate I, Fall 2000

Y University

- Spanish 101: Beginning I, Fall 1999
- Spanish 202: Intermediate II, Spring 2000

Pedagogical Training	Certificate in Educational Technology and Language Instruction, Center for Educational Technology, Middlebury, VT, 2001
	ACTFL Oral Proficiency Interview training, University of X, 2000

Teaching and Research Interests	20th- and 21st-century Latin American literature and film Discursive formations/formulations of cultural identity Literary theory Role of the intellectual in the socio-political sphere Representations of the subject from modernity to globalization
Languages	Near-native fluency in Spanish Reading proficiency in French, Latin, Catalan
Technology	Dreamweaver, Photoshop, Blackboard, iMovie, video digitization
Membership in Professional Organizations	Latin American Studies Association Modern Language Association
Service (University of X)	Advisor, University Council Subcommittee (on staff involvement in the presidential search process), 2004-2005 Ivy Graduate Leadership Summit Lead Programming and Logistics Coordinator, 2004 [Six additional service activities follow.]
References (University of X)	[The names of four references are included.]

Sample Humanities Vita
Conducting a geographically limited search; applying to many types of institutions

NATHANIEL SCHOLAR

Department of English
University of State
City, State, Zip code
Phone number
Email

Address
City, State, Zip code
Phone number

EDUCATION

- **Ph.D, English, University of State, 2004**
  Dissertation: "Dark Wanderers: Gypsies in Nineteenth-Century British Poetry"
  Co-Directors: Name and Name
  Readers: Name, Name, Name

- **M.A., English, X University, 1995**

- **B.A., English, Furman University, 1992**

Other study:

- **Y College, Oxford University, Associate Member / Visiting Post-Graduate, 2003** (art history, nineteenth-century social history)

RESEARCH & TEACHING INTERESTS

- British Romantic Literature & Culture

- Victorian Literature & Culture

- Nineteenth-Century Britain & Exotic Others

- Nineteenth-Century Britain & Religion

- Literature and Visual Arts & Culture

- Study Abroad & International Education

- Service-Learning & Community Engagement

ACADEMIC POSITIONS

- Instructor, University of State, 2005–present

- Name Teaching Fellow, University of State, 2004–2005

- Research Assistant, 2001–2005 for Dr. Name
  (worked on *Three Vampire Tales: Dracula, Carmilla, and The Vampyre* [Houghton Mifflin, 2002] and "Lewis/Gonnod's Bleeding *Nonne*: An Introduction and Translation of the Scribe/Delavigne Libretto," *Romantic Circles* Praxis Series, May 2005 [URL])

- Graduate Assistant, University of State at Oxford Study Abroad, 2003

- Teaching Assistant, University of State, 1995–2003

Scholar 2

- Teaching Assistant, X University, 1993–1994
- Graduate Assistant, X University, 1992–1993

RESEARCH

Publications

- "Out-Gypsying the Gypsies: From Wordsworth's Intimations to Arnold's Immortality," *Studies in English Literature, 1500–1900* (under review)
- "Gypsies under the Dreaming Spires: The 1837 Newdigate Poetry Prize," *Victorian Studies* (under review)

Conferences

- "Not Wordsworthian Joy, but Arnoldian Resignation: Arnold's Attempt to Escape Time," North American Victorian Studies Association, September/October 2005, Charlottesville, Virginia
- "George Eliot's Annunciation: Titian and *The Spanish Gypsy*," Victorians Institute, April 2005, Greensboro, North Carolina
  [Eight additional conference presentations follow.]

TEACHING

Courses Taught

Teacher of Record unless otherwise indicated

- English 3633: Introduction to Fiction (Fall 2006)
- English 3000: Introduction to English Studies (Fall 2001 with Dr. Name, Spring 2001 with Dr. Name, Spring 2000 with Dr. Name)
- English 2321: English Literature since 1700 (traditional and writing-intensive formats) (Fall 2006, Fall 2005, Spring 2005, Fall 2004, Spring 2003, Fall 2002, Fall 2000, Fall 1997 with Dr. Name, Fall 1996 with Dr. Name)
  [The names of six additional courses follow.]

Other Teaching, Invited Lectures, & Workshops

- U. State Writing Center tutor, 2000–2003
- "Matthew Arnold, the 'Disinterested' Poet?" invited lecture, Victorian Literature (English 4321), March 2002
  [Fourteen additional entries follow.]

ACADEMIC SERVICE

- Scorer, Advanced Placement English Language Exam, 2007

- Student Membership Committee, Phi Kappa Phi Honor Society, University of State Chapter 1, 2006–present
- Rater, State Regents' Examination, 1996–present
[Nine additional entries follow.]

SERVICE-LEARNING

- Partnership for a Prosperous City, Education Attainment Committee, City, State, 2006
  A community-university partnership to address causes of persistent poverty in County, State.
- Service-Learning Interest Group (SLIG), University of State, 2005–present
  A working group of faculty and graduate students that examines issues related to incorporating service-learning into academic courses and develops service-learning curriculum recommendations for the university.

COMPETITIVE AWARDS, GRANTS, & HONORS

- Name Teaching Fellowship, 2004–2005
- Honor Society of Phi Kappa Phi (interdisciplinary honor society), 2004–present
[Seven additional honors follow.]

PROFESSIONAL MEMBERSHIPS

- Midwest Modern Language Association
- Modern Language Association
- Nineteenth-Century Studies Association
- North American Society for the Study of Romanticism
- North American Victorian Studies Association
- South Atlantic Modern Language Association
- Victorians Institute

ACADEMIC WEBSITES DESIGNED & MAINTAINED

- University of State Writing Center
  [URL]
  [Entries for five additional websites follow.]

REFERENCES

[The names and contact information of five references follow.]

Sample Humanities Vita
Accepted a one-year position at a small private Master's institution

Esme Scholar

Department of English
University of X
City, State, Zip Code
E-mail

Address
City, State, Zip Code
Phone number
E-mail

Education

Ph.D.   Department of English, X University, City, State, July 2006
Areas of Specialization: Contemporary and Modern British Literature; Women's Writing and Feminist Theory; Gay, Lesbian, and Transgender Studies; Contemporary and Modern American Literature
Comprehensive Examination Fields: Modern British Literature, American Literature 1865-1945, and Contemporary Literature (Passed, Fall 2003)

M.A.   Department of English, Miami University, Oxford, OH, 2001

B.A.   Department of English, Franklin College, Franklin, IN, 1998
summa cum laude

Dissertation

"A highly ambiguous condition": The Transgender Subject, Experimental Narrative and Trans-Reading Identity in the Fiction of Virginia Woolf, Angela Carter, and Jeanette Winterson
Director: Dr. Name
Committee Members: Dr. Name, Dr. Name, Dr. Name

Teaching Experience

Lecturer, Y University, 2006-2007
- ENGL 213: Wayward Girls and Wicked Women in Contemporary Short Fiction
- INTC 231: Gender, Sexuality and Culture
- WRIT 101: "Dude looks like a lady": Gender and American Popular Culture
- ENGL 341: Feminist Approaches to Literature, with Dr. Name
- WMST 101: Introduction to Women's Studies, with Dr. Name

Literature Instructor, X University, 2001-2005
- ENGL 410: Gay and Lesbian Literature
- ENGL 331: British Literature II
- ENGL 110: Literary Interpretation
[Two additional positions listed.]

Publications

"Trans-gendering and Trans-forming the Subjects of Virginia Woolf's *Orlando* and Jeanette Winterson's *Written on the Body*." Under consideration.

"The lesbian in us": Fashioning Identity in the Love Sequences of Edna St. Vincent Millay's *Fatal Interview* and Adrienne Rich's "Twenty-One Love Poems." Under consideration.

"1895: Oscar Wilde Convicted on Charges of Gross Indecency." *GLBT History*. Ed. Lillian Faderman, Horacio Roque Ramirez, Stuart Timmons, and Eric C. Wat. Pasadena: Salem Press, 2005.

"1998: Prosser Publishes *Second Skins*." *GLBT History*. Ed. Lillian Faderman, Horacio Roque Ramirez, Stuart Timmons, and Eric C. Wat. Pasadena: Salem Press, 2005.

"Cather's *Death Comes for the Archbishop*." *The Explicator* 63.2 (2005): 90-93.
[Three additional publications follow.]

Conference Presentations

"'I would rather be a cyborg than a goddess': The Transgender Cyborg and Embodiment in Angela Carter's *The Passion of New Eve*." Fifth Annual Meeting of the Cultural Studies Association. Portland, OR. April 19-21, 2007.

"Collaborative Technology in the Gay and Lesbian Literature Classroom." 94th Annual Convention of the National Council of Teachers of English. Indianapolis, IN. November 18-21, 2004.
[Six additional conference presentations follow.]

Awards and Honors

Dissertation Completion Fellowship, 2005, X University
Graduate Student Teaching Effectiveness Award, 2005, X University
Teaching Graduate Assistantship Appointment Award, 2002-2005, X University
[Seven additional awards listed.]

University Service

Facilitator, 2007 First Year Experience EXPLORE! Retreat, Y University, 2007
Volunteer, Women's Center, Y University, 2006
Assistant Editor, *The Hilltopper: A Journal of Graduate Student Research*, X University, 2004-2005
Assistant Director, Writing Center, X University, 2003-2004
[Six additional entries follow.]

Departmental Service

Personnel Search Committee, Modern British Literature, X University, 2003-2004
Association of Graduate English Students, X University
  • President, 2002-2003
  • Secretary, 2004-2005
[Four additional entries follow.]

Memberships & Affiliations

Phi Beta Kappa
Center for Lesbian and Gay Studies (CLAGS)
Modern Language Association
[Three additional entries follow.]

References

[The names and contact information of five references follow.]

Sample Humanities Vita
Accepted position at a small public college

Curriculum Vitae

Denise Scholar

Address, City, State, Zip code
Home phone; Department phone; Email

Education:

Ph.D. English Literature, University of X, August 2002
M.A. English Literature, University of X, May 1996
B.A. English Literature and American History, Queens College, CUNY, May 1994

Dissertation:

Invisible Woman: Reading Rape and Sexual Exploitation in African-American Literature
Director: Name
Readers: Name and Name

Invisible Woman examines the sexual politics of African-American literature focusing on the literary image of the "unrapeable" Black woman. I detail the history of this literary image and, moreover, argue that the sexually-exploited Black woman was effectively "invisible" to the Black male scholars who formalized the study of African-American literature in the late 1960s and 70s. I explore the cultural reasons why this particular system of silence developed at this time, and I describe its ramifications on the genre today. Further, I assert that although feminist theory has begun to throw light on the subject, this dissertation offers a critique of the existing scholarship. I examine the double-bind facing many Black female authors – how allegiance to race or gender may result in silence.

Academic Employment:

Lecturer, University of X, City, State, Fall 2002-present
Instructor/Teaching Fellow, University of X, City, State, Fall 1995-Spring 2002
Teaching Assistant, Queens College, CUNY, Flushing, NY, Fall 1992-Spring 1994

Courses Taught:

University of X, City, State
    "Writing Seminar in Literature: Race, Gender, and Power in African-American
        Literature"(Fall 2005-Spring 2006)
    "Writing Seminar: Literature & Film – Adaptations" (Fall 2005-Spring 2006)
    "Encountering the City" (Summer 2005)
    "Take Two: Film Featuring Great Literary Works and Their Film Adaptations"
        (Fall 2004, Spring & Summer 2005 – 3 sections each)
    "Introduction to African American Literature" (Fall 2004, Spring 2005 – 2 sections
        each)

Scholar   2

"Crimes in American Literature" (Fall 2002-Spring 2004 – 4 sections each)
"Witches and the Conjure Woman in American Fiction" (Fall 2002-Spring 2004 –
    4 sections each)
"African-American Writers: A Generation of Change, 1955-1975" (Fall 2001,
    Spring 2002 – 2 sections each)
"African-American Writers: A Generation of Change, 1955-1975" (Fall 2000,
    Spring 2001 – 2 sections each)
[The names of five additional courses follow.]

Courses Assisted:

Queens College, CUNY, Flushing, NY
    English 100, Name, Ph.D., Fall 1992, Fall 1993
    English 101, Name, Ph.D., Spring 1993, Spring 1994

Teaching Interests and Experience:

• 19th and 20th century African-American literature
• Constructions of femininity and motherhood in African-American literature and culture
• American History: Episodes of Racism and Sexism in the Courts from 1855 to Present
• 19th and 20th century American literature
• Constructions of femininity and motherhood in American literature and culture
• Black Atlantic literature and culture
• 18th and 19th century British novel
• Constructions of femininity and motherhood in the British novel
• Women's texts and feminist theory
• Folklore and literature
• World history, specifically the Holocaust, the Irish potato famine, the "Comfort
    Women" of the Korean War, the enslavement of Africans, and South African apartheid

Honors, Awards, and Fellowships:

Teaching Fellowship, University of X, City, State, 2000-2002
Mellon Dissertation Fellowship, University of X, City, State, 1999-2000
Teaching Fellowship, University of X, City, State, 1998-1999
Fontaine Fellowship, University of X, City, State, 1997-1998
[Ten additional honors follow.]

Publications:

"Confronting the Myth of the 'Unrapeable' Black Woman in Harriet Jacobs' *Incidents in
    the Life of a Slave Girl*." (under review)
"Slavery's Exploitation and Silence: Re-Reading Rape and Resistance in Toni Morrison's
    Beloved." (under review)

Works in Progress:

"A Voice of Her Own: The Depiction of the Mother in African-American Fiction."
"Motherhood Identities: Feminism, Motherhood, & Possibilities in the Writings of
 Octavia Butler."

Papers and Presentations: (*means item was refereed)

*"Rape and the Inward Journey: A Look at Black on Black Rape in Toni Morrison's *The
 Bluest Eye*, and the Movement from Victim to Self," presented on a panel titled
 "Women and Literature"; *Women and Conflict: Third Annual Women's Studies
 Conference*, Temple University, Philadelphia, PA, April 2004.
*"Slavery's Exploitation and Silence: Rape and Resistance in Harriet Jacobs' *Incidents in
 the Life of a Slave Girl* and Toni Morrison's *Beloved*," presented on a panel titled
 "Ambiguity in the Western Tradition"; *First International Humanities Conference*,
 Temple University, Philadelphia, PA, October 2003
"My Soul Looks Back and Wonders: How my MMUF Brought ME Over," presented on
 a panel titled "How Did My Mellon Minority Undergraduate Fellowship Help
 Me?"; Mellon Minority Undergraduate Fellowship's Tenth Anniversary
 Celebration Conference, Queens College, CUNY, Flushing, NY, March 1999
[Three additional papers/publications follow.]

Committee and Service Work:

University of X Critical Writing Steering Committee on Basic Writing, 2005
3808 Journal (City: University of X Press), Reviewer, 2004 to present
University of X Knitters: Member, 2002 to present
Civil Air Patrol: Major, Aerospace Education Officer, 1999 to present
[Five additional service roles follow.]

Professional Associations:

College Language Association
Modern Language Association
National Association of Black Women Scholars

Languages:

Spanish
French

References:
[The names and contact information of five references follow.]

Sample Humanities Vita
Accepted a one-year position at a mid-size private graduate institution

Natalya V. Scholar
Address
City, State, Zip code
Email
Phone number

Education
University of State, City, State
> Ph.D., Department of Near Eastern Studies, December 2006
>> Dissertation title: *The Written Representations of a Central Asian Sufi Shaykh: Ahmad ibn Mawlana Jalal al-Din Khwajagi Kasani "Makhdum-i A'Zam (d. 1542)*
>> Research Fields: Central Asian Sufism, Central Asian History (especially medieval-early modern), Gender in the Islamic World, Persianate literature
> A.M., Modern Middle Eastern and North African Studies, 1996
> A.M., Russian and East European Studies, 1996
>> Thesis: Identity in Nineteenth Century Turkestan: The Sarts
State University, City, State, summer 1994, 1996-1998
> Department of Central Eurasian Studies: Central Eurasian History, Central Eurasian Sufi orders with Name and Prof. Name
Temple University, Philadelphia, PA
> B.A., *summa cum laude*, 1993. 3.8 GPA, President's Scholar, Phi Beta Kappa, Phi Theta Omega
> Major: History. Foci: Middle Eastern, Russian and Soviet history
Middlebury College, Middlebury, VT
> Summer Russian program, 1987, 1988

Honors and Awards
Outstanding Graduate Student Instructor, Q School of Graduate Studies, University of State, 2005. One of 12 awards out of over 3000 graduate student instructors.
State Teaching Fellow, Center for Learning and Teaching, University of State, 2002.

Scholarships and Fellowships
U.S. Department of Education, Fulbright-Hays Doctoral Dissertation Research Abroad Fellowship, Tashkent, Uzbekistan, July 2000-December 2001.
International Research and Exchanges Board (IREX) Individual Advanced Research Opportunities grant, Sharqshunoslik instituti, Tashkent, Uzbekistan, September 2000-May 2001.
University of State, Department of Near Eastern Studies, Smith Memorial Fellowship, Fall 1998, Fall 1999.
[Five additional scholarships and fellowships follow.]

Teaching Experience
X College (one-year visiting position)
> History 175: Islamic Civilization and the Middle East, 600-1500, Fall 2006
> History 377: Gendered Representations in Middle Eastern History, Fall 2006
> History 176: Islamic Civilization and the Middle East since 1500, Spring 2007
> History 371: Central Eurasia Since the Tenth Century, Spring 2007

Scholar   Page 2

      History 478: Traveling East and West: A Historical Understanding of Islamic and
          European Travel Reports, Spring 2007
University of State
      Department of Near Eastern Studies, Fall Term 2004, Fall Term 2005. "World Religions:
          Judaism, Christianity, Islam." Head Graduate Student Instructor for Professors
          Name, Name and Name (F04) and Professors Name, Name and Name (F05).
          Coordinated professors, 6 graduate students and up to 575 students. Designed and
          maintained Ctools-based course web site. Taught 3 sections per term of up to 35
          students each. Graded Honors section taught by Prof. Name F04.
      [Three additional courses follow.]
State University
      Center for the Study of Global Change, Summer 1998. English as a Foreign Language to
          Russian high school students from Siberia. Responsible for design and preparation
          of language preparation materials in order to improve the students' English enough
          to participate with American HS students.
Tashkent State Economic Institute, Tashkent, Uzbekistan, Summer 1997. English as a Foreign
      Language. Taught beginning/intermediate English 4-6 hours per day, 5 days a week as
      part of an academic summer camp for students in Uzbekistan.

Presentations

"Is Silence Golden? Ecstasy and Sobriety, Singing and Meditation in the Dispute over Authority
      and Group Identities in Early Modern Islamic Mysticism," Z College Department of
      History, March 28, 2006.
[Citations for twelve additional presentations follow.]

Publications

Polishing the Mirror: A Teaching Unit on Central and Inner Asia. With Name. Ann Arbor: Center
      for Middle Eastern and North African Studies, July 2000. (Curriculum unit, approx. 350
      pages, with slides and exercises.)
[Citations for nine additional publications follow.]

Work Experience (excludes teaching)

Department of Near Eastern Studies, City, State
      Graduate Research Assistant
      Winter Term 2002, Summer 2002, Fall Term 2002, Fall Term 2003, Winter Term 2004,
          Spring/Summer 2004. Prepared bibliographies, edited text as assigned by Prof.
          Name. Helped to provide Central Eurasian content in a variety of classroom
          contexts.
      Technical Assistant
      Winter Term 2004. Assisted faculty in AAPTIS 492 (Cartography) to implement
          Coursetool-New Generation web site. Scanned and uploaded materials (text and
          graphics) as needed.
[Twelve additional entries follow.]

Scholar   Page 3

Skills
<u>Languages</u>
Foreign: Russian (speak & read), French (speak & read); three years of Uzbek; four years of Persian (Modern and Classical); two years of Turkish; two terms of Chaghatay; reading knowledge of German.
　　　　Some knowledge of Italian, Spanish, Latin.
Computer: HTML, TUTOR, MicroTUTOR, BASIC, C.
Other:　Proficient in grade 1 Braille, some knowledge of grade 2 Braille.

<u>Computer</u>
Software packages:
　　　　Expert level user of a wide variety of word-processing programs (Word, NisusWriter,
　　　　　　WordPerfect) and spreadsheet/database programs on a variety of platforms and
　　　　　　operating systems.
　　　　Excellent knowledge of Photoshop and Acrobat on a variety of platforms.
　　　　Working knowledge of Powerpoint and a variety of web-page creation software
　　　　　　packages.

Community Service
Michigan Mentorships, Summer 2003, Summer 2004 (working with gifted area high school
　　　　student to develop knowledge about the Middle East).
[Sixteen additional entries follow.]

Affiliations
Phi Beta Kappa
Association for Central Eurasian Studies
Society for Iranian Studies
American Academy of Religion
Middle East Medievalists
North American Association for the Study of Religion
American Historical Association
Council on Undergraduate Research

Sample Humanities Vita
Accepted position at a mid-sized private university

Vijay Candidate

Department of History
University of X
Address
City, State, Zip code

Address
Apartment
City, State, Zip code
Home phone
email@institution.edu

EDUCATION

University of X, City, State
Ph.D., History, August 2005 (expected)
South Asian History
Dissertation: Discourse on Population in India, 1870-1960
Advisor: Dr. Name
Committee Members: Dr. Name, Dr. Name

Jawaharlal Nehru University, New Delhi, India
M.A., History, 1998, Modern India

Delhi School of Economics, University of Delhi, Delhi, India
M.A., Economics, 1996

Government Arts College, University of Kerala, Thiruvananthapuram, India
B.A., Economics, 1993

AREAS OF SPECIALIZATION

South Asia
Imperialism
Comparative Development with emphasis on demography and environment
World History

HONORS AND AWARDS

Annenberg Fellow, University of X, 2003-2004, 2004-2005
Junior Research Fellowship, American Institute of Indian Studies, 2002-2003
Junior Research Fellowship, University Grants Commission, India, 1998-1999
Outstanding Student Award for Highest Grade Point Average in M.A., School of Social
Sciences, Jawaharlal Nehru University, New Delhi, India, 1998
University Merit Scholarship, University of Kerala, Thiruvananthapuram, India, 1991,
1992

Vijay Candidate, 2

TEACHING EXPERIENCE

Graduate Student Instructor
University of X, Department of History
China in the 20th Century, with Dr. Name, Spring 2002
America and the World Columbus Made c1400-1700, with Dr. Name, Fall 2001
China in the 20th Century, with Dr. Name, Spring 2001
Africa since 1800 with Dr. Name, Fall 2000
World at War with Dr. Name, Spring 2000
Gandhi's India with Dr. Name, Fall 1999

University of X Writing Program Instructor
University of X, Department of History
India before Modernity with Dr. Name, Spring 2002
Africa since 1800 with Dr. Name, Fall 2000
Gandhi's India with Dr. Name, Fall 1999

PUBLICATIONS

Book Review. Rudrangshu Mukherjee and Lakshmi Subramanian Eds. *Politics and Trade in the Indian Ocean World: Essays in Honour of Ashin Das Gupta*, Om Prakash and Denys Lombard Eds. *Commerce and Culture in the Bay Of Bengal, 1500-1800*, *Biblio* Vol. IV Nos. 7 & 8, July-August 1999
Book Review. Dharma Kumar. *Colonialism, Property and the State*, *Biblio*, Vol. III, Nos.7 & 8, July-August 1998

ADDITIONAL INFORMATION

Fluent in Malayalam, Hindi, Bengali, French.

REFERENCES
[The names and contact information of three references follow.]

Sample Social Science Vita
Accepted position at a large public research university

SOFIA SMITH APPLICANT

Address   Phone number /Fax; Cell phone number
City, State, Zip code   Email

RESEARCH AND TEACHING INTERESTS

Sociology of education; education reform; social research methods; social stratification; sociology of development; sociology of organizations; social interactions

EDUCATION

University of X, Sociology Department and Graduate School of Education
PhD, Joint degree in Sociology and Education, expected graduation May 2006
- Dissertation: "Institutionalizing Educational Ideologies: Curriculum Reform and the Transformation of Teaching Practices in Rural Northwest China"
- Committee: Name (Chair)   Sociology
            Name   Graduate School of Education/Sociology
            Name   Graduate School of Education/Anthropology
            Name   Graduate School of Education
- Fields: sociology of education; sociology of organizations; teaching, learning and curriculum
- Chinese language and area studies
- American Council on the Teaching of Foreign Languages Certificate of Oral Mandarin Proficiency—Superior, January 2005.

Y International University, City, Country and University of X
MA, Education and Sociology, 2003
- Thesis: "Who will teach the poor and remote? Teacher distribution and job satisfaction in rural China."

University of California, Santa Barbara
BA, Biological Sciences, 1992
- Phi Beta Kappa, graduation with highest honors, College Honors Program
- Chinese language and area studies

COURSES TAUGHT

Sociology Department, University of X, Summer 2005
SOCI 100 Introduction to Social Research

PUBLICATIONS

Applicant, Sofia Smith, & Name (2005). Keeping Teachers Happy: Job Satisfaction among Primary School Teachers in Rural Northwest China. *Comparative Education Review, 50*(2).
[Citations for one published article and one article under review follow.]

INTERNATIONAL CONSULTING

Basic Education in Western Areas Project, Yunnan and Guangxi, China, World Bank and UK Department for International Development
Consultant, October 2005

Sofia Smith Applicant, Page 2

- Assessment of success in achieving the project goals of the strategy for ethnic minority education and the project goals for teacher training

RESEARCH EXPERIENCE

Poverty, Parental Health and Children's Schooling in Indonesia, India and China, UNESCO
Consulting team member, January 2005-present
- Statistical analysis of data from the Indonesian Family Life Survey; the Indian Living Standards Measurement Study; and the Gansu Survey of Children and Families

Gansu Survey of Children and Families, funded by the World Bank and U.S. National Institute of Health
Project team member, June 2002-present
- Coordinator for the design and development of the teacher and principal survey questionnaires
- Training of survey interviewers and supervision of data collection in the field
- Qualitative data collection and analysis
- "China Human Capital Projects at University of X" website design and maintenance.
- Translation of documents from Chinese into English
[Three additional experiences follow.]

PRESENTATIONS

Applicant, Sofia S. *Revolutionizing Ritual Interaction in the Classroom—Constructing the Chinese Renaissance of the 21st Century.* Paper to be presented at the Eastern Sociological Society annual meeting, Boston, MA (February 2006).
[Citations for nine additional presentations follow.]

TEACHING EXPERIENCE IN CHINA

ESL and Western Culture teaching experience at university, high school, primary and kindergarten levels as well as adult education in China and Macau
- Xinhua Primary School, Macau (1997-1999)
- School of the Nations, Macau (1996-1998)
- Shanxi Agricultural University, Shanxi, P. R. China (1995-1996)
- Shanxi Teacher's University, Shanxi, P. R. China (1993-1995)

WORKS IN PROGRESS

Name, Name & Sofia Applicant. The Mediating Effect of Educational Engagement on Student Academic Achievement in Rural Northwest China (for submission to *Comparative Education Review*).
[Citations for four additional works in progress follow.]

WORKSHOPS CONDUCTED

Northwest Normal University, Lanzhou, Gansu, P.R. China
Workshop on Qualitative Research Methods, September 2004

University of X, City, State
Workshops on the use of N4 Qualitative Data Analysis Software, March 2001, October 2001 and April 2003

Sofia Smith Applicant, Page 3

FELLOWSHIPS AND AWARDS

- National Security Education Program David L. Boren Graduate Fellowship for dissertation research in Gansu, China, 2004

[Three additional awards follow.]

DATA ANALYSIS COMPUTER SKILLS

- **Quantitative**: Stata, SPSS and SAS
- **Qualitative**: NUD*IST, NVIVO and Qualrus.

PROFESSIONAL ACTIVITIES AND SERVICE

- Co-founder Comparative and International Education Forum, University of X, Graduate School of Education, 2002-present
- Student Organizations Committee, University of X, Graduate School of Education, 2000-2003
- Reviewer for *Comparative Education Review*
- American Sociological Association—Sociology of Education Section, Asia and Asian America Section
- Comparative and International Education Society
- American Educational Research Association (reviewer for annual meeting 2006)

REFERENCES

[The names and contact information of five references follow.]

Sample Social Science Vita
Accepted position at a large public research university

Dora Alicia Scholar

Department, Institution   Phone number
Address   Fax
City, State, Zip code   E-mail

EDUCATION

Ph.D. in Demography, University of X, expected Summer 2005
      Master of Arts in Demography, 2001
Master in Public Policy, Y University, 2000
Bachelor in Arts with Honors in Economics, Instituto Tecnológico Autónomo de
      México (ITAM), Mexico City, 1996

DISSERTATION

Internal Displacement to Urban Areas: A Case Study in Bogotá, Colombia
Prof. Name, Prof. Name, Prof. Name

AREAS OF SPECIALIZATION

Forced Migration
International Migration from Latin America to North America and Europe
Migration Theory and Remittance Use
Quantitative Research Methods in the Social Sciences

OTHER TEACHING AND RESEARCH INTERESTS

Survey Research Design
Demographic Methods
Economic Development and Poverty Reduction in Urban Areas
Population Aging in Latin America

AWARDS AND FELLOWSHIPS

Graduate Fellowship 2000-2004, University of X, Population Studies Center
Research Fellowship 2003-2004, Population Reference Bureau, Program in Population
      Policy Communication
Graduate Fellowship 2000-2003, National Council of Science and Technology, Mexico
Graduate Fellowship 1998-2000, Y University, Y Public Policy Institute
Graduate Fellowship 1998-2000, Institute of International Education, Mexico
Graduate Fellowship 1998-2000, Banco de México (Central Bank), Mexico

RESEARCH GRANTS

Doctoral Dissertation Grant 2004-2005, Population Studies Center-Mellon Foundation,
      University of X
Research Grant 2002-2003, Population Studies Center-Mellon Foundation, University of X

RESEARCH EXPERIENCE

Principal Investigator (Consultant)
      International Organization for Migration, Colombia Mission
            Colombian International Migration and Remittances Study
            The study includes collection of qualitative and quantitative data at the local and
            national level.

The study is carried out in collaboration with UNFPA, National Department of
Statistics, Ministry of Foreign Affairs, Universities and NGOs.
Methodological and operational design of the study
Interpretation and evaluation

Principal Investigator
　Population Studies Center-Mellon Foundation, University of X
　　Colombian Survey of Forced Migration
　　Methodological and operational design of the household survey to study internal
　　displacement in three selected sites in the city of Bogotá (Colombia)
　　Collection of secondary data

Research Assistant
　University of X, Population Studies Center
　　Latin American Migration Project
　　　Data programming
　　　Research activities
　　　Participation in international conference (Costa Rica)
　　Mexican Migration Project
　　　Data collection at the community level
　　　Research activities
　　　Participation in binational conference (Mexico)
　　Project Director: Prof. Name

　Y University
　　Mexican Aging and Health Study
　　　Assistance in design of questionnaires and collection manuals
　　　Assistance in preparing documentation for National Institute
　　　of Statistics, Geography and Informatics (Mexico)
　　　Assistance in organizing a binational meeting on aging and health

OTHER PROFESSIONAL EXPERIENCE

Staff Assistant, Center for Intercultural Education and Development, Y University
　Summer and Fall 1999

Chief of Procurement Department, State Government of Tabasco, México
　April 1996-July 1998

Oil Fuels Price Policy Analyst Assistant, Direction of Tax Policy and International Affairs
　Ministry of Finance, México, November 1994-December 1995

TEACHING EXPERIENCE

Graduate Student Instructor
　University of X, Department of Sociology, 2000-2001
　　Course title: Quantitative Methods I, Prof. Name
　　Course title: Research Methods for the Social Sciences, Prof. Name
　Y University, Public Policy Institute, 1999-2000
　　Course title: Quantitative Methods I, Prof. Name
　　Course title: Quantitative Methods II, Prof. Name

PUBLICATIONS

Scholar, Dora Alicia and Name (2004). "Wives Left Behind: The Labor Market Behavior of Women in
Migrant Communities" in *Crossing the Border. Research from the Mexican Migration Project*, edited by
Name and Name, Russell Sage Foundation, New York, pp. 172-190.

Name and Dora Alicia Scholar (2001) Aging and Health in México: an integral view, *Estudios Demográficos y de Desarrollo Urbano*, Vol. 16 (3), pp. 519-544. (in Spanish)

PRESENTATIONS

Las Remesas en Colombia: Caracterización de los Remitentes, los Beneficiarios y los Patrones de Uso. XXV International Congress of the Latin American Studies Association, October 7-9, 2004, Las Vegas, NV.

Methodological Design of the Study on International Migration and Remittances in Colombia. Colombian Conference on Migration, David Rockefeller Center for Latin American Studies, Harvard University, April 2004, Boston, Massachusetts
[Ten additional presentations follow.]

RELATED RESEARCH

Determinants of Mexican Labor Migration to the US. Public Policy Practicum. Georgetown Public Policy Institute, Georgetown University, May 2000, Washington, D.C.

Poverty Line for the Rivers Zone. Laureate Bachelor of Art Thesis. Instituto Tecnológico Autónomo de México (ITAM), March 1996, Mexico City

PROFESSIONAL ACTIVITIES AND SERVICE

XXV International Congress of the Latin American Studies Association Congress, Las Vegas, NV, October 7-9, 2004
    Session Organizer: Contemporary Colombian Transnational Migration
    Session Organizer: Internal Colombian Migration: Escaping from Need or Fear?
    Mellon Foundation Grant Support for Travel Expenses for bringing Colombian researchers to participate in the sessions.

PROFESSIONAL ASSOCIATION MEMBERSHIPS

American Sociological Association
International Union for the Scientific Study of Population
Latin American Studies Association
Mexican Society of Demography
Population Association of America

REFERENCES

[Names, addresses, phone numbers and e-mail addresses follow for five references.]

ADDITIONAL INFORMATION

Foreign Language
    Fluent in Spanish

Community Service
    African American Minority Group, Treasurer, Y Public Policy Institute
    Primary School Tutor, César Chávez Charter School, Washington, DC

Sample Interdisciplinary (Humanities and Science) Vita
Accepted one-year position at a small private college

Curriculum Vitae

Zoya Candidate
Address
City, State, Zip code
phone
email

Education

Ph.D., Natural Resource Ecology and Conservation Biology, University of State at X, December 2004, Department of Environmental Sciences
> *Thesis*: Intellectual biography of Aldo Leopold's mature conservation vision--its emergence in his thought; its historical and cultural context; its grounding in ecological science; and its implications concerning how humans think about, use and inhabit land.
> *Preliminary Exam Fields*: (1) History of wildlife management in twentieth-century U.S. (2) History of ecological thought in twentieth-century U.S. (3) Contemporary environmental ethics
> GPA: 3.9

M.S., Wildlife Ecology, University of State at X, 1998, Dept. of Environmental Sciences
> *Thesis*: Effects of habitat fragmentation on predation rates on songbird nests in a highly fragmented landscape (using artificial ground and shrub nests under various field conditions).
> GPA: 4.0

M.A., Linguistics, University of State at Y, 1994
> *Study Focus*: Meaning and communication of abstract scientific concepts in English, by speakers whose first language is not English.
> GPA: 4.0

B.A., Biology, Ithaca College, Ithaca, New York, 1988
> Minor in Music
> *Study Focus*: Succession in pine barren communities; foraging behavior of downy woodpeckers.
> GPA: 3.4

Publications

Books
Candidate, Z., 2006. *Aldo Leopold's Odyssey* [Rediscovering the author of *A Sand County Almanac*]. Washington, D.C.: Shearwater Books/Island Press, 483pp.

Book Chapters
Candidate, Z., Forthcoming 2006. Science, recreation, and Leopold's quest for a durable scale *in* Name and Name. *The Great New Wilderness Debate, Volume II*. University of Georgia Press.

Articles
Forums
Candidate, Z., Name and Name. 2007. *Viewpoint*: Land, ecology and democracy: A twenty-first century view. *Politics and the Life Sciences* 25(1-2): 42-56.
[Citations of two additional forums follow.]
Papers
Candidate, Z. 2007. Finding shade in the noon of science: John Burroughs and Aldo Leopold on science and values. *Wake Robin* Winter Issue 29 (2): 1, 12-15.
[Citations of four additional papers follow.]

Theses and Technical Reports
Candidate, Z. 2004. The Commonweal of Life: Aldo Leopold and Land Health, Ph.D. Thesis, University of State at X.
[Citations of two additional reports follow.]

Presentations

Radio Broadcasts
Candidate, Z. 2007. Aldo Leopold's Odyssey: Rediscovering the Author of *A Sand County Almanac*. WILL (NPR), Urbana, IL. Focus 580, 24 January.

Invited seminars
Candidate, Z. Upcoming, 2007. "Dear Aldo…It ought to make you president": Leopold's land ethic and new ecological vision in the age of global climate change. Aldo Leopold Foundation Shack Seminar Series, Baraboo, WI, 16 July.
[Citations of eight additional submitted talks follow.]

Submitted talks
Candidate, Z. Upcoming, 2007. Land-ethical thought in the 19th century. Association for the Study of Literature and Environment meeting. Wofford College, Spartanburg, SC, 12-16 June.
[Citations of eleven additional submitted talks follow.

Professional Experiences

Post-doctoral Research Assistant, University of State at X, City, Department of Geology, September 2006-February 2007.
> Research and collaboration with Dr. Name on various journal articles having to do with the interfaces of science, policy, and human behavior, particularly pertaining to "megacatastrophes" and catastrophes and the ideal of "sustainability." Additional independent and creative work.

Post-doctoral Research Assistant, University of State at X, City, Department of Environmental Sciences, December 2004-August 2005.
> Research and collaboration with Dr. Name on various journal articles having to do with human-environment psychology, conservation policy, and ecology. Additional independent and creative work.

[Eight additional professional experiences follow.]

Grants

2004: The Name Foundation, Inc., 1 to 1 matching grant for City, State community event featuring speaker Name, $4,100.00.
[Two additional grants follow.]

Professional Services

Society for Conservation Biology student paper award judge, Annual Meeting, 2006.

Search committee member for open track professor in professor in landscape ecology (2006) and landscape spatial analysis (2007), Department of Environmental Sciences, University of State.

Search committee member for assistant or associate professor in wildlife ecology and management, Department of Environmental Sciences, University of State, 2004-2005

External reviewer for *Conservation Biology*, 2004, 2005.

State Department of Natural Resources, Deer-checker for firearm seasons, 1997, 2004.

Professional Memberships

Ecological Society of America, from 2005; The Association for the Study of Literature and Environment, from 2005; American Society for Environmental History, from 2003; The Society for Conservation Biology, from 2000; The American Ornithologist's Union, from 1999; The Wildlife Society, 1997-1999; Teachers of English to Speakers of Other Languages, Inc. 1993-1997

Honors and Awards

Departmental nominee, Graduate Research Award, Department of ES, University of State, 2005 and 2006; Alternate, University of State Graduate Fellowship Award, 2003; Institute of Environmental Studies Graduate Fellow, 2003; Phi Kappa Phi Honor Society, 1998; Participant, Workshop in Outdoor, Natural History, and Environmental Writing, X College, VT, 1997; Gamma Sigma Delta Honor Society, 1998; Outstanding College Students of America, 1987-1988.

References

[The names and contact information for eight references follow.]

Sample Science Vita
Used for application for government postdoctoral fellowship that
requires personal information and other details

Chia-Jen Scholar

PERSONAL INFORMATION
Gender: Female
Date of birth: October 5, 1982
Place of birth: Taichung, Taiwan
Citizenship: US Citizen
Permanent home address: Address, City, State, Zip code
School address: Address, City, State, Zip code
Work address: The XYZ Laboratory, Address, City, State, Zip code
Cell phone number: 246-810-1214 (preferred)
Work number: 123-456-7890
Email: cjscholar@yahoo.com (preferred)
School email: cjscholar@xyzlaboratory.insitution.edu

EDUCATION
University of X, School of Medicine, City, State
PhD Candidate, Biomedical Graduate Studies, Cell & Molecular Biology, Vaccines & Gene Therapy
Started Sep 2003, Expected Graduation May 2008
> Thesis: Studies exploring vaccine prime-boost strategies using adenovirus and adeno-associated virus vectors
> to induce CD8+ T cell responses against HIV-1 at mucosal surfaces

University of Delaware, College of Arts & Sciences, Newark, DE
Department of Chemistry & Biochemistry, University Honors Program
Honors Bachelor of Science in Biochemistry, *magna cum laude*
Started Sep 1999, Degree awarded May 2003
Eugene DuPont Memorial Distinguished Scholar: full scholarship and stipend (1999-2003)
Minors in English and History

RESEARCH EXPERIENCE
University of X
Graduate Student (May 2004 – present, 50-60 hours per week)
- Dr. Name, The XYZ Laboratory, Address, City, State, Zip code, Phone number
  Study *in vivo* immune responses elicited by adenovirus and adeno-associated virus vectors for vaccine
  against HIV-1. Conduct prime-boost studies and characterize systemic and mucosal immune responses in
  mice and non-human primates. Explore immunomodulatory mechanisms in chronic infection, regulatory T
  cells, anergy, and dendritic cell maturation.

Rotation Student (Jan 2004 – May 2004, 20-30 hours per week)
- Dr. Name, Address, City, State, Zip code, Phone number
  Investigated tissue-specific gene expression in p53 knockout mice through RNA isolation and microarray
  analysis. Verified up-regulated gene expression with PCR, Western Blots and immunohistochemistry.

Rotation Student (Sep 2003-Dec 2004, 20 hours per week)
- Dr. Name, Address, City, State, Zip code, Phone number
  Established cells lines to examine the shuttling of endosomal proteins in melanocytes. Utilized fluorescence
  microscopy to determine co-localization of proteins.

Merck & Co.
HPV Clinical Research Intern (May-Aug 2002, 40 hours per week; Sep 2002-May 2003, 10-15 hours per week
through Kelly Scientific)
- Dr. Name, Address, City, State, Zip code, Phone number
  Worked on the recruitment and retention of clinical trials for Gardasil©, the human papillomavirus vaccine.
  Wrote newsletters for patients and designed presentation slides for investigator update meetings.

US Department of Agriculture
Physical Science Technician (Jun-Aug 2001, 40 hours per week)
- Dr. Name, Agricultural Research Center, Address, City, State, Zip code, Phone number
  Determined optimum conditions for lipase-catalyzed production of biodiesel from restaurant grease.
  Designed and optimized assay using HPLC.

Chia-Jen Scholar 2

LABORATORY TECHNIQUES
Immunology: ELISpot, ELISA, intracellular cytokine staining, isolation of lymphocytes from systemic and gut and genital tract mucosal compartments from mice, flow cytometry, immunohistochemistry, fluorescence microscopy
Molecular biology: Western blot, RNA and DNA isolation, PCR, polyacrylamide gel electrophoresis, cell culture

COMPUTER SKILLS AND LANGUAGES
Proficient in Microsoft Word, Excel, Powerpoint, Access, Publisher
Working knowledge of STATA, Maple, Fortran, C, Python
Proficient in flow cytometry analysis programs: WinMDI, FlowJo, Summit
Conversational use of Mandarin Chinese and French

LEADERSHIP ACTIVITES
Graduate Women in Science and Engineering (GWISE), University of X
Founder and co-chair (2006-present)
- Assess the concerns and issues of graduate women in science and address them through professional development, social, and community-building programs; spearhead the effort to advocate for and promote better learning and working environments for graduate women in science and engineering.
Graduate and Professional Student Assembly, University of X
Vice Chair for Student Programs (2007-present)
- Build community within 11,000+ graduate and professional students at University of X by organizing cultural, academic, and social events in collaboration with the Graduate Student Center; plan and coordinate festivities for GradFest07, an unprecedented all-day celebration event for graduate students; help fund-raise and manage an event budget of $85K.
Vice Chair for Internal Affairs (2006 – 2007)
- Served as the internal relations coordinator of meetings and events; developed strategies to enhance both internal and external communications; managed a budget of over $300K.
Philadelphia Partners in Public Health (PPPH), Philadelphia, PA
Secretary (2006-present)
- Manage the logistics of meetings and communications to effectively create a community of partnership organizations in public health.
Graduate Associate at B College House, University of X
Leader of Medical Care/Medical Challenge Suite (2005 – present)
- Design and conduct a series of medical and science career-oriented programs and activities for undergraduate students living in on-campus residence.
Planned Parenthood of Southeastern Pennsylvania, Philadelphia
Volunteer Medical Counselor (2003-2004)
- Obtained medical histories and counseled patients about contraceptive options and prevention of sexually transmitted diseases; assisted physicians and medical technicians in the surgical center.
[One additional entry follows.]

HONORS AND AWARDS
Merck Index Award (2003)
Quaesita Drake Scholarship, University of Department of Chemistry and Biochemistry (2002)
Study Abroad in Paris, France (Summer 2000)
Freshman Honors Program Certificate, University of Delaware (1999-2000)

PROFESSIONAL SOCIETY MEMBERSHIPS
American Public Health Association student member
National Society of Collegiate Scholars
Phi Beta Kappa Society
[Three additional entries follow.]

TEACHING EXPERIENCE
Summer Science Academy, Applied Sciences and Technologies, University of X
Guest Lecturer (Jul 2007)

Chia-Jen Scholar 3

Biomedical Science Group Leader (Jul 2006)
• Assigned scientific articles and facilitated discussions about vaccines and diseases with high school students.
Department of Chemistry & Biochemistry/Academic Services, University of Delaware
Organic Chemistry Laboratory TA (Jan 2003)
• Lectured, prepared, and supervised undergraduate organic chemistry lab sessions.
Organic Chemistry Tutor (2001-2003)
University Honors Program, University of Delaware
Writing Fellow (2001-2003)
• Completed training in composition writing pedagogy and tutored undergraduates in writing sonnets, creative
  pieces, and essays, and assisted faculty in interdisciplinary courses with emphasis in writing.

SCIENTIFIC CONFERENCE PRESENTATIONS
Scholar C-J, Name, Name, Name, Name. AAV vectors as antigen delivery vehicles: Do they cause T cell
unresponsiveness? *Gene Therapy and Vaccines Seminar* (Institution, City, State, 2007).

Scholar C-J, Name, Name, Name, Name. AAV vectors dampen transgene-specific CD8+ T cell responses to
subsequent adenoviral vector vaccine. *Immunologic Memory Keystone Symposium* (Santa Fe, NM, 2007).

Scholar C-J, Name, Name, Name. Systemic administration of chimp-derived adenoviral vector elicits HIV-1 gag-
specific CD8+ T cells in gut lymphoid tissues. *American Association of Immunologists* Annual Conference
(Boston, MA, 2006).

Name, **Scholar C-J**, Name, Name. Adenovirus/MVA Prime Boost Strategies Induce Strong Peripheral and
Mucosal Responses Against an HIV-1 Antigen. *HIV Vaccines Keystone Symposium* (Keystone, CO, 2006).

RESEARCH INTERESTS

Vaccination and cancer prevention	Molecular approaches in product development
Cancer immunotherapy	Clinical trial design and analytic methodology
T cell immunology	Viral epidemiology
Viral immunity	

ABSTRACT
Name, **Scholar C-J**, Name and Name. Innate immune responses to viral gene therapy vectors. *American Society
of Gene Therapy Annual Meeting* (Baltimore, MD, 2006); Abstract.

BIBLIOGRAPHY
Scholar C-J, Name, Name, Name. Recombinant AAV vectors induce transgene product-specific CD8$^+$ T cells that
are functionally impaired. (in press, *Journal of Clinical Investigation*)

Name, **Scholar C-J**, Name, Name, Name, Name, Name. Intramuscular immunization with a chimpanzee-origin
adenovirus vector expressing gag of HIV-1 induces a robust genital gag-specific CD8+ T cell response in mice.
(submitted to *Molecular Therapy*)

Name, **Scholar C-J**, Name, Name, Name, Name, Name, Name. A pre-clinical animal model to assess the effect
of pre-existing T cell immunity on AAV-mediated gene transfer. (submitted to *Nature Medicine*)

Name, **Scholar C-J**, Name, Name, Name, Name. *In Vitro* Neutralization Assays of an Adenovirus Neutralizing
Escape Mutant Do Not Correlate with *In Vivo* Results. (submitted to *Journal of Virology*)

Name, Name, Name, Name, **Scholar C-J**, Name, Name, Name, Name, Name. Targeting of antigen to the
herpesvirus entry mediator augments primary adaptive immune responses. (submitted to *Nature Medicine*)

Name, Name, Name, Name, Name, Name, **Scholar, C-J**, Name, Name, Name, Name, Name, Name. Adenoviral
Vectors Persist In Vivo and Maintain Activated CD8+ T cells: Implications for Their Use as Vaccines. *Blood* 2007
Sep 15;110(6):1916-23
[Four additional publications follow.]

Sample Engineering Vita
Used for applications for postdoctoral fellowships

Siobhán G. Engineer
Curriculum Vitae

University of X Medical Center
Department of Radiology
ABC Laboratories
Address
City, State, Zip code
Phone number
Fax
Email

Education

May 2007 (expected)	Ph.D. Candidate, Bioengineering University of X, City, State Dissertation: "NMR and NIR imaging of phospholipase activity" Advisors: Dr. Name and Dr. Name
May 2001	B.S. Electrical Engineering, *magna cum laude* Minor: Computer Science Manhattan College, Riverdale, N.Y. Advisor: Dr. Name

Awards and Recognitions

2007	Joint M.I. Conference Student Travel Stipend
Nov 2002–Nov 2004	NIH Ruth L. Kirschstein National Research Service Award

[Seven additional awards follow.]

Research Interests

The primary focus of my research deals with investigating various applications of near-infrared (NIR) light, to non-invasively monitor physiologic variables, as well as pathologic and therapeutic processes. My previous work involved the implementation of near-infrared spectroscopy (NIRS) to trans-abdominally monitor fetal cerebral blood oxygen saturation. I have subsequently been investigating the implementation of NIR self-quenching fluorescent probes to analyze the effect of chemotherapeutic drug therapy in prostate cancer. I intend to co-register NIR fluorescence measurements with simultaneous magnetic resonance spectroscopy (MRS) in order to delineate specific cell signaling pathways *in vitro* and *in vivo*. The information gained from this molecular imaging approach may lead to earlier diagnoses and improved management of disease.

Research Experience

Jun 2004–present	University of X, Department of Radiology, Magnetic Resonance Center for Research in Metabolism (MRCRM), Laboratory of Molecular Imaging *Research Assistant* Advisor: Dr. Name Characterized self-quenching NIR fluorescent probes for phospholipase activity.
Sep 2001–Jun 2004	University of X, Magnetic Resonance Center for Research in Metabolism (MRCRM) *Research Assistant*

Engineer,   2

Advisors: Dr. Name, Dr. Name and Dr. Name
Developed a method to non-invasively monitor fetal cerebral tissue blood oxygen
saturation using a continuous-wave near-infrared imager.

2000
(summer)
Y University, Department of Electrical Engineering, Lightwave Communications Laboratory,
City, State
NSF REU Fellow
Advisor: Dr. Name
Development of low-loss alignment and coupling of fibers for optical communication
networks.

1999
(summer)
Z University, Department of Astronomy, Space Sciences Building, City, State
NSF REU Fellow
Advisor: Dr. Name
Orbital planning for X-ray/Gamma-ray Spectrometer (XGRS) instrument on-board the Near
Earth Asteroid Rendezvous (NEAR) Shoemaker spacecraft to develop global maps of the
elemental composition of the surface of asteroid 433 Eros.

Teaching Experience

Apr 2005-
Aug 2005
The Princeton Review, City, State
MCAT Physics Instructor
In-class Physics instruction (26.5 hours) for pre-med students preparing for the MCAT.

Sep 2004-
Jun 2005
University of X, Center for Community Partnerships, Access Science Program
Course Developer, Instructor
Developed an Academically-based Community Service (ABCS) Course, "Bioengineering in
the World," in which X students implement a broad range of bioengineering-related labs
and activities in a local high school physics or science elective classroom.

1999
(summer)
Manhattan College Summer Program
Program Counselor
Prepared minority and women high school students in science, engineering, and SAT.

Publications

Engineer, S., Name, Name, Name, Name, Name. "Effect of errors in baseline optical properties on
accuracy of transabdominal near-infrared spectroscopy in fetal sheep brain during hypoxic stress." *Journal
of Biomedical Optics*, 10, 064001, 2005.

Name, Name, Engineer, S, Name, Name, Name. "Fetal transabdominal pulse oximeter studies using a
hypoxic sheep model." *The Journal of Maternal-Fetal and Neonatal Medicine*, 17(6): 393-399, 2005.

Abstracts and Presentations
Engineer, S., Name, Name, Name, Name, "In Vivo Bio-distribution of an Enzyme-Activated Near-infrared
Probe Highly Specific to Phosphatidylcholine-specific Phospholipase C." The Joint AMI/SMI Molecular
Imaging Conference, Providence, RI, USA, September 8-11, 2007.

Engineer, S., Name, Name, Name, Name, Name, Name, "Design and Characterization of an Enzyme-
Activated Near-infrared Probe Highly Specific to Phosphatidylcholine-specific Phospholipase C." The
Eunice and Irving Leopold Annual Scientific Symposium, March 13, 2007.
[The entries for eight additional presentations follow.]

Professional Memberships and Leadership

Society of Molecular Imaging (SMI)

International Society for Magnetic Resonance in Medicine (ISMRM)

American Society for Engineering Education (ASEE)

International Society for Optical Engineering (SPIE)

Graduate Association of Bioengineering (GABE), University of X
    Vice President (2001), Committee Chair (2002)

Society of Women Engineers (SWE)
    Manhattan College Chapter: Treasurer (1999), President (2000)

Institute of Electrical and Electronics Engineers, Inc. (IEEE)
    Manhattan College Chapter: Vice President (2001)

Engineering Council, Manhattan College: Council Chair (2001)

Student Government, Manhattan College: School Treasurer (1997)

Other Activities

Aug 2006– May 2007	University of X, City, State Career Services Intern
July 2006– present	Amnesty International, Group 707 Yonkers Urgent Action Coordinator
Sep 2004– May 2005	St. Barnabas Catholic Church, Yonkers, NY Confraternity of Christian Doctrine (CCD), 1st Grade Teacher

Sample Science Vita
Accepted position at a large public research university

Mark David Researcher

The Research Institute   Home Address
The University of X   City, State Zip code
Address   Home phone
City, State Zip code   Work phone
E-mail   Fax

EDUCATION

The University of State, City, State
Ph.D. in Immunology, August 2000
Thesis Title: Role of the Interferon gamma/Interferon Gamma Receptor Complex in Signal Transduction
Sponsor: Name, Ph.D.

The University of Florida, Gainesville, Florida
B.S. in Microbiology, May 1996
Minor in Chemistry
Cumulative G.P.A.: 3.71/4.0

RESEARCH EXPERIENCE

Research Fellow, Laboratory of Dr. Name, Ph.D., 2006-Present
The Research Institute & The University of X
City, State
The Significance of Regulatory T cells in Influenza Infection
We are currently examining the role of CD4+CD25+ regulatory T cells during the course of an influenza infection using a combination of regulatory T cell depletion and adoptive transfer experiments.

Postdoctoral Fellow, Laboratory of Dr. Name, Ph.D., 2000-2006
The Research Institute & The University of X
City, State
Factors Governing Regulatory T Cell Activation and Function
Showed that regulatory T cell suppressor function can be mediated through a partial T cell receptor signal. Regulatory T cell suppressor function can mediate the suppression of T cell proliferation, cytokine production, and memory B cell antibody production.
- Generated regulatory and conventional CD4 T cell primary cell lines from TCR transgenic mice
- Maintained colony of TCR transgenic mice- responsible for mating decisions
- Analyzed the capacity of regulatory T cells to become skewed to TH1/TH2 phenotypes using cytokine ELISAs and intracellular staining
- Characterized the phenotype of regulatory T cells through flow cytometry
- Measured the capacity of Altered Peptide ligands (APL) to activate CD4 T cells by 3H thymidine incorporation and CFSE analysis
- Analyzed the capacity of APL activated regulatory T cells to inhibit T cell proliferation in vitro
- Showed that regulatory T cells can inhibit memory B cell responses by in vivo transfer followed by ELISA and ELISPOT analysis

Research Assistant, Laboratory of Dr. Name, Ph.D., 1996-2000
The University of State, Department of Microbiology and Cell Science
City, State
Role of the Interferon gamma/Interferon Gamma Receptor Complex in Signal Transduction
 We showed that the interferon gamma/interferon gamma receptor alpha chain was translocated to the cell nucleus with kinetics similar to that of signal transducer and activator of transcription 1α (STAT1α). These data suggested that interferon gamma, which contains a nuclear localization signal (NLS), likely plays a role in the nuclear translocation of STAT1a, a protein necessary for the activation of CD4 T cells.

- Conducted protein binding studies to analyze the affinity of iodinated interferon gamma (IFN γ) to the intracellular domain of the interferon gamma receptor
- Responsible for the maintenance of human cell lines
- Performed nuclear import assays with permeabilized HeLa cells to illustrate the presence of two NLS sequences in human interferon gamma
- Interferon gamma devoid of primary NLS sequence was expressed in *E. coli* and purified in order to show its necessity in biological function
- The nuclear translocation of interferon gamma/interferon gamma receptor was observed through a combination of immuno-florescence, electron microscopy, western blotting, and immuno-precipitation

TEACHING EXPERIENCE

Undergraduate Residence House, **The University of X**
Senior Fellow, serve as mentor and seminar instructor to undergraduate students in a student residence house capacity, 2003-present.

The University of X Freshman Reading Project**, Discussion Leader** during freshman orientation, 2006.

The University of X Talent Search Program, **Science Instructor** to rising 8th grade students, 2006.
[Five additional teaching entries follow.]

INVITED TALKS

Washington Elementary School Annual Career Day, Keynote Address: Life as an Immunologist, **The School District of City** Washington Elementary School, City, State, 6/08/2006

Lupus Awareness Forum, Lupus: Bridging the Gap from the Benchtop to the Bedside, **University of X,** City, State 2/22/2005

The 2nd Annual Biomedical Postdoc Research Symposium, Degenerate Activation of CD25+CD4+ Regulatory T cells by Analog Peptides, **University of X,** City, State, 11/12/2003
[Six additional invited talks follow.]

HONORS AND AWARDS

The Association of Medical Laboratory Immunologists Travel Award Recipient 2006
Keystone Symposia Travel Award Recipient 2005

Researcher   3

The Graduate School at the University of State Pre-doctoral Fellow 1998-2000
IFAS Pre-doctoral Minority Fellow, University of State 1996-1998

PUBLICATIONS

<u>Researcher M</u>, Name, and Name. (2007) Activation of CD4+CD25+ regulatory T cell suppressor function by analogs of the selecting peptide. *Eur J Immunol.* 37(1): 139-46.

Name, <u>Researcher M</u>, Name, and Name. (2007) Spontaneous auto-reactive memory B cell formation driven by a high frequency of auto-reactive CD4+ T cells. *J Immunol.* In press.

Name, Name, Name, Name, Name, Name, <u>Researcher M</u>, Name, Name, Name, Name, Name, Name, and Name. (2007) CD4+ T cell repertoire dictates disease penetrance in a mouse model of autoimmune arthritis. Submitted.

<u>Researcher M</u>, Name, Name, Name, and Name. (2007) Naturally occurring CD4+CD25+ regulatory T cell selection is dominated by TCR specificity for self-peptides within the thymus. Manuscript in preparation.
[Twelve additional publications follow.]

ABSTRACTS

<u>Researcher M</u>, Name, Name, and Name. 2006. Activation of Self-Antigen Specific CD4+CD25+ Regulatory T Cell Suppressor Function by Cross-reactive Peptides. The 19th Annual Association of Medical Laboratory Immunologists (AMLI) Meeting. Washington, DC.
[Thirteen additional abstracts follow.]

Sample Science Vita
Accepted position at a small private Master's institution

Anthony Scientist, Ph.D.
Address, City, State Zip code
Home Phone; Work Phone
Fax; Email

CURRENT POSITION:
- Postdoctoral Fellow, 2001-present. Mentor: Name, Ph.D., Department of Animal Biology, University of X, City, State. Research focus: I study gene silencing via the Polycomb complex. We characterized a novel domain in Yin Yang 1 that is responsible for Polycomb recruitment to DNA. This recruiting activity of Yin Yang 1 is the first such characterized at a biochemical level.

PREVIOUS TEACHING EXPERIENCE:
- Teaching Assistant, 2002-2004. University of X, School of Veterinary Medicine, City, State. Directed veterinary students (VMD program) in a laboratory project with analysis of clinical samples; evaluate laboratory write-ups; preparation of materials for the laboratory sessions.

- Part Time Lecturer, 2001-2002. Department of Chemistry, State University, City Campus. Taught biochemistry courses and lab sections to a mixture of third and fourth year undergraduates (pre-medical and pre-professional) and M.S. candidates; material included protein structure/function, intermediary metabolism, membrane biology, polynucleotide biochemistry, cell signaling, protein trafficking.

- Assistant Professor (1-year contract), 2000-2001. Department of Biology, X University, City, State. Taught biochemistry, molecular biology courses and lab sections to a mixture of third and fourth year Biology majors (pre-medical and pre-professional); material included protein structure/function, intermediary metabolism, membrane biology, polynucleotide biochemistry, cell signaling, protein trafficking. Taught introductory lab to first year Biology majors; material included basic histology, anatomy and physiology with an emphasis on interrelating structure and function. Taught human genetics course to non-majors; material included fundamental concepts of inheritance, genetic engineering, ethical issues and public policy.

PREVIOUS RESEARCH EXPERIENCE:
- Graduate Research Assistant, 1992-2000. Advisor: Name, M.D., Ph.D. Departments of Biochemistry and Thrombosis Research Center, Y University School of Medicine, City, State. Research Focus: Structure/function analysis of blood coagulation factor IXa EGF2 domain and its interaction with the factor X-activating complex.

Curriculum Vitae – Anthony Scientist, Ph.D.

RESEARCH SUPPORT
- Individual Postdoctoral Award, American Heart Association, July 2003-June 2005.

- Urology Training Grant T-32, October 2001-June 2003.

EDUCATION:
- Ph.D., Biochemistry (2000). Y University School of Medicine, City, State. Advisor: Name M.D., Ph.D.
  Dissertation: Residues 88 to 109 of Blood Coagulation Factor IXa are Important for Assembly of the Factor X Activating Complex

- B.A., Biology (1992). La Salle University, Philadelphia, PA

RESEARCH SKILLS:
- *Drosophila* techniques including husbandry, transgenesis, genotyping, and phenotypic analysis.

- Molecular biology techniques including yeast two-hybrid, chromatin immunoprecipitation, PCR, RT-PCR, subcloning, agarose gel electrophoresis, acrylamide gel electrophoresis, Southern blot, ribonuclease protection assay, and Northern blot.

- Microbial culture techniques including growth and maintenance of *E. coli* and yeast in liquid and solid media, preparation of competent cells, transformation, recombinant protein expression.

- Tissue culture techniques including growth and maintenance of cell lines, transfection, development of stable cell lines, and recombinant protein expression.

- Protein techniques including purification, spectrophotometry, bicinchoninic acid analysis, column chromatography, HPLC, acrylamide gel electrophoresis, *in vitro* translation, GST-pulldown, immunoprecipitation, western immunobloting, ELISA, enzyme kinetic analysis.

ADDITIONAL SCIENTIFIC ACTIVITIES:
- Mentoring. I have mentored many students including undergraduate, graduate, veterinary, and medical. I train students to perform experiments and they learn to work independently. I also discuss the contribution of their work to the broader goal of the lab so they know how they are contributing to the group effort. I have also helped students prepare short research-related seminars and posters to be presented at national meetings.

Curriculum Vitae – Anthony Scientist, Ph.D.

- Biomedical Postdoctoral Council Cochair. The Biomedical Postdoctoral Council (URL) is a group of volunteer postdocs who represent the 800+ postdoctoral fellows at the University's Schools of Medicine, Dental Medicine and Veterinary Medicine. We work with the Biomedical Postdoctoral Programs office to organize and enhance various training opportunities in career development, scientific writing and speaking.

AWARDS and HONORS:
- Honored Researcher, 2004. American Heart Association. The award recognizes the top 10 scoring research proposals, including those by faculty, postdocs, and students submitted to the PA/DE affiliate.

- Second Place, 2001. Twenty-first Annual Erwin Margulies Research Conference Temple University. The award recognizes excellence in research presentation.

PUBLICATIONS:
- **Scientist, A.** and Name. YY1 residues 201-225 recruit the PcG complex to DNA (manuscript to be submitted by Dec 2005)
- **Scientist, A.** and Name. Yin Yang 1 residues important for polycomb-group mediated silencing (Abstract 125.23) ASBMB meeting, Boston MA, June 2004
[Five additional publications follow.]

RESEARCH PRESENTATIONS:
- Oral presentation at the XVIIIth Congress of the International Society on Thrombosis and Hemostasis, Paris, France, July 2001
- Oral presentation at the Twenty-first Annual Erwin Margulies Research Conference, Temple University, Philadelphia PA, June 2001
[Four additional presentations follow.]

SOCIETY MEMBERSHIPS:
- American Society of Biochemistry for Molecular Biology (ASBMB)
- Federation of American Societies for Experimental Biology (FASEB)
- National Postdoctoral Association (NPA)

REFERENCES (submitting letters):
[Contact information of four references follows.]

REFERENCES (additional):
[Contact information of four additional references follows.]

Sample Science Vita
Accepted position at a mid-size public Master's institution

Monique R. Researcher
E-mail address
Department, University of X
Address
City, State, Zip code
Phone number

EDUCATION: **University of X**, City, State
Ph.D. in Physics and Astronomy   *Expected May 2006*
Master of Science Degree in Physics and Astronomy, G.P.A. 3.96   *May 2004*

Cornell University, College of Arts and Sciences, Ithaca, NY
Bachelor of Arts Degree in Physics, Magna cum Laude, G.P.A. 3.83 *May 2001*

RESEARCH EXPERIENCE:

Department of Physics and Astronomy, University of X, City   *May 2003-Present*
Theoretical cosmology. Doctoral thesis research conducted with Drs. Name and Name.
- Demonstrated how stacking weak-lensing signals of galaxy clusters, based on their Sunyaev-Zel'dovich decrement, can constrain cluster physics.
- Chose, generalized, and applied a nonparametric method (the smoothing spline) to reconstruct the primordial power spectrum.
- Tested gravity at megaparsec scales by deriving the matter power spectrum and bispectrum for small deviations from the inverse-square law, and comparing with large-scale structure data.

Department of Physics and Astronomy, University of X   *May-August 2002*
Theoretical cosmology. Advisors: Drs. Name and Name.
- Derived light curves for gravitational microlensing events in the presence of weak external shear.

NASA/New York Space Grant Fellowship, Cornell University, Ithaca, NY   *June-August 2000*
Theoretical astrophysics. Advisor: Dr. Name.
- Calculated hydrogen ionization fraction for a neutron star atmosphere, over a range of magnetic fields for which there are no good electron quantum numbers.

Newman Laboratory for Elementary Particle Physics, Cornell University *January-May 2000*
High-energy theory. Advisor: Dr. Name.
- Studied Plebanski's demonstration that the Born-Infeld electromagnetic lagrangian is the only Lorentz-covariant lagrangian consistent with causality, with the aim to generalize the argument to higher dimensions.

NSF Research Experience for Undergraduates Fellowship, University of Chicago *June-August 1999*
Theoretical condensed matter physics. Advisor: Dr. Name.
- Devised and applied new method to demonstrate the fractal nature of late stages of mineral growth.

Wilson Synchrotron Laboratory, Cornell University   *June-July 1997*
High-energy experiment. Advisor: Dr. Name.
- Performed feasibility study for detecting an exotic B meson decay.

PUBLICATIONS:

Researcher, M., Name, and Name (2006) Stacking Weak Lensing Signals of SZ Clusters to Constrain Cluster Physics. Submitted to *Astrophysical Journal*. E-print: astro-ph/0601254.

Researcher, M., Name, and Name (2005) Smoothing spline primordial power spectrum reconstruction. *Physical Review D*, 72, 103520.

Researcher, M., Name, and Name (2005) Limits on deviations from the inverse-square law on megaparsec scales. *Physical Review D*, 71, 083004.

UNIVERSITY TEACHING:

Summer Science Academy, University of X, City, State   *July 2005*
- Taught lectures on special relativity and quantum interference to advanced high-school students.

Department of Physics and Astronomy, University of X
- Gave invited talk for undergraduate Physics Club on gravity research project.   *February 2005*
- Taught recitation sections for engineering physics, mechanics and electromagnetism. *Sept. 2002-May 2003*
- Conducted labs for engineering physics electricity and magnetism course.   *January-May 2002*

Center for Learning and Teaching, Cornell University, Ithaca, NY   *August 1998-May 2001*
- Tutored all tracks of introductory physics courses. Held office hours for three hours a week.

K-12 AND COMMUNITY TEACHING:

Access Science Volunteership, City, State   *October 2003-Present*
- Co-taught professional development workshops for high-school physical science teachers.
- Initiated after-school Science Fair Club to assist 4th and 5th grade students with their projects.
- Assisted 6th grade teacher to plan and conduct engaging and accurate science lessons.

Science Museum, City, State   *March 2002-June 2003*
- Explained exhibits to visitors as a volunteer in the Interpretive services department.

Explore Our Solar System, Monroe Free Library, Monroe, NY   *August 2001*
- Created and taught a week-long summer science program for children grades 4-6.

Game of Science, Beverly J. Martin Elementary School, Ithaca, NY   *Sept. 1999-May 2001*
- Initiated and ran weekly after-school science enrichment program for grades 3-5.

AWARDS AND HONORS:

- Sponsored by the NSF to attend the **Lindau Meeting of Nobel Laureates and Students** in Germany. *2004*
- **Kieval Prize in Physics**, awarded every year to an outstanding Cornell physics senior who shows unusual promise for future contributions to physics research. *2001*
- **Phi Beta Kappa**, *2001*
- **Robinson-Appel Humanitarian Award**, which recognizes three Cornell students annually who have had significant involvement in community service, and provides support for their projects, which address a community's social needs. Awarded for Game of Science program (see above). *2000*
- **Golden Key National Honors Society**, *1999*
- **College Scholar**, Cornell University, *1998-2001*

REFERENCES:

[The names and contact information of four references follow.]

INTERESTS AND ACTIVITIES:

Plays & Players Theater, Artistic Member and Actress, *September 2003-Present.*
Swing Dance Club, Co-President, *January 2005-Present.*
University of X Choir, *January 2002-May 2005.* Soloist, *December 2003.*
Work in France, Council Exchanges, Assistant High-School English Teacher, *October-December 2001.*
Cornell University Chorus, *1997-2001*. International Tour Manager, *2000.*
Society of Physics Students, Cornell University, President, *1999.*

Sample Mathematics Vita
Accepted position at a large public research university

John Patrick Scholar

University of X
Department of Mathematics
Address
City, State Zip code
Email
Website
Phone

Current Position

I am a lecturer in Mathematics at the University of X. My research concerns analytic, combinatorial, and probabilistic techniques for the analysis of algorithms and data structures; I am also interested in game theory and information theory.

Education

Y University
Ph.D., Mathematics with Specialization in Computational Science, May 2005
　　　　Dissertation: *Analysis of the Multiplicity Matching Parameter in Suffix Trees*
　　　　Advisor: Name, Department of Computer Science

University of Wisconsin-Madison
M.S., Applied Mathematical Sciences, May 2003
　　　　Thesis: *Analysis of a Randomized Selection Algorithm*

Denison University
B.S., Mathematics and Computer Science, summa cum laude, May 1999
　　　　Senior Honors Project: *Mathematical Foundations for Performance Analysis*

Grants

NSF 0603821: Asymptotic Enumeration, Reinforcement, and Effective Limit Theory
　　　　Name and I are Co-Principal Investigators; 2006-2008

Honors

Good Teaching Award (University of X) in Math 104, Spring 2006
Good Teaching Award (University of X) in Math 104 and Math 432, Fall 2005
Actuarial Science Program Scholarship, Y University, Fall 2004
　　　　(scored 10 out of 10 on SOA/ CAS Actuary Course 1 Exam)
Excellence in Teaching Award (Y University), Spring 2004
[Six additional awards follow.]

Experience

University of X
Lecturer
>Math 999: Independent Study and Research in Analytic Combinatories
>>(Supervised study for Graduate Students), Spring 2007
>Math 499: Game Theory (Supervised Study for Undergraduates), Spring 2007
>Math 104: Calculus, Spring 2007

[The names of nine additional courses follow.]

State University-City
Teaching Assistant
>MSRI Summer Graduate Course:
>Analysis of Algorithms and Information Theory, Summer 2004

Y University
Instructor with Full Responsibility
>Math/Stat 371: SOA/CAS Actuary Course 1 Exam Preparation, Spring 2005
>Math 220: Introduction to Calculus, Fall 2004
>Math/Stat 371: SOA/CAS Actuary Course 1 Exam Preparation, Spring 2004
>Math 111: Algebra, Fall 2003
>Math 220: Introduction to Calculus, Spring 2002
>Math 223: Introductory Analysis I, Fall 2001

Guest Lecturer for Five Semesters
>CS 182: Foundations of Computer Science, Fall 2002-Fall 2004

University of State-City
Teaching Assistant
>Math 240: Elementary Discrete Mathematics. Spring 2001
>Math 211: Calculus, Fall 2000

Summer Institute for the Gifted
Instructor
>Drew University: Computer Science, Mathematics; Summer 2002
>Amherst College: Computer Science, Mathematics; Summer 2000, 2001
>Denison University: Computer Science, Robotics; Summer 1999

Book

Combinatorial Game Theory, currently a draft of 71 pages

Refereed Publications

13. The variance of subword complexity, in progress.

Scholar 3

12. A combinatorial study of the ward-parameter (with Name, Name, Name, and Name), in progress.

11. On correlation polynomials and subword complexity (with name), submitted to *Discrete Mathematics and Theoretical Computer Science* – special issue on Analysis of Algorithms 2007.
[Ten additional publications follow.]

Program Committees

Analytic Algorithms and Combinatories, Miami, 21 Jan 2006.

Newsletter Publications

Eight hours with the board, *FOCUS* **23**, 8 (Nov 2003), 15.

Colloquia, Lectures, Seminars

Twelfth Annual Seminar on Analysis of Algorithms, Alden Biesen, Belgium, 7 Jul 2006
Mathematics Department Colloquium, Drexel University, 1 May 2006
Mathematics & Statistics Colloquium, Swarthmore College, 21 Feb 2006
Graduate Student Seminar, Y University, 27 Jan 2006
[The names of ten additional colloquia, lectures, or seminars follow.]

Professional Societies

American Mathematical Society
Mathematical Association of America
    National MAA Committee on Graduate Students, 2003-2009
    How to Apply for Jobs (Panelist), MathFest, Albuquerque, 5 August 2004
    Graduate Student Workshop (Panelist), Spring Meeting of the Indiana Section of
    the MAA, 3 April 2004
[The names of five additional professional societies follow.]

Editorial

Selected by Name to serve as 1 of 3 proofreaders for the following books:
    Selected Papers on Computer Languages, CSLI, 2003
    Selected Papers on Discrete Mathematics, CSLI, 2003

References
[The names and contact information of three references follow.]

Sample Engineering Vita
Accepted position at a small private Master's institution

Curriculum Vitae

Lauren Melissa Engineer, Ph.D.
University of X
Department of Bioengineering, Address, City, State Zip code
Phone; E-mail

Education:

1997-2001   Ph.D., Tumor Biology, Y University
             City, State

1993-1997   B.S., Biochemistry, Mount Saint Mary's College
             Emmitsburg, Maryland

Research Experience:

2004-Present Research Associate, Department of Bioengineering
              University of X, City, State

2001-2004   Postdoctoral Fellow, Department of Biomedical Engineering
             Z University, City, State

1997-2001   Graduate Student, Interdisciplinary Program in Tumor Biology
             Y University, City, State

1996-1997   Undergraduate Research Student, United States Department of Agriculture, Fort
             Detrick, Maryland

1996   Summer Research Student, University of Pittsburgh, Department of Biochemistry
             and Molecular Biology, Pittsburgh, Pennsylvania

Honors and Awards:

2004   Ruth L. Kirschstein National Research Service Award (NRSA) Grant
2001   Second Place Award in Y University Student Research Days Poster Competition
2001   Finalist in Lombardi Cancer Center Research Fair
[Seven additional awards and honors follow.]

Grants Awarded:

Pending Research Support
[Grant Number]   Engineer (PI)

NIH
Adhesion to the Extracellular Matrix, Focal Adhesion Kinase, and Regulation of
Proliferation

> The major goal of this project is to investigate the molecular mechanisms by which cell
> adhesion to the extracellular matrix regulates proliferation in endothelial cells.

> Role: Principal Investigator

Completed Research Support
[Information concerning two previous grants follows.]

Publications:

1. Name, Name, Name, **Engineer LM**, Name, Name. (2005) Activation of ROCK-2 by RhoA is
   Regulated by Cell Adhesion, Shape, and Cytoskeletal Tension. (Submitted)

2. **Engineer LM**, Name, Name. (2005) Adenoviral microarrays: a novel functional screening
   tool. (manuscript in preparation)

3. **Engineer LM**, Name, Name, Name, Name, Name, Name, Name. (2006) An Inhibitory Role
   for Focal Adhesion Kinase in Regulating Proliferation; a link between limited adhesion and
   RhoA-ROCK signaling. *J. Cell Biol.* 174(2): 277-288.
[The names of twelve additional publications follow.]

Textbook Chapters:

1. **Engineer LM** and Name. (2004) Using lab-on-a-chip technologies to understand cellular
   mechanotransduction. *Lab-on-Chips for Cellomics: Micro and Nanotechnologies for Life
   Science.* Kluwer Academic Publishers: 171-196.
[The name of one additional textbook chapter follows.]

Podium Presentations:

1. **Engineer LM**, Name. (2005) Microscale Tissue Engineering: Lessons in Forces, Form, and
   Function. The Society for Physical Regulation in Biology and Medicine, 23rd Scientific
   Conference.
[The entries for five additional podium presentations follow.]

Poster Presentations:

1. **Engineer LM**, Name, Name, Name, Name, Name, Name, Name.
   (2006) An inhibitory role for FAK in regulating proliferation: a link between limited
   adhesion and the RhoA-ROCK signaling pathway. Gordon Research Conference – Signaling
   by Adhesion Receptors.
[The entries for eighteen additional poster presentations follow.]

Invited Seminars:

April 2003   Mount St. Mary's College, Emmitsburg, Maryland. "Cells lying on a bed of microneedles: Sensing cell force."

August 2001   Z University School of Medicine, Department of Biomedical Engineering, City, State. "SPEC1: a link between Cdc42 and integrins?"
[The entries for four additional invited seminars follow.]

Teaching Experience:

Lecturer, <u>Molecules and Cells</u>, Core Undergraduate Curriculum, Department of Biomedical Engineering, Z University, 2002-2004. This course presents modern molecular and cellular biology in the context of potential biomedical engineering applications. Enrollment: 60-110.

Lecturer, <u>Cell Mechanics</u>, Advanced Graduate Elective, Applied Biomedical Engineering Program, Z University. 2003. This course covers current approaches to the study of mammalian cell mechanics. Enrollment: 4-10.

Lecturer, <u>Techniques in Biochemistry and Molecular Biology</u>, Core Graduate Curriculum, Department of Biochemistry, Y University, 2001. This course covers current methods in biochemistry in molecular biology in biomedical research. Enrollment: 20-30.

Professional Activities:

2005-Present Founding co-chair of the University of X School of Engineering and Applied Sciences Postdoctoral Association
2003-2004   President, Z University School of Medicine Postdoctoral Association
2002-2004   Postdoctoral Representative, Department of Biomedical Engineering
2002-2003   Vice President of Archives, Z Postdoctoral Association

References:
[The names and contact information for three references follow.]

Engineer 3

Sample Professional Vita, Theatre
Accepted position at a small private college

Edward K. Dramatist

Theatre Technologist

Address
City, State Zip code
Phone
E-Mail

OBJECTIVE

To become a theatre technology teacher and technical director

EDUCATION

May 2003	MFA	Theatre Technology	State University
1999	BA	Theatre, Scenic Design Emphasis	San Diego State University

PROFESSIONAL EXPERIENCE

2002	Properties Master, Brown County Playhouse, Nashville, IN
2001	Shop Foreman, Brown County Playhouse, Nashville, IN
1999-2000	Carpenter, San Diego Opera Scenic Studio, San Diego, CA
1997-1999	Scene Shop Foreman, La Jolla Playhouse/University of California at San Diego's Mandell Weiss Center for the Performing Arts, La Jolla, CA

[Three additional professional experience listings follow.]

TEACHING EXPERIENCE

2000-2003	Associate Instructor	State University
1997-1999	Stagecraft Practicum Instructor	University of California at San Diego
1996-1997	Interim Shop Supervisor	San Diego State University
1995	Technical Director/Instructor	Serra High School, San Diego, CA

Technical Direction

Old Globe Theatre (1994-2000)

Play On!	Assistant to the Technical Director
Macbeth	Assistant to the Technical Director
Pride's Crossing	Assistant to the Technical Director
Dracula	Assistant to the Technical Director

A Moon for the Misbegotten   Assistant to the Technical Director
[One additional technical direction position follows.]

Master Carpentry & Shop Management

La Jolla Playhouse, University of California, San Diego (1997-1999)

Rent	West Coast Premiere; Director: Michael Greif
Harmony	World Premiere; Dramalogue Award; Director: David Warren
The Captain's Tiger	West Coast Premiere; Playwright in Residence: Athol Fugard
Dogeaters	World Premiere; Director Michael Greif
Light Up The Sky	
Macbeth	
Nora	
Ubu Rock	
Having Our Say	
The Invisible Circle	
Blur	
Not Them!	

[Two additional master carpentry and shop management positions follow.]

Scenic Design

State University (2000-2003)

In the Boom Boom Room	Scenic Design	Director: Eric Anderson
The Love Talker	Co-scenic Design	Director: Rick Fonte
A Moon for the Misbegotten	Scenic Design	Director: Steve Decker

Fault Line Players (1999)

Polyester	Scenic Design	Director: Tim Heitman

[Two additional scenic design positions follow.]

Sound Design & Music Composition

State University (2000-2003)

Art	Sound Effects Sequencing	Director: Murray McGibbon
Lysistrata	Music Coordinator/Composer	Director: Noah Tuleja

[One additional sound design and music composition position follows.]

Stage Management

San Diego State University (1991-1996)

It's a Bird, It's a Plane, It's Superman	Director: Paula Kalustian
Diamonds	Director: Paula Kalustian
Midsummer Night's Dream Assistant Stage Manager	Stage Manager: Jim Baldwin

Properties Master

State University (2000-2003)

Pirates of Penzance
Noises Off
Much Ado About Nothing
Lysistrata
[One additional properties master position follows.]

Carpentry

San Diego Opera (1999-2000)

The Crucible
Alcina
Il Trovatore
A View From The Bridge
The Method
Cosi Fan Tutti
Falstaff
Rigoletto
[Four additional carpentry experiences follow.]

Production Crew

San Diego Opera (1999-2000)

Hansel & Gretel	Run Crew
Il Trovatore	Run Crew
Don Giovanni	Follow Spot Operator
Falstaff	Run Crew
Of Mice And Men	Properties Crew

[Three additional production crew experiences follow.]

REFERENCES
[The names of four references follow.]

Sample Professional Vita, Business
Accepted position at a large public research university

Min Researcher
Phone
Email
Address
City, State, Zip code
Visa Status: US Permanent Resident Application Pending

EDUCATION

University of X
Ph.D. Finance, May 2007 (Expected)

Princeton University
Master in Finance, May 2003

University of Maryland at College Park
M.S. Agricultural Economics, May 2001

People's (Renmin) University, China
B.S. Economics, July 1996

WORK EXPERIENCE

Sanford Bernstein, NY
Research Associate, Quantitative Asset Management Strategy, 02/2003-08/2003

Deutsche Bank Asset Management, NY
Summer Intern, Global Research Center, 06/2002-09/2002

WORKING PAPERS

"Financial Constraints, R&D Investment, and Stock Returns: Theory and Evidence"
(Job Market Paper)
Committee: Name, Name, Name, Name, Name

"Distinguishing Rational and Behavioral Models of Momentum"
Ongoing Research

Internal Capital Allocation and Organization Scope: Theory and Evidence from the Biopharmaceutical Industry

Asymmetric Information and Stock Returns: Evidence from Biotechnology Alliances

Researcher 2

RESEARCH INTERESTS

Corporate Finance, Asset Pricing, Financing of Innovations, High-tech Industries

CONFERENCE PRESENTATIONS

Midwest Finance Association, Chicago, 2006
Eastern Finance Association, Philadelphia, 2006

TEACHING EXPERIENCE

Teaching Assistant, The ABC Business School, University of X, 2003-2006
- Funding Investments, Dr. Name (MBA and Undergraduate)
- Financial Derivatives, Dr. Name (MBA and Undergraduate)
- Trading and Investing, Dr. Name (MBA and Undergraduate)
- Real Options, Dr. Name (Undergraduate)
- Corporate Finance, Dr. Name (Undergraduate)
- Monetary Economics, Dr. Name (Undergraduate)

HONORS AND AWARDS

Dean's Fellowship for Distinguished Merit, University of X, 2003-2007
Best Second-Year Paper (Bessie DeVault Scholarship), University of Maryland, 2000
Graduate Student Fellowship, University of Maryland, 1998-2000
Scholarship for Academic Merits, People's (Renmin) University, 1992-1996

REFERENCES
[The names and contact information of three references follow.]

Sample Professional Vita, Social Work
Accepted position at a large public research university

Curriculum Vitae
Nina Candidate

Education

Ph.D. candidate, Social Welfare, University of X, City, State (2007)
M.S.W., Social Work, University of Texas, Austin, TX (1995)
B.A., Psychology, University of North Carolina, Greensboro, NC (1992)

Grant Experience

Principal Investigator, Children's Bureau, Grants for Doctoral Student-Initiated Research in Child Abuse and Neglect, Children's Bureau (2003-2005)

Title: *A Population-Based Investigation of the Prevalence of Children's Exposure to Domestic Violence and the Co-occurrence of Child Maltreatment*. Research funded by the Department of Health and Human Services. <u>Objective</u>: To develop a typology of domestic violence events, and examine the prevalence and nature of children's exposure to each type. Associated risk factors were also examined, including the co-occurrence of domestic violence and child maltreatment ($50,000).

Research Experience

Research Assistant, Women and Family Project Laboratory, University of X (2006-present)

Psychiatric and Behavioral Consequences for Children of Battered Women. Research funded by the Administration for Children, Youth, and Families. <u>Objective</u>: To interview mother-child dyads across a 10-year period to document the effects of growing up in households with domestic violence. <u>Responsibilities</u>: Conduct secondary analyses of dataset to examine both how children's exposure to domestic violence affects their school achievement and the ways social capital in families is derailed through violence and poverty.

Research Assistant, Field Center for Children's Policy and Research, University of X (2005-2006)

Safe and Bright Futures Initiative. Research funded by the Department of Health and Human Services. <u>Objective</u>: To plan and develop a coordinated community response to children exposed to domestic violence using pediatric healthcare settings as a focal point. <u>Responsibilities</u>: Provided assistance in understanding national research base on children exposed to domestic violence; supported grant writing efforts; co-chaired subcommittee to identify effective service delivery to families experiencing domestic violence.

Research Assistant, Graduate School of Education, University of X (2002-2006)

Building Scientifically Valid Systems to Investigate the Prevalence and Impact of Children Exposed to Domestic Violence. Research funded by the Packard Foundation. <u>Objective</u>: To develop a valid and reliable protocol for documenting the prevalence and nature of children's exposure to domestic violence across two municipalities. <u>Responsibilities</u>: Analyzed and interpreted quantitative data using multiple logistic regression and cluster analysis; developed grant proposals; wrote research summaries.
[Three additional entries follow.]

Teaching Experience

Instructor, School of Social Policy & Practice, University of X (2003-present)

Courses taught (All MSW level): Individuals and Families in the Social Environment (HBSE I); Groups and Communities in the Social Environment (HBSE II); Introduction to Social Work Research; Middle Childhood and Adolescence (Theory); Intimate Violence.

Instructor, School of Social Administration, Temple University (2002-2006)

Courses taught at the BSW level: Senior Seminar in Social Work Practice; Senior Seminar Field Liaison; Human Behavior in the Social Environment; Social Welfare Policy in the U.S. *MSW level*: Practice of Social Service Delivery I & II; History and Philosophy of Social Welfare; Evaluation of Clinical Practice; Human Behavior in the Social Environment.

Instructor, Social Sciences Department, Community College of Philadelphia (2001-2002)

Courses taught: Introduction to Sociology; Sociology of the Family.

Practice Experience

Lead Therapist, Kerr Youth and Family Center, Portland, OR (1997-1998)

Developed treatment plans for adolescent girls in a residential facility; implemented individualized behavior modification programs; managed treatment milieu; supervised team of staff members.

Clinical Social Worker III, Austin State Hospital, Austin, TX (1996-1997)

Provided case management to clients and their families; co-facilitated group therapy with adults diagnosed with anxiety and mood disorders; participated in multi-disciplinary treatment planning. [Two additional entries follow.]

Other Professional Activities

Advisory Board Member, Clinical Network on Children's Exposure to Domestic Violence. Invited to sit on board comprised of representatives of Philadelphia agencies serving children, with the goal of improving the city's response to children exposed to domestic violence (2006-present).

Conference Co-Chair, 5th Annual Cross University Collaborative Mentoring Conference, *Developing Science & Scientists: Integrative Processes for Theory, Research and Practice.* University of X, City, State (2005, May).

BSW Curriculum Committee, Temple University. Invited to participate in committee to review changes to the BSW curriculum in accordance with Council for Social Work Education guidelines (2004-2005).

Publications

Name, & Candidate, N. (in preparation). Dual victimization: A population-based investigation of children who have experienced both child maltreatment and exposure to domestic violence.

Name, Candidate, N., & Name. (in preparation). Parent voices: An assessment validation procedure with Head Start parent partners.

Name, Name, & Candidate, N. (2006). Social capital and school achievement of youth exposed to domestic violence. Manuscript under review.

Name and Candidate, N. (in press). Children's direct exposure to types of domestic violence crimes: A population-based investigation. *Journal of Family Violence.*

Candidate 2

Name, Candidate, N., Name, & Name (in press). Domestic violence and children's presence: A population-based study of law enforcement surveillance of domestic violence. *Journal of Family Violence.*

Name and Candidate, N. (2007). Children's direct sensory exposure to substantiated domestic violence crimes. *Violence & Victims, 22,* 158-171.

[Two additional publications follow.]

Presentations

Candidate, N. (2007, March). *Children's direct sensory exposure to domestic violence and associated risk characteristics. A population based study.* Poster presented to the Society for Research on Child Development, 2007 Biennial Meeting, Boston, MA.

Candidate, N. (2007, January). *A population-based study of children's direct sensory exposure to domestic violence.* Paper presented to the Society for Social Work and Research, Eleventh Annual Conference, San Francisco, CA.

[Nine presentations follow.]

Professional Memberships

Society for Social Work and Research
American Professional Society on the Abuse of Children
National Association of Social Workers
Society for Research in Child Development
American Public Health Association

Professional References

[Names and contact information of three references follow.]

Contact Information

Home Address
Telephone
E-mail

Candidate 3

Sample Fine Arts Vita
Currently employed at a large public research university

Curriculum Vitae
Marcus Artist   Address, City, State, Zip code   Phone number, E-mail address

EDUCATION
1994–1996 M.F.A. X Academy of Art, City, State

1989–1993 B.F.A. Rhode Island School of Design, Providence, Rhode Island

PROFESSIONAL EXPERIENCE
2004–Present Assistant Professor – Department of Fine Art and Visual Communications
University of Z, City, State
Coordinator of the Graduate Program and teaching both academic and studio classes for graduate and undergraduate students.

2001–2004 Visiting Assistant Professor – School of Art
Carnegie Mellon University, Pittsburgh, Pennsylvania
Duties include Teaching Beginning and Advanced Drawing, Graduate Academic and Integrative Seminars, Concept Studios (Time and Space, Senior Project), Cultural Semiotics, and advising Graduate Art students

2000 (Spring) Visiting Lecturer – Art and Art History Department
University of Chicago, Chicago, Illinois
Duties include developing and teaching one beginning and one advanced studio art class for undergraduates and advising the Graduate Art students

2000 (Fall) Full Time Lecturer–Humanities (Art Department)
Delta College, Midland, Michigan
Courses developed and taught include "Drawing 1," "Two-Dimensional Design," and "QuarkXpress Computer Design"

1999–2000 (Fall) Adjunct Professor – Liberal Arts; "Cultural Semiotics"
Center for Creative Studies, Detroit, Michigan
Teaching the history and language of Semiotics and using the systems discussed to analyze different aspects of culture (Advertising, The City, Race, Class, Gender, Media, etc.)
[Two additional positions follow.]

VISITING LECTURES, CRITIQUES, PAPERS
2007
Hosting Panel (with Name) "Painting and Plurality" CAA NYC
Public Lecture for "InWords" – University of Delaware
Visiting Critic – University of Alabama
Visiting Speaker – St. Mary's College of Maryland

2006
Visiting Critic – X Academy of Art
Visiting Critic and Speaker – Pennsylvania State University

2005
Visiting Lecturer and Critic – Cleveland Institute of Art
Co-presented paper titled "The Artist as Media Integrator" for lecture series and upcoming book on "Integrated Media."
Visiting Critic – Carnegie Mellon University MFA Program
Visiting Critic – Rhode Island School of Design
Visiting Lecturer – Mount Holyoke College

2003
Part of the Panel "Teaching Painting in the Post-Digital Era"
Co-presented paper titled "Two Perspectives on Some Shifting Scopic Regimes," South Eastern College Art Association Conference – Raleigh, North Carolina
Visiting Critic – Rhode Island School of Design (Architecture Program)

2003
Visiting Lecturer and Critic – University of Alabama Visiting Critic and Instructor – X Academy of Art *(spring) part 2 – "The Contemporary Sublime, Uncanny, and Abject"*

2002
Visiting Critic and Instructor – X Academy of Art *(fall) part 1 – "The Unit, Repetition and Difference"*
Part of the Carnegie Mellon University Artist Lecture Series
Pittsburgh, Pennsylvania
[Five additional lectures, etc. follow.]

ONE PERSON EXHIBITS
2007   **RetroCircumSpect** (Nov. –Dec.) – Freedman Gallery at Albright College, Reading, Pennsylvania
        Knock (with Name) – Plan B Gallery, Banff Art Center, Banff, Canada
2004   **Nework** – University of Z
1998   **Hooks and Lines and Sinking** – The Urban Institute for Contemporary Art, Grand Rapids, Michigan
        Thinking Out Loud – Big Biscuit Gallery, Detroit, Michigan

SELECTED GROUP EXHIBITS
2007   **Art & Place 2: Material at Hand** – Space 301, Mobile, Alabama
2006   **Mediated** – Clarion University of Pennsylvania, Clarion, Pennsylvania
        Nest – Paul Kotula Projects, Detroit, Michigan
        Art Basil Miami – Paul Kotula Projects, Miami, Florida
2005   **Four Years Later** – Fe Gallery, Pittsburgh, Pennsylvania
        Temporary Alliances – Moore College of Art, Philadelphia, Pennsylvania
        Crafty Bastards – alternative craft fair, Washington, D.C.

Identity – Gallery MC, New York, New York
2004   **Media City 11, International Festival of Experimental Film & Video Art** (collaborative work with Name) Artcite Inc., Windsor, Ontario
Machine Life (collaborative work with Name), The Davies Foundation and Samuel J. Zacks Galleries, Kingston, Ontario, Canada
Video Bodies (collaborative work with Name)
{Twenty-one additional exhibitions follow.]

ARTICLES AND REVIEWS
2007   Sozanski, Edward. "Art: The Power of language as image." *Philadelphia Inquirer*, January 21, 2007
2006   Biro, Matthew. "Contemporary Developments in Drawing." *Contemporary Magazine*, no. 83, 2006. London, England.
Mazzei, Rebecca. "Mutant scribe: Marcus Artist and his unsteady hand." *Detroit Metro Times*, June 7, 2006
Mansen, Ann. "Artists play on words in upcoming exhibition." *Messenger*, Volume 14/number 4, 2006
2005   Shaw, Kurt. "Tragedy Examined." *Pittsburgh Tribune* Review, October 13, 2005
2004   Smusiak, Cara. "Machines come to life at Agnes Etherington." *Queen's Journal*, February 2004, Vol. 131/issue 32
[Nine additional reviews follow.]

GROUP EXHIBITION CATALOGUES and PUBLICATIONS
2007   "InWords: The Art of Language," for the catalogue "InWords," University of Z
2005   "Missing the Point," for the catalogue "Pause: The Work of Brian Bishop," University of Alabama
2004   "Machine Life" catalogue, Queen's University
"100 Creative Drawing Ideas," edited by Name, Shambhala Press
[Three additional group exhibition catalogues follow.]

Chapter 11
Additional Application Materials

About Your Research

Dissertation Abstract

You may be asked to provide an abstract of your dissertation as part of the initial screening process for a faculty position. Or you may wish to provide it with your application whether or not you are specifically asked for it.

Your abstract should conform to the conventions for your field. It is usually one or two pages long. Make the abstract, and therefore your dissertation, sound interesting and important. Use the active rather than the passive construction whenever possible, and stress findings and conclusions where they exist. Rather than saying, "A possible relationship between x and y was studied," say, for example, "Demographic data indicate that x increased as y declined."

Briefly indicate how your research fits into a broader context to answer the implicit "Why should anyone care?" question that may be asked of any piece of research. Someone who reads your abstract should have a clear idea of what your work entailed and want to ask you more about it. Write, rewrite, and seek critiques from your advisor and others in your department until you're satisfied that the abstract will achieve this effect.

Research Statement

Like an abstract, this short summary (usually one or two pages) may be requested as part of the application process. At other times, you may choose to include it to strengthen your application. Preparing this document is wonderful practice for interviews (see Chapter 14, "Interviewing"), because employers are keenly interested in what you plan to do in the future. It is not expected that you will have begun to do research beyond your dissertation or your current postdoctoral work, only that you will have begun to think about it coherently.

If you plan to publish your research as several articles or turn it into a book, you may mention that fact briefly. Be sure, however, to discuss plans for research that extend beyond what you're doing now. If your plans sound simply like extensions of your current work, or if you use phrases like "We do this," then you risk giving the impression that you view your plans as an extension of your advisor's research and that you have not begun to think of yourself as an independent researcher.

Give a brief context for your research interests, including how they fit into work others have done, and then discuss your plan for investigation. It is very important to communicate a sense that your research will follow logically from what you have done and be different, important, and innovative. Describing plans at an appropriate level of generality/specificity may require some rewriting and feedback from faculty members. A research plan so specific that one article could complete it is too limited, but one that includes a whole area of study, for example, "labor economics," is too general. If you will require substantial facilities and/or external funding for your research, include that in your discussion. If you've identified funding organizations likely to support your research plans, indicating that this is the case will make your plan sound more credible.

If this document makes the reader want to ask you further questions, even challenge you, it has done its job admirably, because it has helped make it seem that an interview with you would be lively and interesting. Write as clearly and concisely as you can.

While of course it would be unethical for members of a hiring committee to appropriate a candidate's detailed research plans for their own research, candidates have at least suspected this has happened to them. Find your own balance between talking about your research plans specifically enough to be credible and abstractly enough to protect your interest in your own creative ideas.

Dissertation Chapter or Other Writing Sample

In some fields a writing sample is requested as a matter of course, and you should be preparing one as you prepare your other job hunting materials. In other fields these documents are usually requested only after an initial screening, and it isn't to your advantage to send them unsolicited. In deciding what to send, choose something that is interesting and stands on its own, even if it is part of a longer document. If you send a long chapter, you might want to enclose a note directing readers' attention to a particular section of it, since, in reality, many committee members will skim documents. Check with your advisor and other faculty members to see what work would represent you best. Apart from a dissertation chapter, it is usually better to send published, rather than unpublished, material.

About Your Teaching

Statement of Teaching Philosophy

While the word "philosophy" is often used as part of the name for this document, it is perhaps better thought of as a brief essay that will give a hiring committee an idea of what you actually do in the classroom. You will need to make some general statements, but make sure to include examples that illustrate what you mean by them. If at all possible, describe things you have already done, or at least seen in practice, rather than give examples which are entirely hypothetical. If students responded well to an approach, say so. Avoid clichés and "hot button" words that may immediately cause the hiring committee to identify you as something you are not. However, do not hesitate to express your ideas simply and directly.

For ideas, try to look at statements written by others in your department as well as those written by applicants to your department, if those are available to you. Look at the Web pages of hiring institutions and read their statements of philosophy, missions, and goals to help you get a sense of some of the dimensions which are frequently addressed when people talk about teaching.

Teaching Portfolio

Sometimes, particularly after making a "first cut," candidates are asked for additional materials about teaching, such as a syllabus for a course you have taught or a proposal for a course you would like to teach. Some candidates compile "teaching portfolios," which can include syllabi and other materials developed for courses, comments from students, and self-evaluations of one's teaching. While these can be nice enhancements, they are rarely required and should not be submitted unsolicited at the first stage of application.

However, Web-based versions (discussed in more detail in Chapter 12) should always be mentioned on your vita or in your cover letter. Compared to paper copy, they are much less burdensome for hiring committees.

If you haven't yet begun to compile materials for a teaching portfolio you might begin to do so, as this can be a helpful step in writing your teaching philosophy. It is also a good idea to get into the habit of keeping a record of work you do in the classroom, because teaching portfolios are sometimes required as part of a tenure file.

Evidence of Successful Teaching

Some job ads ask for "evidence of successful teaching." While such a requirement is obviously open-ended, it's a good idea to include something that involves external evaluation of your teaching. You might, for instance, present a faculty member with all your teaching evaluations, if your institution uses them, and ask that person to summarize them into a shorter letter. The author of the letter can interpret whatever numerical system is generally used by your institution. For example, if instructors of a required chemistry course on average receive scores of only 3 on a scale of 5, the person writing the letter can explain that your score of 3.7 is truly impressive. Sometimes candidates themselves put together an information sheet that might include this information as well as quotations from student evaluations. In addition to having a faculty member discuss your teaching, you could also selectively ask a few students to write on your behalf. If you've received teaching awards, you or someone writing about your teaching can put those into context as well.

Video of Your Teaching

As institutions try to control their hiring costs, they increasingly want to know more and more about candidates before paying to bring them to campus. On some occasions, institutions that care very much about the quality of teaching are asking candidates not only to write about their teaching philosophy but also to send a recording of their classroom teaching. Generally, this will be requested after the initial pool of applicants has been narrowed down to a smaller number. While there is no guarantee that you will be asked for a video, if you are concentrating your search on institutions oriented to teaching you should probably go ahead and prepare one so that you can have it ready immediately if it's requested.

You are more likely to be asked for a short recording than for one of a full-length class. If you want to emphasize the breadth of your teaching abilities, you might choose to compile a recording from shorter classroom segments. If you don't care to prepare it in advance of your applications, be prepared to produce one on short notice, if necessary. If you are currently teaching a course, you could easily produce a video quickly simply by arranging for part of one of your regular class sessions to be filmed. If you are not currently teaching, you might want to find someone who would let you use part of his or her class time for this purpose.

Other Things That Might Be Required

If you are in a visual field, such as fine arts or architecture, a portfolio or slides of your work will always be required, as may be an "artist's statement." Their preparation is beyond the scope of this discussion, but take them very seriously. Check with your professional association. For example, the College Art Association, www.collegeart.org, gives excellent advice on slide preparation. Your advisor will also be able to provide you with guidelines. Seek out his or her critiques, and ask others for theirs as well.

Schools with a strong religious identity are likely to ask candidates for a faith statement. This is an opportunity to talk, in a personal way, about your own religious faith and its relationship to your work as a teacher and scholar.

A Note About the Sample Materials That Follow

The following examples, generously volunteered by real candidates, are provided to give you an idea of what such materials look like. We have not modified them in any respect except to change the job candidates' names and current institutions, and correct a few typographical errors. Custom in your own field might well dictate that yours should be quite different in style, language, or appearance.

Sample Research Statement, Humanities

Anita Scholar

Statement of Research

In my research, I am drawn time and again to examine processes of identity-formation. Of particular interest to me is the ever fraught relationship between personal desire and socio-cultural influence in the determination of self-definition. I am also fascinated by the seemingly paradoxical nature of self-definition as a phenomenon that is, at turns, intractably rigid and unexpectedly flexible. I am interested in the relationship between art and society, in the roles that language, race and ethnicity, gender, sexual orientation, political ideology, profession, family, education, and particularly social class, play in determining who we believe we are--and, often more importantly, who we are not. The uses of these self-definitions are also a critical point of inquiry: what are the personal, socio-cultural, and political ramifications of the ways in which we choose--or are led--to define ourselves? These questions always seem to inform the thematic specificity of my investigations. Literature and film are prime vehicles for the study of self-expression and the representation of selfhood, for they take these as their very subjects. I have outlined below two research projects that I hope to carry out upon completing my dissertation. The first is to produce a manuscript for publication based on my thesis; the second is to engage in a book-length study of the literary fictionalization of theoretical discourse.

I. Affect and the Critique of Market Culture

My most immediate postdoctoral research project will be to revise my dissertation for publication. Entitled "Affect and the Critique of Market Culture in Latin American Literature and Film," my thesis explores the work of five novelists and filmmakers from Argentina, Bolivia, Chile, Cuba, and Mexico in an attempt to synthesize a model of globalized subjectivity representative of the broader Latin American perspective. Given the claims of representativity to which this project aspires, my first task would be to expand my treatment of Latin American cultural production significantly beyond these five case studies in order to present a deeper and more comprehensive consideration of the region's literature and film. Ultimately, I would like to arrive at a topical presentation of my study rather than orienting it around emblematic texts. In order to accomplish this, I will need to research other literary genres (e.g., short story, poetry) and include further analyses of representative novelistic and cinematic works.

I would likewise seek to expand my base knowledge of recent cultural production in the United States, especially literary, in order to craft a final manuscript that can rightfully claim to be more comparative in its approach and analyses. Developing and incorporating a more nuanced understanding of U.S. culture would enhance the project not only as a means of identifying with greater clarity the cultural pressures exerted on the South by its eminently influential neighbor to the North, but also as a means of developing a model of convergent and divergent cultural tendencies across the two regions. To what extent do they participate in the same globalized market culture and to what extent do they play distinct roles with distinct perspectives? I have attempted to give these vital questions preliminary answers, but believe they warrant further research of U.S. cultural production.

Finally, I would like to develop a clear distinction between the cultures of modernity/postmodernity and globalization in order to periodize my project's claims regarding the models of subjectivity prevalent in the latter. There are generally two schools of thought with respect to the filiation of globalization with modernist capitalism: the first characterizes post-Industrial Revolution capitalism as one long continuum (Jameson); the second argues that globalization constitutes a dramatic and qualitatively distinct turn in capitalist practice and culture (Beck, Lash). My view is that there is truth in both perspectives and that they are not inherently contradictory. For the purposes of strengthening the foundation of my own project, then, I need to develop a working model of pre-globalized subjectivity that is at once differentiated from its globalized counterpart and reflective of an underlying continuity between the two. To this end, I will explore theoretical approaches to the capitalist culture of the modern and postmodern periods and produce a sufficiently representative survey of their cultural production in the United States and Latin America.

II. The Fictionalization of Theory

A second book-length project that interests me is the phenomenon of the fictionalization of theory in Latin American literature--that is, the self-conscious structuring of fictional texts around the scaffolding of theoretical discourse (I here define "theory" broadly as post-linguistic turn philosophy: structuralism, poststructuralism, deconstructionist thought). Among the authors whose works could be studied in this way are Severo Sarduy (Cuba), Luisa Valenzuela (Argentina), and Diamela Eltit (Chile). These writers, principally novelists, construct their texts on the strength of a conceptual foundation informed by an amalgam of poststructuralist--primarily French--theory. Sarduy, as an emigré in Paris, was involved with the Tel Quel group and attended Jacques Lacan's famous weekly seminars. Valenzuela and Eltit incorporate into their texts feminist perspectives on psychoanalysis (Luce Irigaray, Hélène Cixous) and poststructuralist ideas about canonicity and power (Roland Barthes, Michel Foucault).

These novelists write against or under dictatorships that adopt a repressive or outright anti-intellectual stance toward literary and humanistic thought (Batista, Castro, Videla, Pinochet). In the face of such repression and censorship, it would make sense that authors might reach for highly developed, yet codified, mechanisms of opposition to these regimes. Poststructuralist theoretical discourse is precisely such an instrument: in general terms, as a subset of philosophy, it occupies a privileged position in the humanistic disciplines; in specific terms, as a particular body of thought, it theorizes the cultural dynamics of power, control, and subjectivity that are apropos of these authors' resistance to the socio-political circumstance of dictatorship. This study would interrogate the conditions that give rise to this phenomenon and the changes it signals both in the role of the contemporary Latin American intellectual and in the nature of the long-standing cosmopolitan intellectual relationship between Europe and Latin America.

Sample Research Statement, Social Science

RESEARCH STATEMENT – Lourdes Sociologist

I began doing research as an undergraduate student at the University of California, Irvine. After coming to the University of X for a summer workshop in demography, I began an affiliation with the Mexican Migration Project (MMP) in 1997. I did my fieldwork on a bi-national sample of two rural villages from Guanajuato, Mexico for my honors thesis, which focused on the topic of reciprocity and solidarity among migrants from Mexico to the U.S. Then after entering the doctoral program at University of X, I was able to get a grant from the Mellon Foundation which allowed me to survey a bi-national sample from two additional different-sized communities from the same Mexican state. For all four communities, I administered my own questionnaire about social networks while also administering the ethnosurvey questionnaire developed by Name and Name. At present, I am using the data I collected during this fieldwork for my dissertation.

While I was writing my honors thesis about the relations of reciprocity and solidarity among Mexican migrants, I noticed that the behavior of people within migrant networks was consistent with Durkheim's concept of mechanical solidarity. While working on my Master's thesis at University of X, I extended this observation by documenting the solidarity created among migrants who migrate from rural places of origin has a different social dynamic than the solidarity created by who migrate from urban places of origin. These findings suggested that researchers doing research work on the relationship between migration and social capital needed to pay more attention to rural versus urban origins. Following up on this idea, Name, Name and I decided to write a testing for systematic differences in the characteristics of migrants and the determinants of migration by size of origin community. In this work, we indeed found substantial evidence that those who migrate from urban places of origin do so for various different reasons, and used very different social mechanisms from those migrating from rural places of origin.

I then decided to investigate whether the behavior of solidarity that I observed among migrants from Guanajuato was similar to the solidarity behavior expressed by other Latino groups in the United States. I sought to measure whether the construction of solidarity through social networks led to higher wages among those already living in the United States. After analyzing the Multi-City Study for Urban Inequality dataset, I found evidence to the existence of something unique about the solidarity relations of the Mexican immigrants compared with other immigrant groups from Latin America, such as Puerto Ricans, Dominicans, and Central Americans. My findings also suggested that the solidarity among the Mexican immigrants did not necessarily lead to higher wages.

This prior research work led me to the subject of my dissertation, which seeks to look more closely at the interrelation between social context, social capital, and network structure using the novel social network data that I collected in my Guanajuato fieldwork. By using quantitative and qualitative research methods, my dissertation is seeking to accomplish the following objectives. First, I seek to identify whether there are differences in social network structure and the resulting accumulation of social capital among migrants from rural as opposed to urban communities. Second, I seek to identify which network structures produce more and higher quality social capital. Third, I propose to investigate and empirically confirm two theoretical propositions: the strength of strong

L. Sociologist, Research Statement, 2

ties, and the clique effect. I argue that strong ties produced by clique network structures predominate among undocumented Mexican migrants and that this structure is the most conducive to the cultivation and sharing of social capital. I also argue that urban origin migrants who lack ready access to migrant networks deliberately seek out rural-based clique networks so that they can successfully migrate, find a job, and settle in the U.S.

My dissertation research promises to provide important information for an improved understanding of the concept of social capital and to yield important implications for public policy. My contributions to the understanding of the interrelation between social context, social network structure, and social capital represent a theoretical and methodological advance over prior work, and offer a more concrete and direct elucidation of the concept of social capital, which is often vaguely defined. In making this contribution my goal is to demonstrate the power of the solidarity emanating from clique networks in enabling risky ventures such as international migration. In addition to elaborating the concept of social capital, I also hope that a better understanding of how social networks operate might provide a useful tool enabling policy makers to design social programs for the benefit of disadvantaged migrants.

My future research plans include writing a book and several journal articles based on my dissertation and fieldwork in Guanajuato. I then plan to continue researching the interrelation of social networks and social capital among Latinos. My ultimate goal is to learn how social relations of social solidarity among immigrants lead to upward socioeconomic mobility in the United States. To do this I plan to collect data from migrants of other national origins in the United States, to undertake a comparative analysis of networks, social capital, and social mobility. I believe that one of the most important immigrant groups to consider is Asians, who have been labeled "the model minority." My next project will be to compare solidarity-producing behaviors across immigrant groups, including the various Latino sub-populations (Central Americans, South Americans, and Caribbeans) as well as the different Asian subgroups (Koreans, Chinese, Filipinos, and others).

Sample Research Statement, Science

Research Plan – Anthony Scientist, Ph.D.

My research is easily adaptable for the undergraduate student and will generate many small projects that can easily be completed. My work will grow from my postdoctoral research focusing on a protein, Yin Yang 1 (YY1). YY1 is a mammalian transcription factor that is required for normal embryogenesis. YY1 is structurally similar to PHO, a *Drosophila* protein. The activity of the PHO protein remains elusive, but the *pho* gene interacts genetically with the Polycomb-group (PcG) complex repression system. The similarity between YY1 and PHO led us to test if YY1 is a mammalian PcG protein. We found that YY1 is indeed a PcG protein and interacts with other PcG proteins. Characterizing YY1 as a PcG protein provided new insight into its contribution to mammalian biology.

The PcG proteins are part of a cellular memory system that regulates gene expression during embryogenesis. In order for cells to form the correct adult structures, they must have the correct "program" of gene expression. The PcG complex repression system contributes to this program by silencing target genes. Important targets for the PcG proteins are the homeobox genes that specify positional information in the embryo. Disruption of this system causes aberrant gene expression and transformation of body parts. One important, but poorly understood, property of the PcG proteins is their target gene specificity.

Appropriate targeting of PcG proteins is essential. So, how do PcG proteins find the appropriate targets? Polycomb Response Elements (PRE) are DNA sequences that bind PcG proteins. However, it is not clear how PRE sequences and PcG proteins interact. Nearly all identified PcG proteins lack DNA-binding activity, so other proteins must be responsible. Some *Drosophila* proteins have been implicated as PcG recruiting activities but these have no identified mammalian homologues, so their relevance to mammalian biology is questionable. No mammalian PcG recruiting proteins were identified until our lab's characterization of YY1. In our working hypothesis, YY1 recruits PcG proteins to DNA via its sequence-specific DNA-binding activity (finding PRE sequences within the DNA) and simultaneous interaction with PcG proteins (specific protein-protein interactions). Defining a role for YY1 in recruitment of mammalian PcG proteins will be a substantial advance in understanding the mechanisms of embryogenesis.

My research will investigate the recruitment of PcG proteins to DNA. I intend to use both *Drosophila* models and mammalian models. The PcG proteins have been thoroughly studied in flies because of the power of *Drosophila* genetics and because several PRE sequences have been isolated. *Drosophila* systems have identified interactions among PcG proteins that are important for mammalian systems. *Drosophila* and mammalian PcG proteins are highly conserved and are thought to work through similar mechanisms. One such *Drosophila* protein, Enhancer of zeste [E(z)], is thought to be recruited to PRE sequences by PHO. E(z) has two mammalian homologues – EZH1 and EZH2. Therefore we predict that YY1, based on its similarity to PHO, will recruit these proteins to mammalian PREs. I will investigate physical (protein-protein) interactions between YY1 and EZH1/EZH2 using standard biochemical techniques. Minimal regions for interaction will be identified using deletion analyses. I will also

Research Plan – Anthony Scientist 2

study YY1-EZH1/EZH2 complex binding to DNA using chromatin immunoprecipitation and gel-shift assays. These studies will help define the role of YY1 in recruiting EZH1/EZH2 to DNA.

We do not know if YY1 will be the only protein to recruit EZH1/EZH2. To identify other proteins that might recruit EZH1/EZH2 to DNA, cDNA libraries will be screened using yeast two-hybrid systems. Putative DNA binding proteins will be identified at the sequence level and interesting candidates can be tested as above in biochemical assays. Identification of DNA-binding proteins that also bind to EZH1/EZH2 will help identify biological functions of these proteins.

My research is cross-disciplinary incorporating material that they will learn in biochemistry, molecular biology, genetics, invertebrate biology, and anatomy. The research work can easily be divided among several students so that each student can make a unique contribution. In my experience mentoring students, they learn the techniques in a short amount of time. The research projects that students will work on will provide a valuable learning experience.

Sample Research Statement, Science

RESEARCH STATEMENT

Monique R. Researcher

PAST AND CURRENT RESEARCH

Theoretical cosmology strives to understand the structure and evolution of the universe. Three pieces of this puzzle with which I have worked are the law of gravity on megaparsec scales, the power spectrum of the initial density fluctuations after the big bang, and the mass function of low-mass galaxy clusters.

The law of gravity has been carefully tested and verified only up to solar-system scales. Persuasive evidence now indicates that the universe is not only expanding, but that the rate of expansion is increasing. Often this acceleration is attributed to an unknown particle or field dubbed "dark energy." Some papers (e.g., [1]) propose that the recent accelerated expansion of the universe could be due to changes in general relativity on large scales, instead of new fields or particles. My research [3] places the first constraints on how gravity behaves at megaparsec scales (scales that span clusters of galaxies).

Naturally, one cannot use orbital motion or laser ranging to test gravity at megaparsec scales. We use the evolution of structure formation: how the overdensities in the universe grow with time. This involves modeling matter as a pressure-less, nearly-homogeneous fluid, and computing how density perturbations change under the influence of gravity. The overdensities grow differently under a different law of gravity. We examine a couple of models in which Newton's law is modified at a huge physical scale, and work to first order and second order in the overdensity. We compare the power spectrum for a modified gravity law with observations, thus placing bounds on how greatly gravity could deviate from an inverse-square law on large scales. We find no deviation, but the constraints are weak. We also compute the change in the bispectrum (the fourier transform of the three-point correlation function), which involves second-order effects in the overdensity.

On the small-scale end of things, cosmology also addresses how the initial fluctuations in the universe were created. The most popular theory currently holds that the inhomogeneities were created by the quantum fluctuations of one or more homogeneous particle fields, and then quickly expanded to classical sizes during a period of rapid inflation of the universe. To test inflation and its competing theories, one needs to know the spectrum of the initial fluctuations. However, we cannot directly observe this primordial power spectrum. Until the universe cooled enough for hydrogen to form, the universe was an opaque, ionized plasma. The WMAP satellite has carefully measured the anisotropies in the cosmic microwave background (CMB), the light freed at the last-scattering surface (when hydrogen formed and the universe became transparent, three hundred thousand years after the big bang) [2]. Since the matter and radiation were strongly coupled before the last scattering, we can therefore infer the matter power spectrum at that time. We also know the physics of how the fluctuations evolved during those first three hundred thousand years: it is a complex set of transfer equations that can be computed with CMBFAST [5].

While a power-law primordial power spectrum fits the data very well, there remains the tantalizing possibility that there could be structure in the primordial power spectrum. Any spectral features

M. R. Researcher: Research Statement—2

would shed light on theories of the universe's birth. In my paper [4], we develop and apply a model-independent method to reconstruct the primordial power spectrum. We adapt and apply the smoothing spline method, a nonparametric technique to reconstruct a continuous function from discrete, noisy data. Using Markov Chain Monte Carlo to explore the likelihood of primordial power spectrum shapes, we find no statistically significant indication of deviations from a power-law spectrum. Our results also examine the degeneracy between the primordial power spectrum shape and the values of the cosmological parameters. We find virtually no difference in the matter density value and error when we give the primordial power spectrum a lot more freedom, but the errors on the optical depth and baryon fraction increase significantly.

For my current project, I am developing a method to help determine the mass function of low-mass galaxy clusters. Since the formation of clusters depends exponentially on a function of the matter density and dark energy, their mass function provides a sensitive probe of cosmological parameters. The Atacama Cosmology Telescope will conduct a large survey of galaxy clusters, observing their Sunyaev-Zel'dovich decrement (SZD). The SZD is caused by electrons in the cluster scattering the CMB photons to higher frequencies. It is roughly proportional to the number of ionized electrons in a cluster, which in turn is proportional to the number of baryons; thus the SZD provides an indication of the cluster's mass. However, we do not know for sure how well the baryons trace the mass for low-mass clusters. For high-mass, low-redshift clusters, weak gravitational lensing can provide a good estimate of the total cluster mass. For a small cluster (10^{14} solar masses), however, the weak-lensing signal is weak, especially at high redshifts. My project aims to combine the weak-lensing signals from several small clusters to increase the signal-to-noise, and thus establish the relationship between SZD and mass for low-mass clusters.

FUTURE RESEARCH

There are several natural extensions of my thesis work I will pursue in the near future. I have already derived an expression for the matter bispectrum under a perturbed law of gravity, which provides an independent constraint on the gravitational force law. I will place stronger limits on possible deviations from the inverse-square law by applying the bispectrum expression to observations, and combining it with my previous results from the power spectrum. The smoothing-spline analysis of the primordial power structure could be enhanced by incorporating large-scale structure data. Additionally, in my previous work, I kept the neutrino mass equal to zero. I plan to perform a nonparametric primordial power spectrum reconstruction while treating the neutrino mass and number of species as free parameters. This will explore degeneracies between the neutrino mass and primordial power spectrum shape, and truly test how much the CMB can say about neutrinos (and vice versa). With my current project, I would like to generalize assumptions about the shapes of galaxy clusters (circular lenses with NFW profiles) to stack their weak-lensing signals. I will also explore ways to improve the signal-to-noise of cosmological parameters from cluster surveys. Rather than translating the observational data into a mass function, and using the mass function to constrain cosmology, perhaps we could find a cosmology-constraining function more directly tied to the observations.

On a longer time scale, I plan to explore Lorentz-covariant modifications to the general relativity (GR) lagrangian at large scales. Many scalar-tensor theories of gravity are mathematically equivalent to modifications of general relativity without a scalar field. If I could find a paramerization of a Lorentz-covariant GR modification consistent with data, I could use the power spectrum and bispectrum from large-scale structure observations to constrain the theory. I'm also fascinated by holography: how the dependence of entropy on surface area, rather than volume, might constrain and imply theories of gravity.

I'm also excited to further develop the statistical tools I encountered while working with the smoothing-spline method. The primordial power spectrum reconstruction poses a challenge to the smoothing-spline, because a complicated nonlinear function lies between the data and the desired function. I chose to use a cross-validation method to select the smoothing parameter for the spline. (The smoothing parameter determines the balance between allowing the reconstructed function to bed to maximize the likelihood, without giving it too much freedom to fit noise in the data.) Since cross-validation is computationally expensive, I would like to derive an analytical approximation in this context. There are also alternative methods worth optimizing and exploring further, such as running another Markov Chain in which the smoothing parameter is a free parameter. Additionally, I plan to learn and apply a more rigorous computation of Bayesian evidence. I expect to find many other problems in astrophysics, and possible other fields, that could greatly benefit from these statistical methods.

UNDERGRADUATE INVOLVEMENT

Touching the extremes of human knowledge on both large and small scales, cosmology is an awe-inspiring field with an influx of data, and it offers many exciting and accessible research projects for undergraduates. I would love to involve bright undergraduates in the simple extensions of my past and current research, described above. Further development and application of the smoothing-spline method can provide many important undergraduate-level projects. One example of such a project would be to create a series of two-dimensional images, along with plots of their correlation functions and power spectra, such that they give an intuition for what the power spectrum means. Such projects would allow freshmen to develop tools they would need for research, without requiring more advanced coursework.

REFERENCES

[1] Sean M. Carroll, Vikram Duvvuri, Mark Trodden, and Michael S. Turner. Is cosmic speed-up due to new gravitational physics? *Phys. Rev.*, D70:043528, 2004.
[2] G. Hinshaw et al. First year Wilkinson microwave anisotropy probe (wmap) observations: Angular power spectrum. *Astrophys. J. Suppl.*, 148:135, 2003.
[3] Monique R. Researcher, Name, and Name. Limits on deviations from the inverse-square law on megaparsec scales. *Phys. Rev.*, D71:083004, 2005.
[4] Monique R. Researcher, Name, and Name. Smoothing spline primordial power spectrum reconstruction. 2005.
[5] U. Seljak and M. Zaldarriaga. A line of sight approach to cosmic microwave background anisotropies, *Astrophys. J.*, 469:437, 1996.

MONIQUE R. RESEARCHER. RESEARCHER, DEPARTMENT OF PHYSICS AND ASTRONOMY, UNIVERSITY OF X, CITY, STATE, ZIP CODE. EMAIL ADDRESS

Sample Research Statement, Mathematics

Research Statement   **John Patrick Scholar**

Current and Future Research

I analyze algorithms and data structures using analytic combinatorics and probabilistic methods. I am also greatly interested in information theory (see "Dissertation" below) and game theory (see my Teaching Statement).

My research is currently supported by an NSF grant: Asymptotic Enumeration, Reinforcement, and Effective Limit Theory (2006-2008). Name and I are Co-Principal Investigators. Our goal is the asymptotic estimation of constants for which a multivariate generating function is known. Our research in this direction can be roughly divided into two parts: we use computational symbolic algebra to implement complex analytic methods of analysis; we also continue to apply further techniques of integration of meromorphic forms so that the above analytic methods can be applied to a wider class of generating functions.

Also, I am analyzing the profile of suffix trees. The profile of a tree describes the number of nodes at a certain level of the tree. This parameter is quite powerful because it easily yields a great deal of information about many other parameters of the tree, including depth, fill-up level, height, shortest path, and size. A complete characterization of the profile of suffix trees seems feasible to me for two reasons: Recently, Name (Institution), et al., successfully analyzed the profile of a tree. Also, in my Ph.D. dissertation and in my recent paper with Name (International Institution), I was able to successfully translate several results about trees into new results about suffix trees.

I am collaborating with Name and Name (International Institution) on a problem concerning the unique minima in a collection of independent, identically distributed geometric random variables, where the mean of each depends on the total number of variables. We utilize an exponential diagonal depoissonization scheme.

Name (International Institution) coined the term "scholar-parameter" for the parameter of suffix trees I analyzed in my Ph.D. dissertation. We are working with Name, Name, and Name (International Institution) to analyze the behavior of this new parameter on a variety of other trees, including binary search trees, digital search trees, simply generated trees, and the cumulative scholar-parameter in trees.

Dissertation

My Ph.D. dissertation completed the resolution of an information theory problem: the incorporation of error-correction into an adaptive data compression scheme without the introduction of additional redundancy. Traditionally, adaptive data compression algorithms examine the uncompressed portion of a file, searching for subsequences that occur in a database; compression occurs as subsequences are replaced by pointers into the database. The Lempel-Ziv '77 algorithm is one such scheme with many desirable theoretical and practical properties; its compression ratio is asymptotically optimal, and the algorithm enjoys widespread use. Unfortunately, adaptive data compression algorithms traditionally have no error resilience. Transmission errors in a compressed file are propagated when the file is decompressed (so compressed files are even more susceptible to errors than uncompressed files). The standard remedy is to add redundant bits for error-correction.

My research proves that sufficiently many redundant bits are already present in the Lempel-Ziv '77 algorithm to allow substantial error-correction with no additional overhead. This surprising result is possible because the LZ '77 encoder is unable to completely decorrelate the input sequence. My research was done in collaboration with Name (Institution) and Name (Institution). In my dissertation, I prove that the number of pointers into the database in LZ'77 follows the logarithmic series distribution. My proof includes an extensive analysis and comparison of suffix trees and trees built over independent strings.

Sample Research Statement, Interdisciplinary (Computer Science and Linguistics)

Research Statement

Madeleine Researcher

I am a computer scientist with interdisciplinary research interests in natural language processing and computational biology. The connections between these two fields touch upon core areas of computer science such as algorithms, formal language theory, artificial intelligence and machine learning.

Like the terabytes of text available on the internet, genomic databases contain a vast number of biological data that are given to us in the form of raw, unlabeled sequences. But just as it is necessary to know the grammatical structure of a sentence in order to understand its meaning, it is necessary to know the three-dimensional structure of the corresponding protein in order to understand the function of a gene. Just as native speakers of a language communicate effortlessly, proteins fold quickly and spontaneously into their native structures, even though every sentence and every protein chain has a myriad of possible structures. My research addresses the question of how the hidden structure of such sequential data can be identified automatically. It also addresses the related question of how computational techniques can be used to understand (and ultimately exploit) the accuracy and efficiency of these search processes in nature. Both have important technological applications such as information extraction, natural language understanding, proteomics and drug design.

From a computational point of view, there is a deep, yet generally unexplored, connection between my two research areas, protein structure prediction and natural language parsing. Both tasks require an appropriate representation of the underlying structure (e.g. a formal grammar), a scoring function (a probability model or energy function) that ranks alternative structures of the same input string, and an efficient search algorithm that uses this scoring function to quickly identify the most likely structure among an exponentially-sized set of possible analyses. While protein structure prediction and parsing are typically only concerned with the identification of the desired structure, protein folding and human sentence processing studies are primarily concerned with the nature of the underlying search processes, both of which are equally difficult to observe experimentally. Computational approaches are therefore essential to our understanding, even if the underlying scientific questions are specific to each area.

The fundamental question that motivates my research on natural language is: how can the syntactic representations that are postulated by theoretical linguistics be acquired and processed efficiently? As a PhD student I decided to focus on supervised machine-learning techniques for expressive grammars. The aim of my PhD thesis under the supervision of Name at the University of Y was to develop the first wide-coverage statistical Combinatory Categorial Grammar (CCG) parser. Most statistical parsers use an impoverished linguistic representation that makes it difficult to obtain a corresponding semantic interpretation. CCG is an expressive, yet efficiently parseable, grammar formalism with a completely transparent syntax-semantics interface. In order to obtain sufficient amounts of labeled training data to estimate the parameters of the probability model, I developed an algorithm to translate the analyses in the X Treebank, a one million word corpus of Wall Street journal text annotated with simple phrase structure trees, into CCG. CCGbank, the resulting corpus, is now published through the Linguistic Data Consortium, and has been purchased by a large number of research institutes and universities. Through this work, as well as through many conversations with my colleagues at X, I have developed a strong interest in the linguistic issues that have to be taken into account when designing an annotation scheme for a treebank.

In developing my thesis parser, I was able to show that, contrary to common belief that more expressive probability models are required, the word-word dependency structures that approximate the underlying logical form in CCGbank can be captured with a very simple generative model. Although subsequent work by my former colleagues Name and Name has since shown that other models may achieve higher parsing accuracy, such generative models can still pay an important role in tasks such as language modeling, an area I would like to explore in future work. Since labeled data is expensive to produce, I have also worked on the use of semi-supervised machine learning techniques such as co-training to improve the performance of statistical parsers.

Most research on wide-coverage parsing with linguistically expressive grammars has concentrated on English. However, the need for expressive grammars is much greater in languages with free word order, such as German. I have recently developed an algorithm to translate the German Tiger corpus, a treebank of comparable size to the X Treebank, but with a very different syntactic annotation, into CCG, and plan to create a statistical parser that is trained on this data.

As a postdoctoral research fellow with Name at the University of X and Name at the University of State, City, I have also developed a strong research interest in protein folding and structure prediction. I am currently using simplified lattice models of protein structures to investigate the parallels between parsing and protein folding. In the theoretical and computational protein folding literature, there is a widespread assumption (sometimes contested by experimentalists) that folding is guided by a hierarchical search. Our paper in Proteins demonstrates that standard dynamic programming techniques used in statistical parsing provide an efficient implementation of such a search process. We develop a new folding algorithm that is based on the standard Cocke-Kasami-Younger (CKY) chart parsing algorithm. Unlike standard methods such as Monte Carlo or Molecular Dynamics simulations, CKY explores and returns all possible folding routes simultaneously. We show that a "computational folding rate" that is based on the combinatorics of this search process predicts important features of the known physical folding process. We also show that our algorithm defines a sequence-specific "chart energy landscape" whose shape determines the speed of the folding process.

I am currently extending this folding algorithm to obtain a continuous-time Markov chain that models the complete kinetics of a hierarchical folding process, including misfolding and unfolding events. Such kinetic models, or master equations, are often used in protein folding studies. However, current techniques typically require not only prior knowledge of the folded structure, but also exhaustive enumeration of all possible intermediate structures. The dynamic programming technique that I am currently developing improves upon this in a number of crucial aspects: because the states and transition rates of this model are obtained directly from CKY and do not require exhaustive enumeration, it can be applied to much longer sequences than is currently possible. Furthermore, because this model captures only those folding and misfolding events that arise in a hierarchical search process, it will provide a more stringent test of the hypothesis that protein folding is guided by a hierarchical search process.

Even though lattice models are important tools that allow us to understand the essential properties of complex systems such as proteins, the goal of my research is to understand the folding processes and predict the structures of real proteins. Future work will therefore extend both the search algorithm and the kinetic model to more realistic, off-lattice, representations of real protein sequences. The main challenge for realistic simulations of protein folding lies in the amount of computing time required. Here, we will be able to exploit the fact that CKY consists of many small search processes for short chain fragments that are easily parallelizable.

I also plan to investigate how recent advances in machine learning techniques that have been successfully applied to estimate parse selection models can be applied to learn energy functions from the structures in the Protein Data Bank. I believe that this may lead to more accurate coarse-grained energy functions that can be used in combination with CKY as a first pass to speed up folding simulations.

I would also like to investigate how the ways in which physicists think about processes such as protein folding, in particular the concepts of energy landscapes and transition states, which are commonly used to

Researcher, M., Research Statement, 3

explain why the folding speed of proteins varies so much between sequences, could be applied in models of human sentence processing to explain why the processing difficulty of sentences has similar degrees of variance.

Although, at first glance, protein folding and natural language parsing do not seem to have much in common, I strongly believe that as computer scientists, we are in the best position to identify and exploit the underlying connections between them.

Sample Statement of Teaching Philosophy, Humanities

Anita Scholar

Statement of Teaching Interests

My teaching interests, though diverse, nevertheless reflect a central and persistent curiosity regarding how people define themselves. Can these self-definitions ever be said to be entirely autonomous, or are they always in some measure born of socio-cultural forces that seek to mold the members of their group in a similar likeness? What role(s) do language, class, race and ethnicity, gender, sexual orientation, political ideology, profession, family, and education play in determining who we believe we are--and, often more importantly, who we are not? To what ends do we use these beliefs about ourselves and others? Convictions regarding identity are among the strongest motivating forces for human action; striving to understand how and why those convictions of self-definition come into being may help us comprehend not only who we think we are, but also why we act the way we do. I have always been drawn to literature and film as media that privilege as a classic narrative the development of the subject and, often, the self-conscious interrogation of identity. Certainly, information regarding self-definition may be gleaned from any aspect of human affairs. To my mind, however, nowhere else are these queries more readily explored than in a format which sets out expressly to probe the dimensions of the subject and lays bare an inner dialogue regarding the most profoundly and fastly held assumptions about how to answer the questions of who we (believe we) are and by what means we may acquire--or fashion--that knowledge.

One course I would like to teach would explore the representation of the globalized subject in Latin American literature, film, and cultural criticism. Such a course would examine works that emphasize the experience of a predominantly affective--as opposed to thinking--self as their primary narrative vehicle and suggest that the native capacity for emotion is the human subject's last line of defense against the encroachment of dehumanizing market forces. A course along these lines would focus on Latin American literary and cinematic works (e.g., novels by César Aira and Diamela Eltit; films such as *Suite Habana*, *21 Grams*, *Dependencia sexual*), though I would also like to incorporate U.S. film to give the course a comparative bent (e.g., *Fight Club*, *A.I.*, *Eternal Sunshine of the Spotless Mind*). I would complement these primary works with a careful selection of critical perspectives on globalized culture (e.g., Étienne Balibar, Don Slater and Fran Tonkiss, Scott Lash, Alberto Moreiras, Francine Masiello, Gilles Deleuze) and the studied observation of everyday media and advertising culture (e.g., journaled reactions to television, the *New York Times*, *El País*, NPR programming, advertisements). How does market culture seek to shape our sense of self? How do we react to and against those demands? The principal objective of the course would be for students to develop a model of subjectivity as dictated by the globalized market, and another of counter-subjectivity formulated in resistance. Requirements would include several brief reaction papers throughout the semester, an observation journal, and a final research paper or exam.

A second course would explore the profile of the Cuban Revolutionary subject since the fall of the Soviet Union and the ensuing "período especial en tiempos de paz" of extreme economic hardship. Many critics have forecasted the inevitability of economic and cultural liberalization in the wake of this crisis, yet the success of an initial stage of highly regulated neoliberal reforms has been followed by the unexpected constriction of those same measures and the renewal of hard-line Communist political practice and rhetoric. However, the influx of tourism and the outflux of emigration have contributed to a growing awareness of global culture within the island that compounds the intense circumstance of relative immobility on a national scale--that is, of a nation stuck in time and place, because of its adherence to an anachronistic socio-political model and the attendant need to restrict the movement of its populace. This course would seek to provide students with the tools to analyze the relative successes and failures of the Castro regime through a comparison of its goals (e.g., Fidel Castro's "Palabras a los intelectuales," Che Guevara's "El socialismo y el hombre en Cuba," Mikhail Kalatozov's *Soy Cuba* [*Ya Kuba* / *I Am Cuba*]) with its current cultural report card (e.g., Tomás Gutiérrez Alea's *Fresa y chocolate*, Juan Carlos Tabío's *Lista de espera*, Antonio Eligio Fernández's "Mundo soñado," Zoé Valdés's *La nada cotidiana*, Antonio José Ponte's "El abrigo de aire," Reina María Rodríguez's *...te daré de comer como a los pájaros...*, Orishas' "Qué pasa"). Students would consider how works in diverse media (literature, film, music, art, political discourse) reveal a composite--and complex--portrait of contemporary Cuban subjectivity and how it is situated with respect to a globalizing world. Requirements would include brief reaction papers, a class presentation, and a final research paper.

These two courses reflect the current directions of my research but by no means represent the boundaries of my broader teaching interests, which most immediately encompass twentieth- and twenty-first-century Latin American literature (novel, story, poetry, essay) and film. I also hope to develop courses that bring U.S. Latino and non-Latino cultural production into their scope of study. My goal is to bridge what strike me as profoundly artificial--though undoubtedly efficacious--disciplinary divides among Latin America, the United States, and the Latino U.S. I would like to design survey courses on the Spanish-speaking Caribbean (particularly around issues of diaspora and homeland), the Southern Cone (treating memory, violence, exile, and political ideals), the Latin American Vanguard, and the Latin American novel and short story. My training as a generalist (through coursework, exams, and teaching) has also prepared me to teach more panoramic surveys (e.g., Latin American literature from colonial times to the present). This capability is further enhanced by the very personal circumstance of visits and brief residences in Chile, Mexico, Cuba, and Spain. As a scholar and pedagogue, I view as a personal imperative the constant expansion of my knowledge and expertise. I hope that this priority will become manifest, over the course of my professional career, in a teaching portfolio of diverse content and perspective.

Sample Statement of Teaching Philosophy, Humanities

Lucille Scholar
Statement of Teaching Philosophy
University of X

Teaching as Revision

Adrienne Rich defines revision as "the act of looking back, of seeing with fresh eyes, of entering an old text from a new critical direction."[1] Understanding and explicating old texts in new ways is the cornerstone of my teaching philosophy. Whether a student is approaching a classic of English literature for the first time, or learning to re-examine a familiar tale from a fresh perspective, teaching literature requires both teacher and student to find new ways of understanding texts that have been read for many years. I use discussions of scansion, stylistic choices, socio-historical context, psychoanalytic theory, and literary history, as well as a focus on specific aspects of the text in order to estrange students from familiar texts and thereby to enrich the students' understandings of them. Learning can only take place when a student or scholar is faced with an aspect of a text that they do not already understand. When teaching Virginia Woolf's *To the Lighthouse*, I spend a considerable amount of class-time identifying the characteristics of Woolf's idiosyncratic style and then discussing the effect that her style has on the reader. I pair the novel with essays written by the theorists of the Wellesley Stone Center, such as Judith Jordan and Jean Baker Miller, in which they propose a model of psychological health and subjectivity based on empathy and connections to other people. Such a model is not only based on women's experiences, but also dovetails perfectly with Woolf's characterizations of Mrs. Ramsay, Cam, and Lily Briscoe. Certain other texts, such as fairy tales, seem at first to be transparent, but by presenting students with early versions of the tales which they think they know, I bring them face to face with stories in which active heroines, rape, and violence are regular occurrences, forcing them to question exactly how the "simple" stories they thought they knew came to be, and what the significance of their final forms may be.

After studying different forms of pedagogy, I have worked hard in order to make my classroom a space in which students can build on one another's ideas, where developing an understanding of a text is a co-operative group project, and in which disagreement is fruitful rather than combative. Many students are intimidated by an adversarial approach to discussion, and I do not wish anybody to be silenced in my classroom. One of the most successful techniques I have found to elicit co-operative responses from students is the list method. Simply put, rather than asking my class a question, I provide a topic of focus, and everybody is welcome to contribute observations about the text that would help to illuminate its approach to that particular topic. During a class devoted to Toni Morrison's *Beloved*, for instance, I might present the topic of "Recognition," and students would discuss the importance of recognition in the novel, and various methods which the characters use to recognize each other (songs, scars, hats, etc.). When a student makes an observation, I validate her or his point by noting it on the board. By the end of a successful exercise, the board is usually covered with students' points, and criss-crossed with arrows indicating how they relate to one another. As students become more sophisticated over the course of the semester, I include more and more group work, culminating in an optional extra-credit assignment in which groups of students teach a twenty-minute lesson themselves.

Teaching college students how to read always involves an element of revision, as they revisit and hone skills that they have already developed over the course of a lifetime. By illuminating new reading techniques and new aspects of literature, a professor can help her students make what had seemed old into something new. Students can thus help develop a more in-depth understanding of both their own abilities as well as the objects of their study.

---

[1] Adrienne Rich, "When We Dead Awaken: Writing as Re-Vision," *Adrienne Rich's Poetry and Prose: Poems, Prose, Reviews, and Criticism*, ed. Barbara Charlesworth Gelpi and Albert Gelpi (New York: Norton, 1993), 167.

Sample Statement of Teaching Philosophy, Science

Teaching Philosophy—Anna Chemist

In 2005, distinguished scientist Richard Zare wrote an editorial for *Chemical and Engineering News* about teaching chemistry. His short essay, along with the subsequent responses, prompted me to think seriously about my experiences as a student, a teacher and a researcher during the formulation of my teaching philosophy. The main point of Zare's essay was to discourage teaching focused on memorization, especially as it relates to standardized test success, and instead to focus on the scientific method and the skills necessary to be successful in research. I think the latter can frequently be translated into life skills, and yet, a certain amount of memorization is necessary to succeed in chemistry. I feel both of these methods have merits and should be part of teaching and learning in any classroom, whether graduate or undergraduate.

My experiences with these two teaching methods, teaching towards problem solving and teaching towards memorization, have shaped my philosophy. As an undergraduate, courses beyond organic chemistry mainly consisted of take home and open book exams. The professors could ask difficult and time-consuming questions akin to problems experienced in a research laboratory. However, memorization of Bragg's Law or commonly used integrals was not required. Returning to in-class exams in graduate school was sometimes a struggle because it necessitated memorizing formulas that classmates from different backgrounds already knew. Yet, students, such as those I taught as an undergraduate, were at ease working on different experiments from their classmates and solving a wide range of problems. The students I taught during graduate school contrasted with my undergraduate teaching and learning experiences. I encountered juniors and seniors who had already completed a number of science classes and should have been able to solve most of the "thinking" questions I posed to them. They sometimes succeeded, but more often than I expected, they were unable to proceed without my guidance. These same students could easily draw the structure for any molecule I asked about, clearly revealing an imbalance between memorization and scientific inquiry. As a result, I think a combination of these two approaches would best prepare students for their future problem solving and scientific pursuits.

In the classroom, I believe textbooks and traditional lectures coupled with modules based on related topics of interest and current literature would be valuable to graduate and undergraduate students. One such module program has been developed by a colleague. In working through several of these modules, it became clear how easily they could be integrated into a variety of chemistry courses. In addition, I would be eager to develop my own modules, focusing on environmental problems. Variation is an excellent way to attain and maintain the attention of students. Further, the combination of these different approaches can lead to more critical thinking in the classroom.

I believe most graduate students are in need of a guiding force more than a strict lecturer. One of my favorite classroom moments in graduate school was presenting a journal article of my choosing during our course on chemical dynamics. This assignment was incredibly valuable to me as it allowed me to think outside of the textbook and gave me the opportunity to carefully review the current literature. I chose a paper that turned into an idea for a project to attempt in the research laboratory in the following years.

Beyond my ideas regarding classroom pedagogy, I believe that everyone can learn chemistry. For undergraduates especially, relating chemistry to my interest in the environment is an excellent way to achieve this ideal, as environmental issues intersect with many subjects. As an undergraduate, my exploration of environmental issues led me to disciplines varying from biology to political science. I continued to pursue this interest by taking courses in environmental law and chemistry following graduation. This subject lends itself to the creation of a cross-listed courses with topics reaching from molecules, reactions and dynamics, to policy and law impacting scientific research and vice versa. The problem solving, visualization and analytical skills that students gain from exposure to chemistry greatly enhance their education.

Sample Statement of Teaching Philosophy, Science

TEACHING STATEMENT

Monique R. Researcher

Pursuing deep insights in the physical sciences and mathematics brings me immense gratification. Even more rewarding, however, is to share my understanding and discoveries with others. I have sought out opportunities to share my enthusiasm for physics at all levels, from running after-school elementary science programs to giving talks to my colleagues about my research. At the university level, I have established and taught recitation sections for both mechanics and electromagnetism. I also tutored all levels of introductory physics throughout college.

I have two main goals when teaching quantitative sciences: to teach the thinking process to solve problems, and to inspire the wonder that drives science. Physics and its related sciences are especially effective at teaching critical thinking skills, such as the ability to synthesize information and decipher truth from nonsense. Physics occurs all around us all the time, yet it is not transparent, and cannot be learned by rote techniques. It requires playing, experimenting, deducing, extrapolating from what you know to new scenarios and testing that extrapolation. The wonder of physics lies in the amazing things physics can do and describe, from how a bicycle or television works to phenomena at femtometer or gigaparsec scales. Beyond piquing curiosity, I seek to convey the power of physics to explain and predict diverse phenomena with a few universal concepts. Of course, students need to learn the terminology and information and be able to use the right equation for a problem, plug in numbers, and get an answer. However, if this is all the students take away, I will not have met my goals.

Guided discovery provides the means to achieve my teaching objectives. Since my goal is to teach a thought process, not a collection of facts, I intend to give students a chance to play with ideas and arrive at realizations of their own. I believe concepts are best mastered through "inquiry-based" learning, but physics would take forever to learn if students simply pursued their own questions and ideas. They need guidance to explore questions in ways that lead to powerful realizations. My lecture style involves asking a series of guided questions, as demonstrated by the example social relativity lesson summarized below. I try to pose and encourage questions that build up to the concepts I wish to convey, and actively engage students in finding the answers. Whenever possible, I prefer to use activities and demonstrations to raise and resolve questions. Before recitations on accelerating elevator problems, for example, I would borrow a large spring scale and a weight from the demo lab. I tend to respond to relevant questions by breaking them down into simpler questions and guiding the students to the answer. I like to encourage teamwork and peer teaching, especially in labs and office hours. One of the best ways to learn a concept is to explain it to someone else.

Preparation is key to a successful lesson. I enjoy the process of reducing an old, familiar concept back down to its building blocks, and coming up with different ways of building it up. I never learn a subject so well as when I get to teach it. My most successful lesson plans serve as flexible outlines with multiple explanations and approaches to the material. In the classroom, I try to let the students' real-time reactions determine which approaches to take and how fast to proceed. My favorite curricula have lessons that both build on one another and revisit ideas in multiple contexts. Since I believe the power of physics lies in the interconnections among ideas and phenomena, I like to seek them out and emphasize them. For instance, when teaching adiabatic expansion in a heat engine, I would point out that the same physics explains the cooling of the universe as it expands.

My volunteer service from high school through graduate school shows my dedication to science education and outreach. In tenth grade, I arranged to teach science to a fourth-grade class once a week. In college, I served as President of the Cornell Society of Physics Students (SPS), started an SPS outreach program for which I received the Robinson-Appel Humanitarian Award, advised freshmen physics majors, and organized an undergraduate research information session. I have worked with [city] public school teachers through Access Science at the University of X, and volunteered at the Y Institute Science Museum. In addition, my theater experience, which includes performing in over forty plays since childhood, has helped cultivate my stage presence and speaking ability. I am always learning and working to improve my teaching, and I actively seek feedback from my students and colleagues and keep journals on my teaching experiences. As a professor, I will further hone my teaching skills both in the classroom and supervising student research (see Research Statement), and I would involve undergraduates in science outreach to local schools and the community.

MONIQUE R. RESEARCHER. RESEARCHER, DEPARTMENT OF PHYSICS AND ASTRONOMY, UNIVERSITY OF X, CITY, STATE, ZIP CODE. EMAIL ADDRESS

Sample Statement of Teaching Philosophy, Mathematics

Teaching Statement   **John Patrick Scholar**

"Scholar Makes Calculus Worth Learning"

The title of a Facebook webpage – designed by my students of their own accord, soon after my arrival at the University of X – hopefully says it all. My goal is to foster students' intellectual well-being. My love of teaching (undergraduates and graduate students) complements my love of research.

When teaching undergraduates, I make math accessible even for non-math majors. I try to explain each topic in a variety of ways, knowing that everybody has a unique way of absorbing material. I not only write equations and draw graphs, but I also use auxiliary Maple presentations every day. As I discuss each topic, I consistently ask for feedback from the students throughout my lectures. By making the students feel welcome and at ease, the class atmosphere is very conducive to learning mathematics. I give very demanding homework assignments and exams, always encouraging students to extend themselves mentally. Students frequently say that my class was their favorite – and (more important) that they learned a great amount of material too!

Experience

During Spring 2006, I administered advanced oral examinations to two combinatorics graduate students. In Fall 2006, I taught a graduate Combinatorial Analysis and Graph Theory course. I also helped teach a summer graduate course at MSRI on Analysis of Algorithms and Information Theory.

During my first semester at University of X, I developed the math department's first Game Theory course. Advanced undergraduates, they mastered combinatorial (perfect information) games and also von Neumann/Nash (strategy) games. I also conducted one-on-one, customized reading courses in game theory with four undergraduates and one graduate student.

Throughout my career, I have won numerous awards based on student evaluations. In calculus courses at University of X, my students consistently have the highest scores (on common exams), suggesting that my students are digesting a larger portion of the material (as compared to students in other sections). I am always delighted to see my students succeed as a result of their hard work.

Student Comments

Comments from students I taught at University of X, Y University, and State University-City can be found on my website: URL

Sample Statement of Teaching Philosophy, Interdisciplinary (Computer Science and Linguistics)

Teaching Statement

Madeleine Researcher

Computer science is an exciting subject to teach. Although today's undergraduates grew up with the internet, and take the way in which computers have transformed our personal and social lives for granted, many might start college thinking computer science is just programming. But because computational approaches and algorithmic ways of thinking that lie at the heart of computer science are having a profound impact on virtually all academic disciplines and industries, tomorrow's computer scientists need not just excellent technical skills, but also the ability to apply their expertise to a wide range of other domains. This is particularly true for areas such as artificial intelligence and machine learning, which draw heavily on, and at the same time change, the way we think about human and animal learning and behavior, and provide general tools that allow us to process and extract information from vast amounts of data on a scale that would otherwise be impossible.

My own fields of research, computational biology and computational linguistics, both require computer scientists who not only master their own discipline, but also have a profound understanding of the theories and methods that are used to study language and biological systems, as well as biologists and linguists who are proficient in the use and development of computational techniques and models. Educating students both at the undergraduate and graduate level to work in such interdisciplinary and rapidly evolving fields is therefore particularly challenging, especially if the students have different backgrounds and interests. When I was a PhD student, I was the teaching assistant for a graduate-level course in statistical natural language processing that was attended by students whose first degree was in computer science, in linguistics, or in a completely unrelated discipline. While it was difficult to present the material in a way that would be both accessible to all students and interesting, it also created a unique opportunity to engage students and let them teach each other. In 2006, Name, Name, and I developed and taught an advanced course at the International Summer School on Language, Logic and Information (ISSLLI), in which we introduced advanced undergraduate and beginning graduate students from a variety of programs across Europe to current research on the extraction of linguistically expressive grammars from large corpora. I have not been able to engage in formal teaching activities beyond occasional talks and lectures at the University of X because I have been spending large fractions of my time away from [city] at the University of State-City and because my current visa status prevents me to take on additional work beyond the project I am employed on. I am therefore very much looking forward to obtaining a position that will allow me to get back into teaching.

At the undergraduate level, I would be happy to teach any introductory course in computer science and programming, algorithms and data structures, as well theory of computation, artificial intelligence and machine learning courses. At the advanced undergraduate and graduate level, I can teach machine learning, natural language processing, bioinformatics and computational biology courses. More specialized graduate seminars I would be happy to develop for students interested in computational biology could cover computational studies of protein folding, and the applications of formal language theory and grammars to the study of biological macromolecules. For students interested in natural language processing, I would like to offer seminars on expressive grammar formalisms, grammar extraction, tree-bank design, wide-coverage statistical parsing and related topics.

Sample Statement of Teaching Philosophy, Theatre

Edward K. Dramatist

Statement of Teaching Philosophy

Beyond the fundamental concepts of stagecraft, it is my goal to facilitate the students' acquisition of life-long skills in Theatre Technology. This will prepare them to function in a Theatre environment, whether they choose to become actors, directors, or stagehands. I also hope to help students develop problem-solving strategies in order to prepare them for the tasks that many of them shall face as Theatre professionals. In order to effectively teach students, there are several responsibilities that I must undertake. It is important for me to engage the students. Their study of Theatre Technology should not be perceived as a requirement, so much as a useful part of their overall Theatre education. It is also my responsibility to relate the subject matter of my courses to my students' efforts in Theatre. This serves to reinforce learning with the students' current endeavors. Finally, it is my charge to provide a safe environment for a student to learn, both in terms of physical safety and the ability to try, fail, and learn from their mistakes. A good instructor compellingly relates materials to the student. A great instructor also makes the student feel confident and capable.

Achieving these goals requires that the instructor take efforts to combine classroom learning with practical experience. Lectures should take advantage of the productions occurring at the school or in the community. The instructor should often relate a given topic to a current production and show students the technology in use. When a demonstration of the technology is not readily available, the instructor should use anecdotal examples of other productions in order to illustrate his point. In addition, assignments that allow a student to define aesthetics while remaining within given technical parameters should be assigned in order to create a synthesis of the art of Theatre with its technology. Supplemental to lecture and class projects, laboratory assignments that familiarize the student with technology should be a core part of any stagecraft curriculum. Concurrent with class work, students should be given roles in production that provide experience in a Theatre environment. In addition to receiving practical experience, students are likely to learn and retain more in this model. It is my hope that students will be able to experience a degree of pride in their work while participating in a "Hands-On" learning environment, thereby enhancing their educational experience.

My effectiveness as an educator is largely based on the achievement of my students. Testing students becomes a fundamental part of this evaluation. As a Theatre Technology educator, it is important to me that all students walk away from my class having retained at least the basic vocabulary of Theatre Technology. Conventional testing will be employed to that end. However, I also want students to learn problem solving and collaborative skills. Projects will be assigned in which students utilize these skills, stimulating their growth and development.

The study of Theatre Technology has many benefits beyond learning how to support a production technically. It is my belief that students who are taught Theatre Technology learn skills that transcend Theatre. Students of Theatre Technology learn time management skills, how to collaborate in a team setting, and problem solving skills that can be applied in virtually any profession. While developing the next generation of Theatre Technologists, we are also developing the life skills of all of our students by giving them the opportunity to build upon them.

Sample Teaching Portfolio, Social Science
Condensed version includes cover sheet and introductions for each
section

Teaching Portfolio ~ Eli Candidate

Contents

    1. Statement of teaching philosophy and methods
    2. Syllabi of recent courses
    3. Sample teaching materials
    4. Student assessments

1. Statement of teaching philosophy and methods

I do not believe in the much-vaunted "student-centered classroom," which risks becoming sometimes a formula for patronizing and spoon-feeding students who instead need to be taken out of their comfort zone and challenged. I respect the students and the process enough to have high expectations of them and to help them meet those expectations. So I try to create a *learning-*centered classroom. The dynamics of the learning-centered classroom are such that while the instructor is responsible for selecting, contextualizing, and illuminating materials that will challenge and stimulate the students, all in the class are held responsible for engaging critically with those materials to the best of their varying abilities and thus for pushing the learning process forward individually and collectively. The instructor should be learning alongside the students, and in fact one of the great joys of teaching for me is that I learn something new every time I step into the classroom. Even an introductory survey class provides an opportunity for the instructor to explore familiar texts and concepts anew, to experience them through the fresh eyes of the students encountering them for the first time. That constant openness to learning keeps the instructor fresh and the classroom experience dynamic. More advanced courses challenge the instructor to explicate complex issues as clearly as possible. It is there that the good teacher and good researcher meet, where the researcher hones her ability to convey the ideas that excite her with both lucidity and passion.

My core methods for achieving this outcome are threefold: materials, classroom management, accessibility.

Materials need to be chosen carefully – a good syllabus takes a lot of thought and planning. The syllabus needs to convey clearly what the expectations are of how students should engage with the materials. For an introductory course a sound textbook can be a useful backbone, but there is no reason students even at this level should not also be engaging with the best work in the discipline in the form of additional journal articles. More advanced students should be introduced to not only more challenging work within the discipline but also, where appropriate, primary source materials – for example, reading the charter of Hamas as part of a discussion of Islamic radicalism. Where audio-visual materials provide genuine added value – where, for example, a few minutes of video can maximize class time by conveying succinctly what would otherwise take much longer – they provide useful variety and enhance the learning experience. But AV should never be allowed to become a gimmick, a substitute for thoughtful teaching.

Good *classroom management* comes from both the application of strategies learned from more experienced teachers and from direct experience. The instructor must assert authority from the start of a course, and earn respect by displaying both knowledge and readiness to engage honestly with students' questions and concerns. An instructor who projects too casual an image from the start will find it harder to manage the classroom experience; one who has authority and respect will be able to loosen up later if that is appropriate and useful for the classroom dynamic,

E. Candidate, Teaching Portfolio 2

and if that is necessary to ensure a perception of approachability. The most important challenge is to engage the more reticent students in discussions. As well as seeking them out directly for comments, useful strategies are pairing them with more confident students for in-class exercises, asking them to read out a particularly good answer or part of an answer from their written work, or assigning them more prominent parts in role-play exercises, where these are appropriate.

It goes without saying that an instructor needs to be *accessible*, particularly for those students who are less confident about raising questions or concerns in class. In the internet age, students are comfortable asking questions by email and often that is a reasonable way of doing business, provided the instructor makes clear what the students are entitled to expect in terms of turn-around time. But where there is a research component – and I have a preference for research papers over exams where feasible – there should be at least one and ideally two face-to-face meetings outside class time. Providing time limits are set and adhered to, this is not burdensome. Indeed, such meetings can be enriching for the instructor as well as the student, where the relationship becomes more one of mentoring.

A final and important issue: teaching is and should be fun. Students and instructor both benefit if the instructor enjoys what they do. In common with most teachers, I believe, I find grading sometimes a chore, depending on the assignment. But all other aspects of the process – researching and preparing a new syllabus, or refreshing an existing one; engaging the students as a group in class or individually; honing teaching technique by being prepared to take risks and make mistakes; being surprised by the unanticipated question – are stimulating and often exciting. I have taught in a variety of settings – college classrooms of course, but also high schools and church groups as part of the outreach efforts of the Middle East Center, and even my son's pre-school class – and I have been challenged by each new situation, and enjoyed all of it. I plan to maintain that attitude as I advance in the profession.

2. Syllabi of recent courses
International Politics: POLS 141 M College – "International Politics," Fall 2006 – *an introductory level course designed to introduce students, mainly freshmen and sophomores, to key concepts and substantive issues in the study of international politics*

International and Comparative Politics: POLS243 M College "International Politics of the Middle East," Spring 2007 – *a course designed for students with some knowledge of international or comparative politics, in which they will apply different theoretical approaches to key issues in the politics of the modern Middle East, built around four issue areas and including a research component*

Area Studies/History: INTS 715-910 Business School, University of X ~ International Program: "History of the Modern Middle East," May 2006 – *an intensive one-month seminar for students in the highly-competitive dual MA/MBA program, designed to provide essential historical and cultural background for students who would spend the rest of the summer in an immersion program in the Middle East and provide a basis for their further studies*

3. Sample teaching materials
Lecture notes and Powerpoint slides for a guest lecture in Professor Name's course PSCI275-401, "Muslim Political Thought," Spring 2006, on Mustafa Kemal Atatürk, founder of the Turkish Republic. The challenge was to address a group of students of political theory, mainly

E. Candidate, Teaching Portfolio 3

upperclassmen, whose knowledge of Middle East history and politics might vary widely, and in under an hour to convey:
- the essential historical context of the transition from Muslim empire to secular republic;
- the challenges this presented to the political thought of the chief actors and intellectual currents in that drama; and
- relevance of those challenges and issues to contemporary Muslims and students of Muslim political thought.

The presentation opened with a short opening sequence from a rather propagandistic biographical film about Atatürk, which conveyed briefly and forcefully his significance for the emergence of modern Turkey as well as the official account of his ideology. The lecture then proceeded, supported by the Powerpoint presentation, to put the man and the moment in historical perspective, mixing text and photographs, the latter much appreciated by the students who were used to a heavy emphasis on text, given the nature of the course. The arc from concrete historical developments to the abstract principles at stake was designed to ground the latter, making them more accessible and demonstrating their relevance to real-world problems.

Feedback from the students was positive. One member of the class has since sought my help and advice in applying for a Fulbright teaching fellowship in Turkey, inspired by the lecture, she says, to a strong interest in the country – two of my students in previous classes have been awarded Fulbright fellowships for study in Turkey, a letter from one of whom appears in part 4.

4. Student assessments

Anonymous student assessments of performance as TA in:
- PSCI 001 "Introduction to the Study of Politics" in Fall 2001 under Professor Name and Spring 2002 under Professor Name
- PSCI 150 "International Relations in Theory and Practice" under Professor Name
- PSCI 253 "International Politics of the Middle East" under Professor Name

Anonymous student assessments of performance as Instructor in INTS715, "History of the Modern Middle East," May 2006.

Letter from Name, recent graduate, concerning my performance as teacher and mentor.

Sample Teaching Evaluation Summary, Humanities

Anita Scholar

Statistical Course Evaluations Summary

Department of Spanish, University of X

UNIVERSITY OF X	Instructor Rating (1-4)	Course Rating (1-4)	
Spanish 219: "Contextos de la civilización hispánica"	3.9	2.7 (pilot semester)	Fall 2001
Spanish 140: Intermediate II	3.8	3.2	Spring 2001
Spanish 130: Intermediate I	3.9	3.5	Fall 2000

Y UNIVERSITY	Instructor Rating (1-9)	Course Rating (1-9)	
Spanish 202: Intermediate II	8.12	7.64	Spring 2000
Spanish 101: Beginning I	8.57	8.22	Fall 1999

Chapter 12
Web Sites

As more and more people use the Internet as their primary means of finding information and communicating, some job candidates are constructing their own Web sites. This practice is now common in both technical and nontechnical fields. Job candidates who take the time to construct professional sites carefully report that potential employers are interested and impressed.

A typical site might begin with a homepage that links to a vita, a statement of research interests, publications, sites one has prepared for courses or other professional purposes, other professional sites (such as those maintained by one's professional association), and, perhaps, sites reflecting personal interests. The vita is also typically linked. For example, one might be able to click on an advisor's name and find a document with an entire list of that person's publications, or click on the name of the degree-granting department and be linked to a graduate catalog or the department's recruitment materials.

For candidates in fields where visual materials are important, a Web site offers an outstanding opportunity to make it easy for an employer to view work, rather than dealing with cumbersome slides or portfolios. For example, candidates could provide a complete set of photographs of a portfolio, diagrams of molecular structures, patented drawings for a new mechanical device, a clip from a documentary video, CAD-generated perspective drawings of a new building, or archival photographs of the ritual objects analyzed in a dissertation.

Obviously preparing a good site can become quite time consuming, and one is rarely required as part of an application. Since at this point a Web site will not substitute for any of the written materials you need to prepare, before you set out to construct one to use in your job search, decide how many people are likely to view it, how helpful it is likely to be to you, and, therefore, how elaborate you want to make it.

Constructing a Web Site

If you decide you want to take the time to construct a site, here are some things to consider:

- Browse through other people's sites for inspiration before you start to construct yours.
- Keep the site current. Make sure that all the links are to current addresses. If you find that the connection to a particular site is slow, you might want to put a warning to that effect on the menu, so that the reader's first attempt to use your page doesn't result in a frustrating wait.
- Remember that millions of people worldwide have the potential to view your site. Even though site pages are frequently used as expressions of personality, including humor only one's friends might find funny, don't include anything unless you want it to be seen by the chair of the search committee at your first-choice school!
- As with a vita or any other job search materials, review your site carefully, making sure it is perfect.
- You may tailor a vita to specific applications. However, because of the universal access to your site, if you have more than one version of it, anyone who views one may also view the others. This form of presentation requires you to present a more uniform view of yourself.
- Make sure the menus have a clear and obvious sense of organization. If you include many links to other sites, group them in ways whose logic is immediately apparent to the reader.
- Give some thought to the danger of having materials "stolen" or otherwise misappropriated. It may not be advisable to put up any material you have not already published or given in a public forum. You also may have some concerns about the use of your ideas. For example, your statement of research interests may prove inspirational to someone in your field with whom you view yourself as competing. Add a copyright symbol and a phrase such as "Not to be copied or distributed without permission" to everything you post, unless you don't care if someone else uses it.

A Note About the Sample Web Sites That Follow

The following examples, generously volunteered by real scholars, are provided to give you an idea of some of the wide variety of ways in which a site may be designed. Since they are public documents, we have not changed the authors' names.

Sample Humanities Web Site

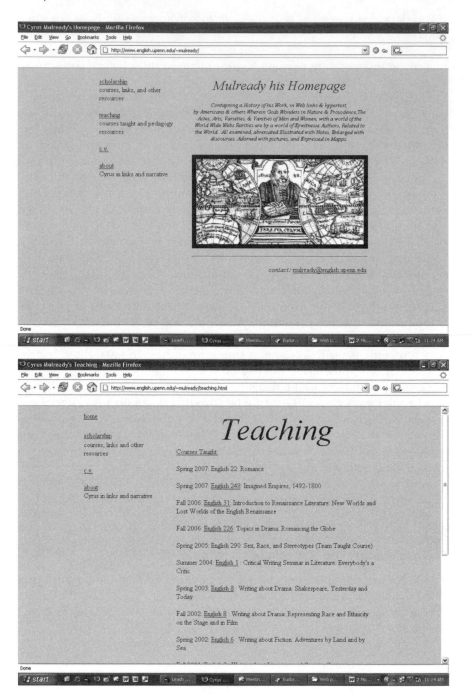

Sample Mathematics Web Site

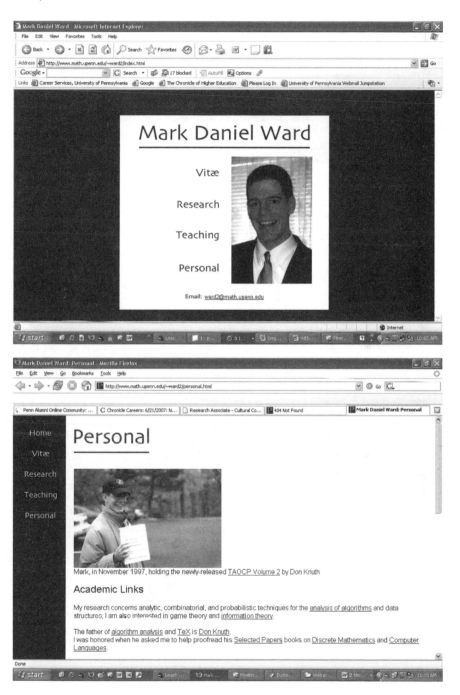

Sample Education Web Site

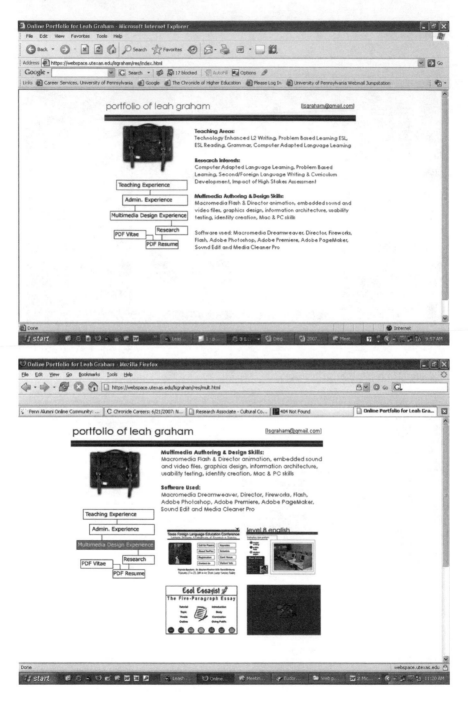

Chapter 13
Job Hunting Correspondence

Always include a cover letter or letter of interest when you send your vita to an employer. It is your opportunity to highlight your experience and expertise relevant to the specific institution and position.

Never send a form letter. Whether you will stress the potential of your research, the success of your teaching, or your enthusiasm for the mission of the institution will depend on the hiring priorities of the employer. The more you learn about the institution and department, the greater the chance that you can write a letter which will make you look like not only an outstanding candidate, but also one who will be a good "fit" for the position.

It is essential that your letter be interesting and well written. How you write, as well as what you say, will be scrutinized carefully. Use simple, direct language and no unnecessary words or sentences. If you are an international scholar and English is not your first language, have a native speaker read your drafts to ensure that the diction sounds natural. Appropriate language may be somewhat less formal than that you would use in your home country.

Proofread several times to be sure spelling and grammar are perfect. Your letter should be printed in a readable typeface. Use a high quality printer. If your department or laboratory encourages job candidates to use departmental stationery, do so.

Cover Letters

Salutation

Use a formal title such as "Dr." or "Professor" even if you know the individual, because the letter normally will be read by many people. If an advertisement indicates that you should respond to "Search Committee," "Dear Committee Members" is an appropriate salutation.

First Paragraph

Explain why you are writing and indicate how you learned about the position, for example, "At the suggestion of Professor Jones . . ."; "I would like to apply for the position of Assistant Professor which was advertised in the October 6 issue of *The Chronicle of Higher Education*"; or "Thank you for taking time to speak with me yesterday about your unexpected need for a Visiting Lecturer."

Middle Paragraph(s)

This is the heart of your letter. Your vita describes your accomplishments up to the present. Your letter refers to these, but extends them into the future by demonstrating that you understand the requirements of the position and will be able to meet them. After reading your letter, ideally the search committee will be able to visualize you in the position and doing a great job.

Discuss how your achievements and qualifications relate to the specific requirements of this position. Let the department chair or search committee know what you have to offer without repeating your vita word for word. Explain your interest in the institution/position. In general, at a major research university, it is most important to stress your interest in the research done by the members of the department; at a small college, it is also helpful to express an interest in the institution. If you are familiar with and enthusiastic about the kind of students a school attracts, say so.

One easy way to organize the heart of your letter is to use the structure of the ad. For instance, if the ad discusses four desired qualities and mentions two main responsibilities, explain that you have those four qualities and how they relate to performing the two responsibilities successfully. If you use this approach, be subtle enough that your letter doesn't sound mechanical. Don't abandon complex sentence structure in favor of bulleted phrases, as hiring committees often look at a cover letter as an indication of a candidate's ability to write.

Final Paragraph

Offer to provide extra materials or additional information, or give the URL if they're posted to a Web site. Indicate how you can be reached and your availability for interviews at conferences or on campus. If you would be available for an interview at your own expense because you've already planned to travel to a particular location, mention that. Finally, thank the reader for his or her consideration.

Letters in the humanities tend to be longer (up to three pages) than those in the sciences and social sciences (one or two pages). Have your advisor and others read your early letters to make sure that you are expressing yourself appropriately for your field. If your campus career center offers services to doctoral students and/or postdocs, counselors there may also be available to critique drafts.

Thank You Letters

Thank you letters are another important form of job hunting correspondence. You should write one promptly any time anyone spends time talking with you about your job search, whether informally or in an interview. These letters can be brief and should be sent promptly after your meeting or interview. They can reiterate your enthusiasm for a position or convey information you neglected to mention during an interview. However, they should mainly express your appreciation of and interest in what was discussed during the meeting. If you have been regularly communicating with the hiring department by e-mail, it is appropriate to send a thank you that way. Otherwise take the time to use paper.

Letters Accepting or Declining Offers

In writing a letter of acceptance it is common to restate the conditions of employment agreed upon, particularly because they may have changed in the negotiating process. When declining an offer, thank the search committee and mention how much you enjoyed meeting them and visiting their campus. Academia is a small world and you never know if one of these people will be in a position to help your career in the future.

A Note About the Sample Letters That Follow

The following examples, nearly all generously volunteered by real candidates, are provided to give you an idea of what such letters look like. Other than to change the names of individuals and institutions, we have tried to modify them as little as possible. They should be regarded as excellent, but not necessarily perfect.

As you will see, they vary in style. Write your own letters in a style that both is appropriate to your field and feels natural to you.

Sample Cover Letter for a Humanities Faculty Position

Date

Dr. Name, Chair
Department of English
The University of Z
City, Province, Postal code, Canada

Dear Professor Name and Members of the Search Committee:

I am writing to apply for the tenure-track assistant professorship in Renaissance Drama that you advertised in the MLA Job Information List. I am currently at the University of X, where I hold one of the English Department's two Postdoctoral Fellowships. I received my Ph.D. from X in August of this year after completing my dissertation, *Romancing the Globe: Romance, English Expansion, and the Early Modern Stage*, under the direction of Professors Name, Name, and Name.

Romance has been given a long and complex history in English literature, but not as a dramatic genre. In *Romancing the Globe*, I trace this bias to the co-opting of the term "romance" in nineteenth-century studies of Shakespeare: first by Coleridge to distinguish Shakespeare's works from those bound by classical strictures, and later by Edward Dowden to designate the fourth and last generic division of Shakespeare's canon—the "romances" (for Dowden, *Pericles*, *The Tempest*, *Cymbeline*, and *The Winter's Tale*). Critics and editors to this day rely on Dowden's "romance" as a classification of Shakespeare's "late plays," and thus sustain the notion that romance is dominantly a Shakespearean genre, one issuing (to use Dowden's titular phrase) from "Shakespeare's Mind and Art." Rather, I argue, these plays belong to a dramatic kind that is not only pre-Coleridgean, but pre-Shakespearean. The "stage romance," as I have called it, is a genre that dates back to the earliest years of the commercial theater in sixteenth-century London. Building on the work of earlier bibliographers, I have identified more than forty plays from the period, many now lost, that adapted popular prose romances, pseudo-histories, and other fantastical tales to the stage. Yet due to the narrow application of the term "romance" in dramatic criticism, the generic kinship of these plays has gone unremarked.

In my account, the genre of stage romance develops as a response to England's broadening horizons in this period of expanding overseas commerce and exploration. Plays such as the anonymous *Clyomon and Clamydes* and Thomas Dekker's *Old Fortunatus* bear witness to the stage's attempt to translate the geographic and temporal leaps of narrative romance into the circumscribed space of the stage. At the same time, the influx of romance into English drama challenged the foundations of traditional dramatic theory and form, evinced by Sidney's influential *Defense of Poesy*, where he targets the "gross absurdities" of plays that violate the unities of time and place. To demonstrate the emergence of "romance" out of a global history of expansion rather than a developmental account of authorial biography, my chapters focus on specific formal elements: the representation of time and space in *The Tempest*, the dramatization of narrative in *Old Fortunatus*, the use of a Chorus in *Henry V* and *Pericles*, and the transfer of romance from commercial stage to court entertainment in Milton's *Comus*. Drawing on materials from early modern cartography, literary theory, historiography, travel writing, and racial theory, these chapters relate the transformations in dramatic form to the social and historical issues raised by England's expansion into new territories.

Candidate   2

My research involves me in the vibrant current debates about the impact of overseas expansion on early modern culture. The first chapter of my dissertation, "'Affric of the one side, Asia of the Other': Sidney's Unities and the Staging of Romance," has been accepted in a collection, edited by Valerie Wayne and Mary Ellen Lamb, *Staging Early Modern Romance: Prose Fiction, Dramatic Romance, and Shakespeare*. I am currently at work revising my dissertation toward publication, a process that will allow me to explore more fully a range of issues that were incipient in the thesis: the interplay of history and romance in the period, the geography of the eastern Mediterranean in romance, and the migration of stage romance to other genres in the seventeenth century. Furthermore, I have recently discovered two little-known stage romances in manuscript, *Tom a Lincoln* and *The Fairy Knight*, which will be integrated into the book. I have also done preliminary research for a second book-length project that will explore the travels of various early modern books overseas: from a copy of Foxe's *Acts and Monuments* that Sir Francis Drake carried with him during his circumnavigation to seventeenth-century performances of *Hamlet* and *Richard II* aboard an English ship on the coast of Sierra Leone.

In my experience as a graduate instructor, I taught a broad range of courses, from dramatic representations of race to travel and adventure writing. In one course, *Shakespeare: Yesterday and Today*, I emphasized the status of the period as both "early" and "modern," a world at once strange to us and enticingly contemporary. My students explored this paradox in units that paired modern adaptations and appropriations of Shakespeare's plays with a broader historical study of the period's social, theatrical, and print culture. My efforts as a teacher were recognized in 2003, when I was one of nine graduate student instructors in the College of Arts and Sciences to receive the Dean's Award for Distinguished Teaching.

As a postdoctoral fellow in the University of X's English Department, I have developed a series of courses that grow out of my interests in romance, drama, travel narrative, and the literature of empire in early modern England. I am currently teaching a survey course, *New Worlds and Lost Worlds of the Renaissance*, that works to complicate traditional conceptions of the "Renaissance" through readings of texts ranging from Shakespeare's *Richard III* and *Titus Andronicus* to More's *Utopia* and Amerigo Vespucci's New World epistles. These readings prompt classroom discussions and writing assignments in which students evaluate traditional formulations of the historical period (the Renaissance, the Age of Discovery, the Reformation, the Late Medieval), as we explore the competing (and sometimes contradictory) social and historical energies that spurred cultural production. In an upper-level seminar I will teach this spring, *Imagined Empires, 1492-1800*, we will study texts that present overseas conquest and empire as an imaginary enterprise. Course readings will include romances, travel narratives, utopias, novels and plays that, in many cases, deal only peripherally with Europe's expansion abroad. In the seminar, we will work to explore how these "imagined empires" are connected to the period's broadening of geographic space.

I have enclosed my *curriculum vitae* and book prospectus. Thank you for your consideration. I hope to hear from you soon.

Sincerely,

Oliver Candidate

Sample Cover Letter for a Social Science Faculty Position

Office of Population Research
Address
Z University
City, State Zip

Date

Chair, Search Committee
Department of Sociology and Anthropology
Large State University
City, State Zip

Dear Chair of the Search Committee,

I am writing regarding the tenure-track position of Assistant Professor of Sociology. I learned about this position through Professor Name at the University of X, where I am currently completing a doctoral program in demography with the support of a Mellon fellowship. I expect to fulfill all the degree requirements by August 2005.

In the description of the position you indicate that you are seeking a specialist in social demography with the ability to teach social statistics at the graduate level. My training as a researcher on international migration from Latin America and the Caribbean to the United States under the direction of Professor Name would contribute to the research agenda of your department. In addition, my experience as a teaching assistant for quantitative research methods under the direction of Professors Name and Name has provided me with the knowledge and familiarity to teach graduate courses on research methods in the social sciences.

I am aware that research methods courses are required in the Comparative Sociology M.A. and Ph.D. programs offered by your department. As a social statistics teacher, I will ensure that students learn statistical tools and understand how valuable they are in explaining complex social behaviors.

Although I have done research on comparative international labor migration from Mexico and the Dominican Republic to the United States, and recently from Colombia to the United States and Spain, my dissertation explores a different area within the field of migration. It investigates the consequences of forced internal migration in Colombia, with particular emphasis on internally displaced persons who resettled in the outskirts of Bogotá.

My study focuses on the effects of internal forced migration on gender and household composition, socioeconomic characteristics, and labor trajectories. For this purpose, I have designed research instruments to collect quantitative and qualitative data on non-migrants, migrants, and forced migrants in three diverse areas of the periphery of Bogotá. This study also allows me to explore literature on urban development, social stratification, and assimilation. Given the research interests of your faculty members, I will be a suitable candidate in collaborating with them on their research efforts.

Scholar   2

As a professional demographer, I have presented my research at the Population Association of America meetings, the Latin American Studies Association Congress, and other academic meetings in the U.S., Mexico, Costa Rica, and Colombia.

I am convinced that internal conflict has had long-term effects on war-ridden countries and their neighbors too. Allied countries are also at high risk of receiving large migration flows as a result of their intervention. My research experience on international and forced migration will allow me to explore even further the impact of conflict on development and international migration. In an effort to enhance the academic dialogue on the effects of civil conflict I organized two sessions at the Latin America Studies Association Congress, in October 2004, one on internal and forced migration in Colombia and the other on international migration from Colombia. In addition, I am putting together a research agenda on international migration patterns from Guatemala, El Salvador, Haiti and Nicaragua--countries with a history of social unrest--to neighboring countries and the United States.

I look forward to discussing the position with you in the next few weeks and to visiting your department for an interview, if you decide to pursue my application. My curriculum vitae is enclosed; my letters of recommendation will follow under separate cover. Please feel free to contact me if you need more information. Thank you for your consideration. I look forward to hearing from you.

Sincerely,

Dora Alicia Scholar

Sample Cover Letter for a Social Science Faculty Position
Letter is written to an institution where candidate has been an adjunct

DOERTHE M. CANDIDATE, M.A., RPA
* * *

Department of Anthropology
University of X
Address
City, State Zip code
*
Phone
Email

Date

Search Committee Chair
Human Resources
Community College of J
Address
City, State, Zip code

Dear Committee Chair and Members:

I am writing to apply for the full time, tenure track position in Anthropology in your department. I am a doctoral candidate in Anthropology, with a specialization in historical archaeology, at the University of X and will graduate in May 2006.

I have considerable teaching experience in a variety of settings. I have taught social science courses at three area universities and colleges--including the Community College of J--and one foreign college, have supervised crucial parts of field schools for three programs, and assisted in several courses at the University of X. In addition to other social science courses, some involving my own specialties in historical archaeology and North America, I have regularly taught both Introduction to Anthropology (ANTH 101) and Cultural Anthropology (ANTH112) for the Community College of J and sometimes teach Physical Geography (GEOG 101) as well. I teach the College's Cultural Geography (GEOG 103) Distance Learning Web-course. The anonymous reviews of my students, both at CCJ and elsewhere, are consistently laudatory and reflect my commitment to undergraduate education in the social sciences.

I am strongly committed to undergraduate education in the social sciences. The social sciences, particularly anthropology, help construct ways to understand and analyze the world. Critical thinking and writing are inherent components of this, and are skills students will use in both their educational and professional future. Case studies of other cultures promote cultural relativism and tolerance, both crucial abilities in modern America, as well as help us to understand our own culture. The modern world is one of interconnection and independence; people who can think and write critically, appreciate diversity, and grasp some of the components of culture are uniquely suited to succeed. I believe that learning anthropology at the undergraduate level, especially in the Community College of J setting, will help students reach their goals.

My dissertation examines the intersections of gender, culture, and power through material culture and social space. I have conducted archaeological survey and excavation, historical research including primary documents and oral history, and used anthropological theory to examine a farm owned by two sisters from 1876 to 1920 in southern Michigan. I am using the physical space and material culture of their lives to consider the ways culture is constructed and negotiated between individuals within the

Candidate--2

social space. This project contributes to our understanding of how gender and power were expressed in the past, and illuminates aspects of how they are encoded in the modern world. At the Community College of J, I will draw on these ideas to help students better understand the social world around them--and better negotiate it to achieve their goals.

I am also an energetic member of the university and professional community in anthropology and archaeology. I have an active publication record, including articles, book reviews, co-authored and contributed pieces and a brief monograph. I currently serve as Chair of the Gender and Minority Affairs Committee of the Society for Historical Archaeology, and have served as a member of two University of X Anthropology Graduate Group Committees. I have organized and chaired a symposium for the Society for Historical Archaeology, and have presented papers at numerous other professional meetings.

I believe I will be an asset to your department and to the Community College of J. I would welcome the opportunity to discuss this position with you further. I look forward to hearing from you.

Sincerely,

Doerthe M. Candidate
Department of Anthropology
University of X

Sample Cover Letter for a Biomedical Faculty Position

Anthony Scientist, Ph.D.
Address
City, State Zip
Telephone
Email

Date

Dr. Name and members of the search committee:

This application is in response to the advertised position of Assistant Professor, Molecular Genetics in the Biology program. Presently, I am completing a postdoctoral position at the University of X in the lab of Name, Ph.D. I am prepared to start a position as an independent scientist and eager to come to the College of State.

You are seeking a candidate with strong teaching skills. I have experience teaching undergraduate students at peer universities (Y University and State University City campus) in the classroom and in the laboratory. I have taught a number of courses in molecular biology and a course in genetics. The students have given me excellent evaluations and I have included some in my packet. My teaching experience includes major and non-major as well as graduate, veterinary and medical students. I also interact with individuals of diverse backgrounds including students and postdocs from all continents.

You are also seeking a candidate with strong scholarship. I have mentored a number of students through short research projects (typically one semester in length) in the lab. The students were successful in these projects and some will contribute to manuscripts to be published in the near future.

In addition, I support the values in your mission statement. First is the emphasis of breadth in the curriculum. I have included a wide range of material in my courses because I think it is important for the teacher to expose the students to the many possibilities in science. You also require depth in the curriculum, and it is here that student research projects allow for exploration of their own interests. Finally, you are committed to the positive development of southern [state]. As a lifelong resident of [city], and a frequent visitor to [nearby region], I know firsthand that the college is located in a unique and precious environment.

Thank you in advance for consideration of my application.

Sincerely,

Anthony Scientist

Sample Cover Letter for a Biomedical Faculty Position

Date

Name, Ph.D
Vice President for Laboratory Science
Cancer Institute at University Medical Center
Address
City, State Zip

Dear Dr. Name:

I am writing in reference to the advertised position of Assistant Professor in the CI at University Medical Center, advertised in the September edition of *Science*. I am currently a research fellow at the Research Institute completing studies examining the selection and activation of naturally occurring CD4+CD25+ regulatory T cells. I welcome the opportunity to engage in translational research of human cancer. I am also interested in any teaching opportunities that may be conducted in conjunction with this postdoctoral appointment.

It was while obtaining my B.S. in Microbiology and a minor in Chemistry, at the University of State, that I began undergraduate research in the laboratory where I eventually obtained my Ph.D. in Immunology. My thesis project, completed in 2000, entitled "The Role of the Interferon gamma/Interferon Gamma Receptor Complex in Signal Transduction" was an examination of events subsequent to the internalization of the extra-cellular, interferon gamma/interferon gamma receptor complex, and its possible significance in signal transduction. As a result of my graduate research work, I served as primary author and co-author on a number of publications. I was also given the opportunity to present my research findings in the form of poster presentations and during invited talks. In addition to the research experience obtained during my pre-doctoral work, I also served as a laboratory instructor for both the undergraduate core Microbiology laboratory class for microbiology majors and the graduate level Immunology laboratory class at the University of State. As a graduate student, I was also selected to serve on a four-person committee responsible for organizing the 2000 Graduate Student Research Symposium of the Microbiology department at the University of State.

In order to further enhance my research experience repertoire, as a postdoctoral fellow my research focus shifted from intracellular protein trafficking to animal model disease (mouse) and T cell activation (both CD4+CD25- effector and CD4+CD25+ regulatory T cells (Treg)). In a primary author publication, recently accepted for publication in the *European Journal of Immunology*, we generated data that corroborates data by others suggesting that CD4+CD25+ regulatory T cells may play a role in tumorigenesis. Specifically, we show that CD4+CD25+ regulatory T cell suppressor function, unlike the proliferation of CD4+CD25- effector T cells (possessing the same T cell receptor (TCR) peptide specificity), can be activated by weakly cross-reactive peptide analogs of the peptide that the TCR of the T cell is specific for. These data suggest that Treg suppressor function can potentially be activated in an environment (such as infection or cancer) where high expression of "altered self" ligands occurs, thus modifying the immune response. As a postdoctoral researcher my duties also included the training of graduate students and laboratory technicians. My record of assisting in the training of graduate students and technicians is evident in my co-authorship of several manuscripts both published, and in the process of being published.

I welcome the opportunity to conduct research related to the translational research of human cancer, in particular pediatric oncology. I also welcome the opportunity to apply for, and seek external funding. My appointment to the CI at University Medical Center would permit me the opportunity to contribute my experience in protein transport, signal transduction, animal model disease, and regulatory T cell selection and function to the field of tumor research.

Researcher 2

Please find the attached C.V. with references. I thank you for considering me for employment within the CI. I will be visiting family in [city] this week (October 10-14) and will be able to discuss career opportunities and/or give a presentation of the work to be published in the *European Journal of Immunology*. I look forward to hearing from you. I can be reached by phone: 321 123-4567 or email: mdresearcher@institute.university.edu.

Sincerely,

Mark David Researcher

Sample Cover Letter for a Mathematics Faculty Position

Date

Dr. Name, Head
Department of Mathematics
Y University
Address
City, State Zip

Dear Dr. Name,

I am responding to the posting on Y University's Mathematics website for an Assistant Professor position. My research concerns analytic, combinatorial, and probabilistic techniques for the analysis of algorithms and data structures; I also have experience in game theory and information theory. Y is my top choice for a tenure track job. My interdisciplinary research complements the interests of Y's faculty in Mathematics. Currently, I am a Lecturer in Mathematics at the University of X. Also, I am the co-PI on an NSF grant with Name in Asymptotic Enumeration.

I was also enticed to apply to Y in 2001 as a graduate student, when State University-City, closed the Center for Mathematical Sciences. I transferred to Y, where I completed my Ph.D. in 2005. The reason I selected Y in 2001 remains valid today – Y has a very firm commitment to interdisciplinary research in applied mathematics. For instance, Y has a Center for Computational and Applied Mathematics and a graduate program in Computational Science & Engineering. At X, I am currently teaching a graduate course in Analytic Combinatorics; this would be a beneficial addition to the curriculum at Y. I am also qualified to teach Y's current graduate probability courses. I envision augmenting Y's Ph.D. qualifying exam topics by creating an "Applied Discrete Mathematics" exam. At X, I developed a new course in game theory for advanced undergraduates; I also conducted one-on-one, customized reading courses with individual undergraduate and graduate students in game theory.

In addition to the desirable research and teaching environment at Y, I am enamored with [city]. It would be ideal to return there to raise my children (Madeleine and John).

Since Y is my first choice for a tenure-track position, Y is the only place I am applying to this year (both Mathematics and Statistics). I am able to stay employed at X through Spring 2008 if necessary.

I am enclosing an AMS cover sheet, my vitae, research and teaching statements. Letters of recommendation are being sent separately via postal mail. Thank you very much for your consideration. I look forward to communication with you soon.

Sincerely,

John Patrick Scholar

Sample Cover Letter for a Social Work Faculty Position

date

Name, Ph.D.
Chair, Faculty Search Committee
University of Y
School of Social Work
Address
City, State, Zip code

Dear Dr. Name,

Please accept the enclosed materials as my application for your Assistant Professor position in the School of Social Work. Currently, I am completing my doctoral studies at the University of X in the School of Social Policy & Practice under the mentorship of Name, Name, and Name. I was excited to hear about the opening in your department because of the faculty's deep commitment to the welfare of children and families.

As an undergraduate I majored in psychology because of my interest in child development. To augment my classroom learning, I volunteered to work in an after school program for children living in foster homes. These children all had histories of severe physical abuse and neglect, and I was shocked by the effect this had on their mental health. I wanted to continuing working with children who were experiencing trauma in their homes, and to that end I pursued an M.S.W. with a concentration in practice with children and families at the University of Texas at Austin.

My interest in helping maltreated children led me to select a field placement with Child Protective Services to develop an understanding of this problem from the front line. I observed the often devastating effects of children experiencing trauma in their most proximal environment. This experience also revealed the extensive problem of children exposed to domestic violence. As I began to ask questions about this population, I found that children exposed to domestic violence were often invisible to service providers. There were no established policies or procedures specifically targeted to this issue, and no systematic data were being collected on the number of children affected. After being told that domestic violence in the home was not something addressed by child welfare workers, I decided to focus my career on fostering intervention with and responses to children exposed to domestic violence.

My commitment to understanding the scope of children exposed to domestic violence inspired me to seek employment at a shelter for battered women. I developed a program for the children that provided opportunities for them to talk about their experiences. This work provided many personal case studies and gave me a better understanding of the developmental impact of domestic violence on children from infancy through adolescence. I realized this was a very complex problem with heterogeneous effects. I began to wonder if the shelter population, who make up a small percentage of children exposed to domestic violence, were representative of all exposed children. I was determined to find the answer to this and other questions about these children, but I found the literature to be inadequate. I could not find accurate statistics on the number of children affected, and most of the studies conducted were focused on the shelter samples. I was motivated to obtain research training to contribute to the burgeoning scholarship on children exposed to domestic violence.

I sought a Ph.D. program where faculty was engaged in population-based child welfare research. At the University of X I pursued research mentoring from Name. His research used a developmental epidemiological model to inform the study of prevalence of children exposed to domestic violence. This project developed a standard and reliable protocol used by police officers to collect data on

Candidate   2

children exposed to domestic violence across two major municipalities. My involvement on Dr. Name's research team solidified my commitment to research in children's exposure to domestic violence. Through this involvement I enhanced my Ph.D. training with courses in advanced statistics learning how to use census data and Geographic Information Systems. These skills increased my ability to pose a richer set of questions examining the prevalence of children's direct sensory exposure to domestic violence.

I used my acquired research knowledge and skills to successfully obtain a competitive, two-year federally funded research grant. The findings from this work showed that children's sensory exposure to domestic violence is a multifaceted concept that needs to be defined more precisely. These results prompted me to develop a dissertation research agenda to examine both what children are being exposed to and how they are exposed. Although these children are often described as passive witnesses of horrific events, my practice and research experience indicated this is not an accurate representation of their role. The children I worked with at the shelter often reported calling for help or intervening in the violence. I wanted to develop a more comprehensive understanding of the ways children are involved in domestic violence events with a more representative sample. I examined children's sensory exposure, and developed an empirical taxonomy of children's involvement in domestic violence across an entire municipality.

I am seeking a university faculty position to continue my research commitment to children who have experienced trauma in their primary context. My goals are to further investigate the risks that often co-occur with domestic violence and poverty, such as child maltreatment, community violence, parental substance abuse, and parental mental health problems. Understanding the variability of such stressors can provide an understanding of the impact of different configurations of risk and has important implications for policy and practice. Finally, I want to continue working within a population-base to develop interagency child welfare plans to serve children and families in their communities.

I have had rich opportunities to teach at both the University of X and Temple University. I have taught across curriculum sequences in policy, research, and practice to both BSW and MSW level students. I particularly enjoy teaching both research and practice, and helping students understand how each domain can inform the other. My clinical work has sensitized me to the complex nature of research activities with vulnerable populations. I have come to appreciate the real-world disconnections that exist between research, policy, and practice. As practitioners and policy-makers help meet the compelling needs of children, they are often forced to intervene without a sufficient knowledge base to support their practice, particularly for underserved populations. My commitment is to facilitate future students' understanding of the perspectives of researchers, practitioners, policy-makers, and the children and families they serve.

I feel fortunate to have pursued my passion and purpose through high-quality training with researchers committed to family violence. I am interested in the University of Y because of your reputation for rigorous and relevant work that bridges research, practice, and policy for children and families. Your program provides an excellent context for developing my own research agenda across an urban setting, with many opportunities to work with top scholars in child welfare. I look forward to the opportunity of talking with you further about the fit between my goals and skills and your institution's current needs.

Sincerely yours,

Nina Candidate

Sample Cover Letter for a Theatre Faculty Position

Edward K. Dramatist

Address

City, State, Zip code

Phone number

E-mail address

Name

Theatre Arts Department

W College

City, State, Zip code

Dear Mr. Name,

I was excited to see your posting for the position of Technical Director/Assistant Professor. I enjoyed reading "The 16 Reasons to Study Theatre Arts at W College" on your web page and found your curriculum and department objectives compelling. I feel that my skills and personality are a good match with your program. I am writing to express my interest in the position.

Currently I am finishing State University Department of Theatre and Drama's intensive Theatre Technology MFA. I expect to graduate in May of 2003. At State University, I am a Teaching Assistant in theatre technology, and responsible for teaching stagecraft in a laboratory setting to our undergraduate students. In addition, I have taught a stagecraft practicum at U.C. San Diego, while fulfilling my role as Scene Shop Foreman of The La Jolla Playhouse and the U.C.S.D. Mandell Weiss Center for The Performing Arts.

While at State University and San Diego State University, I have designed scenery and sound for several productions, as well as received extensive training in all areas of theatrical design and technology. Beyond the classroom, I have worked for several professional and regional theatres as a carpenter, stagehand, scene shop foreman, property master, and assistant to the technical director.

Please consider my enclosed resume and vita. I would very much like the opportunity to speak with you more about this position.

Enthusiastically,

Edward K. Dramatist

Sample E-mail Cover Letter for a Postdoctoral Research Position

Date

Dear Dr. Name:

I am writing to you as a candidate for a postdoctoral research position.

I am currently finishing my fourth year in the laboratory of Dr. Name in the Department of Genetics at the University of X School of Medicine. I anticipate finishing my graduate work in the beginning of 2007. Arranging my postdoctoral plans in advance will give me the flexibility to apply for several postdoctoral fellowships prior to starting in the lab.

The majority of my work in the Name lab has utilized the *Drosophila* eye as a system to analyze the defects associated with the particular mutant I have characterized (see attached Research Summary). During the course of this work I have developed an interest in the various developmental aspects of the *Drosophila* eye. I have read some of your work involving dock, as well as the utilization of the eye for neurodegenerative disease modeling. I find both of these areas very interesting, and would like to learn more about the various projects in your lab.

I have attached my curriculum vitae, research summary, and list of references as Word documents.

Thank you again for your consideration. I look forward to hearing from you.

Sincerely,

Daniel Researcher
Dr. Name's Lab
Address
Phone, E-mail address, fax
Attachments:
DResearcherCV.doc
DResearcherResSummary.doc
DResearcherReferences.doc
[Note that candidate's name appears in the name of each document, so the recipient can easily identify and file them.]

Sample Thank You Letter Following an Interview

Applicant's Address
E-Mail Address
Date

Search Committee Chair Name
Department of Theater Arts
Selective College
Address

Dear Dr. Name,

Thank you for arranging such an excellent opportunity to become more familiar with your campus and department. I particularly appreciate your timing my visit so that I could see a student production. The enthusiasm of your students and the range and depth of the opportunities your department offers them are impressive. The visit confirmed both my interest in joining you and my belief that I would be able to make a contribution to the department that would be consonant with your current goals. I'll be following up on Dr. Name's suggestions about funding sources for expanding the curricular offerings in Asian theater.

I'm enclosing my travel receipts. As you know, I'll be in London until March 29, but I'll check my e-mail daily. Thank you again for the visit. Please convey my thanks to everyone who helped make my time on campus so stimulating and enjoyable.

Sincerely,

Hernando Applicant

Sample Acceptance Letter
Letter summarizes negotiations for laboratory start-up

Candidate's Address
Date

Dr. Name, Provost
Small (Religious) College
Address

Dear Dr. Name,

I am happy to accept your offer for the tenure-track position of Assistant Professor of Biology at a beginning salary of $50,000 (I successfully defended my thesis and will have the Ph.D. by May 2008). I am thankful for this opportunity and eager to serve God by my full-time mission in the Small College community.

Since this is an appropriate time, I would like to raise a few questions.

1. Thank you for the information regarding the medical coverage and benefits package. The base salary, as you mentioned in your letter (2/27/08), should be changed to $50,000 in the contract since I will have the Ph.D. before I begin my position. Also, I am presently covered under my husband's insurance plan. Is there a way to relieve Small College of the obligation to pay for my health insurance and instead use that money toward salary, moving expenses, research, etc.?

2. According to your letter (2/27), the date of my appointment is August 21, 2008, while the date on the letter from Dr. Name states August 1. Which is correct?

3. As we discussed in our last meeting, while my main interest is in teaching in the classroom, I am also interested in the prospect of allowing students at Small College the opportunity for small-scale biological research. Undergraduate research experience is almost as indispensable as computer-literacy is for students nowadays, as you know. Therefore, I have spent time discussing my ideas with Dr. Name and have come up with a request for several items to see this through:

Cell-biology lab for undergraduate research (involving the new lab space that will be created in the room adjoining the animal colony room). My research involves using cell-culture and pharmacological assays to investigate the effects of different agents on the intracellular replication of the protozoan parasite *Toxoplasma gondii*. I have many small projects feasible for undergraduates to do that will generate results. Dr. Name has a few pieces of equipment needed for some cell-culture work such as laminar flow hoods (to maintain sterile conditions). However, an essential item that I need to maintain my parasite and cell cultures is a CO_2 incubator, which costs approximately $8,300. Dr. Name has told me that he could benefit from this incubator as well because it would allow him to use mammalian cells (which I will obtain through my collaboration at the University of X) for different experiments in his Cell Biology course.

Another piece of equipment which is necessary for the long term is a small –70 degrees Celsius freezer (~$6,000) for storage of cells and parasites. Dr. Name has told me that he would also benefit from this freezer since the bacterial cells and some other materials he uses in Comparative Molecular Investigations must be stored at –70 degrees Celsius.

Other miscellaneous items (like a small refrigerator, clinical centrifuge, etc.) would be nice to purchase at some point after the essentials are taken care of. It would also be helpful to have $3,000 or as much as can be spared for the purchase of general reagents, plastic ware, etc. Fortunately, I will be collaborating with my thesis adviser at the University of X for several supplies, taking some of the burden from Small College.

I realize that the amount of financial support I am requesting may appear to be high, but I believe that not only will my students benefit (through application of my research in the classroom and through independent student research), but Dr. Name and his students will benefit as well. Even biochemistry majors might be interested in getting this research experience. I believe that these measures can move the Biology department at Small College to the place it wants to be. Finally, I emphasize that the focus of this request is to further *student* research – if I want to do my own intensive research in the summers at the University of X I know that I can. I am not trying to create a University of X lab at Small College, but hope to give Small College students the tools so they can learn about how the scientific method is actually used and to inspire in students an appreciation that science reveals the majesty and greatness of God!

Thank you for meeting with me a second time and for your support and prayers during my decision-making process. I am so thankful to be officially joining the Small College family. Please keep me informed of answers to my questions. I would be happy to talk with you further if you have additional questions for me. Thanks again and God Bless.

Sincerely,

Joy G. Successful-Candidate

Sample Letter Declining an Offer

Candidate's Address
Date

Dean Name
School of Education
University of Z
University Address

Dear Dean Name,

As we discussed by phone, I must regretfully decline your offer of the position of Assistant Professor as I am accepting a position at the University of Q, where I will have a joint appointment with the Center for Educational Assessment.

While there are fewer people in my field of research at the University of Z, I nevertheless found this a very difficult decision because I so much enjoyed my meetings with you and your colleagues. I was impressed with the school's collective sense of direction, and with the faculty's extraordinary dedication both to its own students and to students in the broader community. I'm honored that you asked me to join you.

I thank you for your consideration and generosity in answering all my questions and hope that our paths will cross again in the future.

Sincerely,

Stacey Hire

Part IV
Conducting the Search

Chapter 14
Interviewing

The academic interviewing process may encompass three different types of events: the short half-hour to hour-long screening interview at an annual conference or convention which serves as the central job clearinghouse for a field, the phone interview, and the all-day or several-day interview on campus which may follow a successful conference or phone interview. If you are invited to interview for a job as a result of your direct response to an advertisement, an all-day campus interview may well be the first and only stage in the interviewing process. If you interview a lot, you may experience everything from highly structured interactions in which all candidates are asked essentially the same questions, to interviews in which you, as the candidate, must provide all the structure.

While there are many similarities between kinds of interviews, each presents its own challenges. At a conference interview you have a very limited amount of time to stand out in a field of candidates, often under rushed and stressful conditions. In this setting you need to be prepared to present your qualifications succinctly and interestingly. An all-day campus visit is a far more complex event. It usually requires a presentation and involves more people, a greater variety of social situations, and more ambiguity.

Any sort of interview, however, is far more like ordinary professional conversations than different from them. Any time two people meet each other, they form an impression of each other. An interview differs only in that the evaluative dimension is more explicit. Whenever you encounter an unanticipated situation, do what you would ordinarily do in a professional setting, and it is likely that your impulse will be correct.

In ordinary conversation, if you are asked a question you do not understand, you ask for clarification, rather than panic. If you say something that produces a puzzled expression on your listener's face, you ask whether there is something you can clarify. If a question spontaneously occurs to you as a result of something the other person has said, you ask it. If you can't answer a question, you say so. All these responses are appropriate in an interview. Most interviewers are far more impressed by candidates who appear confident and candid than by those who appear to be trying to give the "right" answers. While you should always give the interviewer the opportunity to take the lead, many people who conduct interviews are far more comfortable if the candidate feels free to volunteer information and ask questions.

Areas You Will Need to Discuss

In any interview for a faculty position, be prepared to address these concerns: your current research, your teaching, your future research plans, and your interest in the institution to which you are applying. If you are interviewing for a research position, your research will be the main topic of conversation.

Your Dissertation/Postdoctoral Research

Be prepared to explain your work to the variety of people you may encounter in an interview, from world experts in your area of specialization through the person outside the department, such as a dean, whose work may have been in another discipline entirely. Practice particularly the way you will explain your work to those totally unfamiliar with its context. The effort you will need to make to be concise and to explain relevance in that case may well also improve your more technical presentation to experts in the field.

You could discuss your work for hours, but prepare to begin with a brief summary (about a paragraph long). It should leave the interviewer with the impression that he or she knows what you did (be clear); the work was interesting (speak with enthusiasm, and mention interesting findings or conclusions early in your discussion); the work was important (discuss how your work relates to other work and suggest areas for future exploration). Once you've captured this level of interest, further discussion becomes much easier.

Approach this discussion, not as a student seeking the approval of more senior faculty members, but as a colleague in the field who, in this case, is an authority. No one who is interviewing will know more about your research topic than you do. Some candidates find that if they think of themselves as teaching about their research, rather than merely reporting on it, their presentation becomes more confident, lively, and interesting.

Your Future Research Interests

It's imperative that you appear to have some. For example, merely saying that you plan to publish your dissertation isn't enough. You may be so immersed in it that it's hard to look beyond its completion. If so, set time aside to think about what you might do next. The effort will be worth your time. A candidate who says, "I haven't thought about that yet," when asked about research plans places himself or herself at an enormous disadvantage. Prepare to discuss your ideas at a convincing level of detail. Try to convey enough enthusiasm about your ideas that you will carry your audience along with your enthusiasm and interest.

If you will require external funding to do your research, be aware of probable funding sources. In some cases it may even be impossible to continue your research without external funding. Even if such funding is not essential at the moment, your discussion of possible outside resources demonstrates that you are a candidate who is planning for future research needs. Many departments are under so much financial pressure that they may particularly welcome new faculty members who show promise of helping to support the department.

For positions in science and engineering at major research institutions, you will be expected to be able to tell the hiring committee your projected start-up costs. This can also be true for some social science fields and at other types of institutions. To do this credibly you need to have, in addition to a sound research proposal, a good estimate of what external funding will be available, and a budget for personnel, space, equipment, and materials the hiring institution will need to provide to get you started. Often candidates need to work harder to get adequate space than adequate budget.

Teaching

A hiring department's interest in this topic will vary, but most will have at least some degree of interest in what you do in front of a class. Before the interview, read through the department's course offerings in the catalog. Indicate which of the current courses you would be prepared to teach, as well as discussing any new courses you might offer in relation to the department's current offerings. Be prepared to discuss your approach to teaching and successful teaching experiences you have had, giving specific examples wherever possible. When you discuss a course, be able to suggest the text you might use. It is helpful to find out in advance what is currently in use in the department. Even if you would not plan to use the same text, it is neither necessary nor wise to disparage the current choice.

Don't forget that junior faculty members are often expected to carry a great deal of the introductory teaching load. If this isn't your great joy in life, you needn't pretend that it is, but try to convey the impression that you will do introductory teaching competently and with good humor. Make sure you are prepared to discuss using technology in teaching and involving undergraduates in research, as you are likely to be asked about both topics.

Your Interest in the Institution

Major research universities may consider it obvious that you would like to work for them, and a small liberal arts college in a remote location may press you more on the topic of why you want the job. But your enthusiasm for the department and the job is always important. After all, the people who are interviewing you work there, and it is not flattering to them if you seem to find their jobs uninteresting. You usually need to convey interest most strongly at less prestigious universities and at four-year colleges of all descriptions. The latter tend to pride themselves on distinctive institutional personalities and to hire people they believe will fit in.

Research the department before the interview. Look closely at the department's Web site so that you have a good sense of the individuals who work there as well as the curriculum they offer. Use library databases and the Web to learn about the research of faculty members. Read catalogs and college guides to learn about the school. The informal guides to college written for high school seniors are particularly useful in conveying the atmosphere of an institution. Use word of mouth to find out how others view the school.

In general, departments are looking not only for a candidate with outstanding independent research potential, but also for an outstanding colleague who will enrich the department, not simply by being present, but also by interacting productively with others. Be prepared to talk knowledgeably about faculty members' research. Try to search out and explore in advance areas of potential collaboration with faculty in the department.

During the interview, you do not need to be insincere to convey enthusiasm. Just talk about what you do find attractive about the institution. If there are no reasons at all that it appeals to you, why are you interviewing there?

Illegal Interview Questions

It may be helpful to you to know that employers cannot lawfully ask you questions that lead to illegal discrimination on the basis of race, sex, age, religion, national origin, physical disability, or, in many states, sexual orientation. However, they may be asked anyway, particularly in social situations. Try to respond to such questions calmly, answering the concerns they raise without necessarily volunteering the information they request.

Question   Do you plan to have children?
Answer: I see that you're concerned about my commitment to this position. Let me tell you about my research plans for the next several years. I plan to pursue them, whatever other personal decisions I may make.

Question: Did you grow up speaking Spanish?
Answer: Are you interested in hiring a native speaker for this position?

Some illegal questions are asked out of ignorance; some are a mistaken way to try to get information about one issue by asking about another (a common example is asking about a spouse's job in order to determine how long you are likely to stay in a position). Others may be asked not with the intention to eliminate you but with the intention to inform you of all the services offered to faculty, such as child care or help with a partner's job search. Try to react to them nonconfrontationally and to use them as another way to demonstrate your professionalism. Do not feel obligated, however, to provide information that you cannot legally be asked to give.

Question: What does your spouse do?
Answer: (If you feel that providing the information might work to your advantage.) We're fortunate that he's a systems consultant, and can work anywhere.

If you are very uncomfortable with the direction a question is taking, you may politely ask the interviewer why that question is important and how it relates to the position you are seeking. This should alert the interviewer that you feel the question is inappropriate. Be aware, however, that there is some risk associated with this approach.

Question   Are you married?
Answer   Can you tell me how you feel that that would be important for the position we're discussing?

Sometimes it is to your advantage to volunteer information your interviewers may hesitate to request. The law can regulate what is viewed as appropriate to ask, but it does not eliminate employers' concerns, legitimate or not. For example, if you have a physical disability, your interviewers may appreciate it if you explain how you work with it. (If you do have a disability, be sure you are familiar with the protection afforded you by the Americans with Disabilities Act.) If you are much older than the average job candidate, it may be helpful to volunteer remarks that will give the impression that you can work comfortably with younger colleagues. Be alert to comments that may reveal a concern.

Comment   We were all impressed by the years you had spent in business before you got your Ph.D.
Response: Yes, I really enjoyed those years. I feel fortunate to have the opportunity to prove myself again in a new field. (Indirectly

addresses concern that age and experience may make him or her unable to work comfortably in a junior position.)

Bizarre Interview Questions

Some questions, while not illegal, are inappropriate and weird. "What motto do you live by?" "What is the meaning of life?" "Tell us a joke." While you won't often be asked the likes of these, if you do a lot of interviewing, you may occasionally encounter one. In most cases the rest of the hiring committee will find the question as odd as you do. Try to respond cheerfully and matter-of-factly, but don't be constrained by the question. For example, if you can't think of a joke, say you enjoy laughing at other people's. Then, if you can, steer the conversation back to a more appropriate topic.

A Note About Attire

Wear something that conveys a professional appearance and won't detract attention from what you have to say. In general for both men and women this means something with a jacket. However, there is wide variation by field. In some cases a suit is virtually required and in others it is overkill. In some fields dressing with flair is an asset and in others a liability. Dress more casually for informal events that may be planned as part of an all-day visit. If you have the opportunity, watch what is worn by candidates who are interviewing with your own department. Also ask for advice from the best-dressed members of your department. Quality and professionalism are more important than variety. Invest in one good outfit and use changes of shirts or accessories to avoid being a rerun of yourself from one day to the next. Have a portfolio or briefcase, even if it is an inexpensive one, to keep track of papers and handouts.

When All Else Fails

It happens to nearly everyone. Nervousness about how you are doing in an interview interferes with showing yourself at your best. This is why some people interview better with departments they are less interested in. Your preparation for the interview should include enough sleep or exercise or whatever else lets you approach it in as relaxed a fashion as possible.

If you pay too much attention to "body language" during an interview, you will probably distract yourself from the points you are trying to address. However, be aware of how you tend to show nervousness (tapping feet, clasping hands, or whatever) and during the interview occasionally notice how you are behaving. If you are not sitting in a fairly open, relaxed position, change to one. Sitting with your arms crossed or holding your hands creates a closed, uncomfortable impression, and sitting more confidently will probably make you feel more confident as well. It's fine to gesture as you would in any other professional conversation. Holding your breath is a common nervous reaction that makes your speech choppy. Remember to breathe as you speak, and you will appear more relaxed.

Learn to use introductory "structuring" phrases which will let you buy time before trying to answer a question that throws you. They are better than twisting your hands or saying "um." For example:

- That's an interesting question. Let me take a moment to decide how best to respond to it.
- We need to consider several factors. First . . .
- I've never considered it from that point of view, but perhaps . . .
- I'd be glad to tell you about it.
- I'm sorry, but I'm not sure I understand your question. Do you mean . . .

You are expected to be somewhat nervous, but if you feel nervousness is getting in the way of expressing yourself clearly or is making your interviewers uncomfortable, it is best to make a direct reference to it. Paradoxically, the minute you admit you are nervous, you are likely to become less so, as well as to relax the interviewer. Examples of "defusing" statements might be

- Excuse me for speaking so rapidly. I've been looking forward to the chance to speak with you.
- Excuse me, but let me take a second to collect my thoughts. I'm a little nervous, because I'm so interested in this opportunity.
- Let me begin this explanation again. I can see that I didn't express myself clearly.

Preparation

Advance preparation, of course, will let you approach interviews with less nervousness and even with some enjoyment. Learn enough about the institution to feel you have a basic understanding of its size, mission, selectivity, and student body. Know what courses and programs the department offers and the research interests of the faculty. If you can't find key information on the Web and in the library, feel free to get in touch with the department and ask for additional materials.

The end of this chapter includes a list of typical questions. Chapter 15, "Off-Site Interviews: Conference/Convention and Telephone Interviews," and Chapter 16, "Campus Interviews," have checklists for these interview situations.

While you certainly don't want to memorize your responses word for word, it is helpful before any interview to fix in your mind the main points you would like to make, given the probable interests of the employer. Prepared with the knowledge of what you wish to discuss, you can use even unexpected questions that come your way as an opportunity to discuss the ideas that you wish to convey.

Many departments or university career services offices offer practice interview sessions. If yours does, plan to take advantage of the sessions. If it doesn't, try to organize one. Ask a faculty member to give you an individual interview. If you have access to recording equipment, taping an interview will give you the clearest possible idea of how you come across.

In addition, departments provide an excellent forum for delivering the presentation you plan to give at a campus interview. Take advantage of this opportunity, welcome feedback, and add final polish to your interview presentation.

Questions That Might Be Asked in an Academic Interview

Not all of these questions will apply to everyone. For example, a current postdoc is unlikely to get too many questions about his or her dissertation. However, it is likely that you will be asked some, if not several, of these questions.

About Research

- Could you tell us about your current research?
- Why did you choose your research topic?
- Can you tell us briefly what theoretical framework you used in developing your research?
- Of course you've read _____? (names an unfamiliar article/book related to your dissertation).
- If you were to begin it again, are there any changes you would make in your dissertation?
- In doing your research, why didn't you _____? (This question can take many forms. You are being asked to respond appropriately to an intellectual challenge to your work.)
- What contribution does your dissertation make to the field? Is it important?
- You realize that several members of this department tend to approach the subject from a very different perspective than does your advisor . . .
- Tell me about your dissertation (asked in a meeting with a dean who knows very little about your field).
- Why didn't you finish your dissertation sooner?
- I see you have very few publications . . .
- What are your research plans for the next two/five/ten years?

- What are your plans for applying for external funding over the next few years?
- When will you have sufficient preliminary data for a grant application?
- What facilities do you need to carry out your research plans?
- How do you see your research fitting in with the department?
- Who would you collaborate with?
- What kind of start-up package do you need? (This question applies primarily to people in fields where research requires expensive resources.)
- Do you have the permission of your mentor to take this work with you? (This question applies primarily to postdoctoral fellows applying for faculty positions.)

About Teaching

- Are you a good teacher?
- How do you feel about having to teach required courses?
- What is your approach to teaching introductory _____?
- How do you motivate students?
- How would you encourage students to major in our field?
- In your first semester you would be responsible for our course in _____. How would you structure it? What textbook would you use?
- Many of our students are probably (more/less academically talented; older/younger) than those you've become used to at your institution. How successful would you be with them?
- What is your teaching philosophy?
- If you could teach any course you wanted to, what would it be?
- Have you had any experience with the case study method?
- What do you think is the optimal balance between teaching and research?
- Have you had any experience with distance learning?
- How would you involve undergraduates in your research?
- Have you taught graduate or professional students?
- Have you supervised any graduate students, rotations, or research projects or taught specialized skills?

About Your Willingness to Participate in the Department and School

- Can you summarize the contribution you would make to our department?
- Are you willing to become involved in committee work?
- Why are you interested in our kind of school?
- What institutional issues particularly interest you?

About Your Career and Personal Choices

- If you have more than one job offer, how will you decide?
- How do you feel about living in a small college town like this in an isolated rural area?
- I can't imagine why a young person like you would want to go into this field . . .
- I understand your spouse is completing his/her Ph.D. What if you receive job offers in different locations? (This question is not legal in most contexts, but you should be prepared for it.)
- What do you do in your spare time?
- Who else is interviewing you?
- What will it take to persuade you to take this job?
- What kind of salary are you looking for?

Do You Have Any Questions for Us?

The right answer to this is always yes, or you risk appearing uninterested. Prepare some questions in advance, but, above all, ask questions that show a response to what you have learned from the interviewers and that are lively, rather than formulaic.

Questions about salary and benefits are not appropriate now. Wait until you are offered a job to ask about these matters.

These are some questions you might prepare to ask. Have a few questions ready and know that you need to get a sense of thr faculty members with whom it would be more appropriate to talk about certain things, for example, tenure.

- What do you like best about the students at Institution X?
- In what direction do you expect the department to go in the next five years?
- I hear that the school is revising its core curriculum. How will those changes impact this department?
- How is teaching evaluated?
- How are graduate students funded in this department?
- What constitutes service in this department? In this school? Follow-up: How much service is expected of junior faculty members?
- Could you tell me more about the tenure requirements at this institution?

Chapter 15
Off-Site Interviews: Conference/
Convention and Telephone Interviews

Challenges of the Conference or Convention Interview

Conference interviews may be relatively unimportant in your field. In many disciplines, however, preliminary interviews for most of the entry-level jobs in the country are held at the annual meeting. You may be one of ten or more well-qualified candidates on a long interview schedule, interviewing under conditions of stress and possible confusion. So what do you do? First, reassure yourself that other job candidates face the same situation. Practice before the convention so that you can convey key information succinctly and make the most of limited time. Practice ensures that when the interview arrives you can relax and respond flexibly to interviewers, knowing that you're prepared for whatever arises.

Be prepared to be interviewed by a group. Three to six department members is a typical size, but the number varies. When you schedule your interview, ask the person who is arranging it how many people will probably interview you, so that you have some idea of what to expect. You may have interviews in hotel public areas set aside for that purpose. Some departments will have taken suites of rooms for interviewing. Others will interview in an ordinary hotel bedroom.

While you may be happy to interview with everyone who wants to talk to you, be realistic in scheduling interviews. Allow enough time to get from one location to another, bearing in mind that interviews may run behind schedule. Don't book yourself so tightly that you arrive late and disheveled to speak with the institution that is your first choice. Don't hesitate to reschedule an interview if you find that two are too close together.

Of course the main function of a national convention is to share new research in the discipline. If you have already agreed to give a talk, be sure to schedule your interviews so that you have enough time to relax and gather your thoughts beforehand.

A national convention provides you with the opportunity to have both scheduled and chance meetings with scholars in your field. Making the most of these encounters will be to your advantage, not just in this job search but throughout your career. If networking is a concern for you, you might want to take a look at Chapter 6, Conference Presentations and Networking.

Keeping Your Audience Engaged

Important as the job interview is to you, it may be less interesting to members of the interviewing team. They may be preoccupied with other aspects of the conference, be tired, and find that interviewing a long series of candidates is not their preferred occupation. Make every effort to be engaging! You are very likely to be asked to discuss your research. Try hard to give a succinct introduction to your subject and to gauge your audience's immediate reaction, adding more or less detail as their responses suggest.

During each interview, try to introduce something that will make you memorable. This could be some striking aspect of your research, the fact that your advisor used to be a member of this department, the fact that you're trilingual, or anything else that will help people remember who you are. Even if one member of a group does nearly all the talking, address your responses to everyone and try to make eye contact with everyone in the room.

Dealing with Difficult Situations

At a convention you may encounter other situations that do not conform to a script for the perfect interview. There may be schedule confusion, department members may float in and out of the interview suite, or an interviewer may have had too much to drink. Anything you can do to appear unruffled will work to your advantage. Try not to let annoyance at an interviewer's behavior get the best of you.

Always feel free to act in a way that maintains your sense of personal dignity. If anything inappropriate occurs (for example, if an interviewer keeps pressing you to have a drink when you don't want one), realize that setting personal limits is appropriate and will serve you well in the long run: "Thanks, no. I'd like to begin to discuss the position you advertised."

In the extremely unlikely event that you find yourself in what you regard as an impossible interview, in which all your best efforts do not dissuade the interviewer from creating a humiliating situation, feel free to terminate the interview, as calmly as you can: "I'd like to discuss the position, but now doesn't seem to be a good time," or, "There doesn't seem to be a good match between our interests, so I won't take more of your time. Thanks for inviting me to the interview." In such a case check immediately with your advisor or someone else from your department who is attending the conference. If anything seriously inappropriate has occurred, it may be possible to arrange another interview under better conditions.

Usually, however, convention interviews are hectic but professional. Try not to get annoyed at minor issues and to keep a sense of humor. Everyone else will be interviewing under the same stressful conditions, and things won't go perfectly for anyone.

A Desirable Dilemma: Early Offers

Occasionally, in fields in high demand, candidates have received immediate invitations to campus interviews, or even job offers, as a result of convention interviewing. While most candidates long for just this sort of dilemma, and the attention can be flattering, try to keep a sense of perspective. You may feel you have little to lose by accepting another campus visit, but stop short of exhausting yourself by making numerous trips to places where you have no interest in working.

If you receive an offer before you feel you have had a reasonable chance to explore the market, express pleasure at having received it, but explain that you need more time to make up your mind, and negotiate for as long as you can before you need to make a final decision. Don't let the overtures affect your perspective to such an extent that you begin to seem arrogant, an attitude that can quickly alienate even those who were initially very enthusiastic about your candidacy.

Conference/Convention Interview Checklist

Before the Interview

Get all the details straight when you arrange for the interview:

- The logistics of arranging interviews vary from convention to convention. Find out from your own department how yours works.
- Clarify the time and place for each interview. If possible, find out how many people will interview you and learn and memorize their names.
- If interviews will be held at more than one hotel, make sure that you know how you will get from one to another, and how long it will take, so that your schedule is realistic.
- Make sure you have the name and phone number of the contact person in case you need to reach him or her before the meeting.

Learn about the institution, department(s), and interviewers:

- You may have limited time for research, especially if you have many interviews scheduled. In the time available, try to learn something about every school and become fairly knowledgeable about the ones that interest you most. Most of what you need to know should be on the institution's Web site.

- The many readily available college guides written for high school seniors will give you a quick profile of the institution.
- Conduct Web and library database searches for information on publications by department members.
- Ask everyone who might know something about the institution to discuss it.
- Learn whether the department stresses teaching or research and how it presents itself to the world.

Prepare for the interviews:

- Decide what you want to convey.
- Practice answering questions with a friend, a faculty member, or your university career counselor. See Chapter 14 for sample questions.

Bring:

- Extra copies of your vita and other materials you submitted to the search committee.
- Copies of your dissertation abstract and statement of research plans.
- Other materials you may wish to show, if time permits: syllabi, reprints, abstracts of articles. You will not necessarily distribute all of these, but you will be prepared with them should you need them.
- Whatever accessories or repair materials (buttons, glasses, or an extra pair of contact lenses) you might need, to avoid last-minute sartorial disasters.
- Depending on current airline policy, try to avoid checking anything important through on the airplane. Bring the essentials (written materials and interview clothing) in carry-on luggage.

During the Interview

If possible, begin by shaking hands with the interviewer(s), even if you need to take the initiative to do so. If schedule problems cause you to arrive late for an interview, apologize, and then try to forget it and begin on a calm note. If you don't catch a name when you're introduced to someone, have it repeated, so that you know it. Do your best, and concentrate on the conversation with the interviewers and the ideas you are trying to convey, rather than on how well you are "performing."

When your interview ends, briefly summarize your interest in the position and what you feel you could contribute to it. Keep it short. If possible, shake hands with the interviewer(s) when you leave.

After the Interview

A timely, brief thank you note is a courtesy that can reinforce your interest in the position. It is normally not necessary to write to each person you have spoken with. A note to the person who chaired the search committee is sufficient; in this note, you can ask the chair to convey your thanks to the others.

Some faculty members will find an e-mail thank you perfectly acceptable, or even preferable. Others will find a paper letter more respectful. Use your judgment based on impressions you've formed in the interview and on communication you've received from the department.

Challenges of the Telephone Interview

As budgets for interviewing candidates shrink, departments are increasingly doing a first round of telephone interviews before choosing candidates to invite for campus visits. These are not impromptu calls, but conversations scheduled in advance just as a face-to-face interview would be. They save you the trouble of dressing up in your best professional attire, but present you with the difficulty of establishing rapport with interviewer(s) without an opportunity to rely on visual cues. Often the interviews are arranged as conference calls, presenting you with the need to recognize different individuals quickly based on their voices.

You should handle this conversation as you would any other interview, but it will be particularly important to be animated and expressive in your conversation, since the interviewers will know you only by your voice. One seasoned faculty interviewer has suggested smiling as you speak. Assuming the physical expression, even though the interviewers can't see it, will help you assume an appropriate tone of voice. Feel free to ask for more than a normal amount of feedback if it will help you get to know the people you are talking with. For instance, if someone asks you a question without identifying himself or herself, feel free to clarify the person's name. Taking notes as others speak may help you keep individuals straight.

Non-native speakers of English should take note that telephone interviews are sometimes used to assess language ability. Interviewers can often tell if a candidate is reading answers and may ask unexpected questions to test one's ability to speak extemporaneously.

Telephone Interview Checklist

Before the Interview

Get all the details straight when you arrange for the interview:

- Clarify the time for the interview. If possible, find out how many people will interview you and learn their names. Memorize them.
- Make sure you have the name and phone number of the contact person in case you need to reach him or her before the interview.

Learn about the institution, departments, and interviewers:

- It is as important to prepare for a telephone interview as it is for any other kind. See the suggestions above for conference/convention interviews.

Prepare for the interview:

- Decide what you want to convey.
- Practice answering questions with a friend, a faculty member, or your university career counselor.
- Send to the department copies of materials you might otherwise bring to an interview to discuss such as syllabi, reprints, abstracts of articles. You will not necessarily have time to discuss all of these, but you will be prepared with them should you need them.

Arrange for the logistics of the interview:

- Make sure you won't be interrupted during your interview, by your children, your call-waiting, another phone, or anything else that beeps or rings.
- Collect and have near the phone copies of all the material you may wish to refer to during the interview.

During the Interview

If you don't catch a name when the interviewers are introduced, have it repeated, so that you know it. You may wish to jot down names and any other identifying information you are given; no one will see if you refer to these notes during the conversation.

Do your best, and concentrate on the conversation with the interviewers and the ideas you are trying to convey, rather than on how well you are "performing." However, since you won't have visual feedback, don't hesitate to ask if you are making yourself clear, if the interviewers would like to hear more about a given topic, or if they would like to move on to another subject.

When your interview ends, briefly summarize your interest in the position and what you feel you could contribute to it. Keep it short.

Since you can't shake hands with the interviewers, try to say good-bye to each individually, if there are few enough of them for this to be practical.

After the Interview

As after an in-person interview, send a brief thank you note.

Chapter 16
Campus Interviews

Challenges of the Campus Visit

By the time a department invites three to five candidates for a visit, it has determined that all are in some sense competent. During the interview the search committee tries to assess such intangibles as "potential," "fit," and "tenurability." On campus, it is as important to be prepared to be convincing and concise as it is at a conference. In addition, the abilities to respond flexibly to the requirements of unpredictable situations, to talk comfortably with others in informal, unstructured meetings, and to convey interest in the institution to which you're applying will help you land the job.

As institutions increasingly view tenure-track hires as major financial investments, campus visits for these positions have become quite long, sometimes extending to three days. While the minimum requirements of a campus interview are usually a presentation to faculty and interviews with several faculty members, a visit might also involve teaching at least one class, one to several group faculty interviews, meetings with graduate and undergraduate students, several individual meetings, meals, a reception, and entertainment.

You may meet individuals ranging from a dean to a junior representing the departmental majors' club, from genuinely stimulating potential colleagues to the curmudgeon who makes it his or her business to ask all speakers to relate their presentations to his or her own field of thirty-year-old research. Flexibility and a sense of humor will serve you well. Be prepared for potentially problematic aspects of the visit.

The Presentation and Its Question Session

The importance of an excellent seminar, also called a job talk, can hardly be overemphasized. An outstanding seminar can make up for many other shortcomings, but a poor seminar is seldom forgiven. The seminar is used as an opportunity to assess a candidate's research; how he or she handles questions and thinks on his or her feet; how he or she performs in the classroom; and even whether he or she has a sense of humor and a stage presence that suggest he or she will be successful at conferences, in the classroom, and in other professional forums. Pay particular attention to giving the context and motivation for your research. Within the first five minutes you should convince your audience that your work is important.

It is important that you speak enthusiastically about your work. Some job candidates find it helpful to think of their work as an engaging narrative that will draw the audience in. During the talk, try to establish eye contact with everyone present. Avoid speaking in a monotone as it will both put people to sleep and communicate your own boredom with your research. Instead, use your voice to highlight the most exciting aspects of your project. If some members of the audience seem uninterested or even fall asleep, don't let that bother you. If you are using slides, don't rush through them. (For further suggestions on slide presentation, see Chapter Six, Conference Presentations and Networking.) Make sure that your presentation has a clear and marked ending. You'll want to have a strong conclusion so that your audience will know that you're finished and will leave with a clear picture of your research.

In the question period following a presentation, the department chair may field the questions or the candidate may have to do it. You may receive questions that leave you at a loss, point to a weakness in your work, or are challenging to the point of hostility. Stay calm and don't let yourself be put on the defensive. Be confident enough to admit that you don't know something. Respond to even unreasonable questions reasonably. Be prepared to venture reasonable hypotheses. Practice in advance how you might respond to even the most off-the-wall questions about your presentation. Know that, in some cases, how you respond during the question and answer session is as important as the talk itself. Your potential colleagues want to see how well you can think on your feet.

The Teaching Demonstration

In many cases you will be asked either to teach an actual class or to give a teaching demonstration. This is particularly common at teaching-focused institutions, but certainly not limited to them. When the interview is scheduled, find out who will be part of the teaching demonstration. If it will be students in an actual class, find out what they have been studying. If it will be a group of faculty and/or students convened to watch you teach, treat those people as you would if they were class members. Plan to stay close to the teaching style that works best for you. If you normally give dynamic lectures, don't use the campus visit to experiment with small group work. If you shine at creating class discussions, plan an interactive session. If the group is small enough and time permits, feel free to ask everyone to introduce themselves to you before you begin.

Interviewing with Faculty and Administrators

It is likely that you will meet one-on-one with many, if not all, of the members of the department. If you are interviewing at a small school you will also meet with faculty in related disciplines. Be able to talk about the unique contributions you can make to the department with both your research and your teaching. Show that you understand the department's goals, and demonstrate what you can add to them.

At a large institution it is possible that you will meet with a dean, and at a small institution it is likely that you will meet with a provost or even a president. Although these people will probably not be in your field, you'll want to talk about the importance of your research and teaching in an engaging manner. In addition you might want to ask them big picture questions such as the mission of the university and where the department fits within that.

You may meet many people throughout the day without having a very clear idea of who is critical to the decision to hire you. Simultaneously you may begin to tire of hearing yourself discuss the same subjects over and over. It's extremely important that you be enthusiastic about these topics with each new person that you meet. Everyone who meets you will want to form his or her own impression of you. So tell your story again to each new person with as much zest and interest as if it were for the first time. Also, when the opportunity presents itself, ask those who are interviewing you about their work. Most people will be happy to talk about their interest. This will give you a chance to be "off" for a few moments and help you get a sense of your potential colleagues.

Social Events

Social occasions are usually part of a campus visit. Realize that they are also part of the screening process. Follow your hosts' lead in deciding how much to talk shop and how much to talk about topics of general interest. It is a good idea, however, to seize every reasonable opportunity to discuss your work and your field. You can also appropriately ask questions during these times. Your hosts will appreciate it if you make yourself good company: ask questions of others; initiate conversation; laugh at other people's jokes; and display an interest in the people you are with.

If you have no personal objection to doing so, have a drink if others do, but don't drink enough to affect your behavior. Alcohol and interviewing can be a risky combination. One compromise is to have a glass of what is offered, but to drink only part of it. Particularly beware of "confessional" impulses. However friendly your hosts, do not confide that you are here just for practice, that you can't wait to put distance between yourself and your advisor, or any other statement that later you are almost sure to regret having made.

It is easier to handle these occasions if you are very outgoing than if you are shy, but shy people can convey their interest and intelligence through active questioning and perceptive listening. You must push yourself to be an active participant in the occasion. It is better to risk some less than perfect remarks and come across as an individual rather than as a quiet, inoffensive presence, so bland that no one is sure what you are like or what you really think.

Your Opportunity to Learn About the Institution

Interviewing is a two-way process. Even as others are assessing your candidacy for the position, you have an opportunity to learn about the institution and to decide whether or not you want to work there. Both schools and departments have their own institutional cultures. You are most likely to thrive in a department and school in which there is a reasonable measure of fit between you and the others who work and study there. Take advantage of your time on campus to learn everything you can.

Location and Physical Setting

Gauge your own reaction to the appearance of the campus. Does it strike you as lively and inviting? Or do you feel that it is impersonal? In the middle of nowhere? Impossibly urban and congested? It's unlikely that you would choose a job entirely based on its physical setting and appearance, but it is important to be able to visualize yourself as at least reasonably comfortable going to work there every day. Look carefully at the office(s) and/ or research facilities, particularly the ones where you would be working. Do they appear adequate? If laboratory or computer facilities are particularly important in your work, your hosts will be likely to offer you a tour or demonstration of them. If they do not, however, and such facilities are important to you, ask.

The Department

Probably the single most important thing you will learn on a campus visit is what the members of the department are like. These are the people with whom you will interact on a daily basis, who will be available for discussion of ideas, and who will ultimately evaluate your performance. Will you be glad to be part of this group? It is certainly important to keep an open mind and to remember that first impressions are necessarily somewhat superficial. Nevertheless, your reactions to these individuals are some of the most important data you can gather during your visit.

Pay attention to how people appear to relate to each other. Does the departmental atmosphere appear lively and collegial? Extremely hierarchical? Are there obvious divisions between competing factions? Do people appear enthusiastic about where they are and what they are doing, or is there a pervasive sense of cynicism and discouragement?

Students

If you meet students, graduate or undergraduate, during an interview, take these meetings seriously. If students are part of the interview, it is very likely that their opinions will be factored into the decision-making process. If you are particularly interested in teaching and your visit does not include any planned meetings with students, ask faculty members to describe both students and classes. If your visit includes any free time, you may want to spend it at the student union or other campus gathering place. Listen to what students say to each other. Introduce yourself and ask them questions. Pick up copies of the student paper and of any other student-produced publications. They will give you a feel for current campus issues.

The Institution

At a university, probably you will feel you work in your department and your school more than at the institution as a whole. At a college you will probably feel that the college itself is your employer. When you visit, you will probably spend at least some time with someone who represents a unit larger than your prospective department. Use this as an opportunity to evaluate the role that the department plays in the broader picture. Is it strong and respected? Slowly eroding? The bright, brash new kid on the block?

As you learn throughout the day, feel free to comment positively on what you are learning. For example, if your first interview of the day is with someone who devotes a great deal of time to describing the school's excellent computer resources, in the next interview you can explain that you were impressed with them and go on to explain why these facilities would be particularly advantageous in your own research. If you notice an extremely collegial atmosphere throughout the day, and at the end of the day the chair asks what you think of the department, by all means say that you've observed a lively exchange of ideas and are very attracted by that kind of atmosphere. Hiring committees like to know that you have read their institution correctly and can picture yourself functioning well in it.

On-Campus Interview Checklist

Before the Interview

Get all the details straight when you arrange for the interview.

- Find out the length of the interview days and what meetings to expect during them. Most institutions will send you a schedule. A sample interview schedule is included at the end of this chapter.
- If you do not already have a complete job description, ask to have one sent to you.
- Will you be making a presentation? If so, on what? How long? To whom? How should it be delivered? What audiovisual or computer facilities will be available to you? If you want to use a particular kind of equipment, don't hesitate to inquire about it.
- Will you be expected to teach a class? If so, to whom? On what? What has been covered so far this semester? If you would like to use audiovisual materials, find out what equipment will be available.
- Confirm all travel arrangements. When planning travel, allow more than enough time to compensate for flight delays or traffic jams. Find out how reservations should be booked (if you need your tickets paid for in advance, try to negotiate that with the department). Save all receipts.
- Make sure you know the name of the person who has called you, where you are to arrive, how you will be met, the name of the person who will meet you, and all relevant phone numbers.
- If there is enough time before the interview, ask to have any materials that would help you learn more about the school and department sent to you.
- If you encounter unavoidable delays while traveling to the interview, call as soon as you can and explain why you will be delayed.

Learn about the institution and faculty.

- Use Web sites. In addition to specific information, try to get a sense of the campus culture.
- If you are visiting an institution where sports are a major part of campus life, learn the names of the teams, both at the campus you are visiting and at your own institution, and how they are playing this year. Sports are sometimes used as icebreakers.
- Use Web and library searches for information on publications by members of the department. Try to learn the names of everyone in the department, so you can address them by name during your visit.
- Ask everyone who might know something about the institution to discuss it.

Practice both interview questions and your presentation.

- Rehearse how you will respond to questions about your research, teaching and interest in the institution. See Chapter 14 for sample questions.
- Time your talk to ensure that it's the right length.
- Be sure your slides, handouts, and/or other presentation materials are ready in plenty of time. As a back-up, e-mail your presentation materials to yourself.
- Develop a "cocktail party length" brief summary to give to those outside the department.

Bring:

- Extra copies of your vita and any other materials you submitted to the search committee.
- More than enough handouts. Make sure they look good.
- Samples of syllabi for courses you designed, reprints, abstracts of articles. You will not necessarily distribute all of these during the day but you'll be prepared with them if you need them.
- Whatever accessories or repair materials (buttons, glasses or an extra pair of contact lenses) you might need to avoid last minute sartorial disasters.
- Something to do during delays in traveling.
- Whatever you need (running clothes, escapist novels) if you'll be nervous the night before the interview.
- Depending on current airline policy, try to avoid checking anything important through on the airplane. Bring the essentials (written materials and interview clothing) in carry-on luggage.

During the Interview

Remember that each new person you meet hasn't heard your story yet. Be prepared to tell it again and again with enthusiasm.

Be sure to get to the room in which you will give your research talk a few minutes early so you can collect your thoughts and make sure any technology you need is working.

If someone asks you if you have any questions for them, make sure you do. You can build on what you learn throughout the day to formulate your questions.

If you don't catch a name when you're introduced to someone, have it repeated, so that you know it. Shake hands when you meet someone.

Acknowledge everyone present in a group interview, and, if possible, say goodbye to people individually when you leave.

If the day includes social events, follow your hosts' leads in deciding how much to talk about professional, and how much about social, topics.

At the end of the day, find out when a decision will be made, and when you may call if you haven't heard anything. Find out if you should turn in receipts then or send them later.

After the Interview

Take care of any extra receipts.

Write a thank you note to the main person who arranged your day. You can ask that person to convey your thanks to others. Reiterate your interest in the position. It isn't necessary to write to everyone with whom you spoke.

Sample Interview Schedule
For positions in the sciences it is common to have a return interview; in other disciplines it is customary to have one 1–3-day interview.

First Campus Interview

Itinerary
DR. MARK DAVID RESEARCHER
Interdisciplinary Program in the Biomedical Sciences
University of Y, City B, State

Arrive in City B on Sunday February 18th at 2:16pm. He will be picked up by Dr. X.

Lodging at the ABC Hotel

Dinner with Professor Y at 6:30pm

Monday February 19th

7:30 – 8:45 am Breakfast with Dr. A. Pickup in the hotel front desk area.

9:00 – 9:30 Dr. B

9:30 – 10:00 Dr. C

10:00 – 10:30 Dr. D

10:30 – 11:00 Dr. E

11:00 – 11:30 Dr. F

11:30 – Noon Dr. G

Noon – 1:00pm Lunch with Graduate Students and Post Docs

1:00 – 1:30pm Dr. H

1:30 – 2:00pm Dr. I

2:00 – 3:00pm Dr. J

3:00 – 3:30pm Dr. K

3:30 – 4:00 pm Prepare for seminar

4:00 – 5:00pm Seminar 'The Selection and Activation of Regulatory T cells'

6:00 pm Dinner Dr. L and others

Tuesday February 20th.

Check out at 8:30am – Dr. X

Departure at 11:15am

Return Campus Interview

Itinerary
DR. MARK DAVID RESEARCHER
Interdisciplinary Program in the Biomedical Sciences
University of Y, City B, State

Wednesday, March 7

10:15 AM	Depart City A	US Airways Flight 1234

12:22 PM   Arrive City B

Dr. X will pick up Dr. Researcher at the airport and transport him to the hotel.

ACCOMMODATIONS:
ABC Hotel
CONFIRMATION NUMBER 1111

Thursday, March 8

11:00 AM   Meet with Dr. B, Chair, Department of Microbiology and Cell Science
1223 Science Building

2:00 PM   Meet with Dr. N, Associate Dean for Research
456 XYZ Hall

3:00 PM   Meet with Dr. P, Associate Dean for Academics
123 XYZ Hall

Friday, March 9

CHECK OUT OF HOTEL

7:30 AM   Pick up at front of hotel by Dr. Y and transport to XYZ Hall

8:00 AM   Meet with Dr. P, Associate Dean for Academics
123 XYZ Hall

8:30 AM   Transport to airport by Dr. Y

10:00 AM   Depart City B   US Airways Flight 9876

11:50 AM   Arrive City A

Chapter 17
Job Offers, Negotiations, Acceptances, and Rejections

In a tight job market, candidates worry primarily about receiving any acceptable job offer. However, job offers produce their own challenges.

Once an offer is made, you may face a difficult decision about whether to accept it at all. If you are considering an offer, you may have to agree on a timetable for acceptance, decide on your first choice, encourage a first choice school to speed up their hiring process because you have to meet a deadline for accepting another offer, negotiate salary or working conditions, and deal appropriately with schools that you accept and reject.

First, make sure that you really do have an offer. The department member who tells you confidentially that you're the committee's first choice or the chair who says that the department is virtually certain that funds will be approved are not offering positions, merely expressing optimism. A job offer becomes a real offer when a salary and term of appointment are attached to it and when someone has put it in writing. If you turn down a job for which an offer letter states a position and a salary in favor of one for which you've been told, "We're as good as certain that the funds will be available," know that you're taking a calculated risk. At the end of this chapter are two sample offer letters.

Timetable for Accepting a Job Offer

Getting Final Information

When an offer is made is the time to get any additional information that you feel may be necessary to make a good decision. Now that the school is "selling," you can feel free to ask your most probing questions. Be prepared to ask them when you receive an offer, even if you need to schedule another time to talk more extensively. It is not a good idea to call the department again and again asking a different question each time.

Consider visiting the institution a second time to take the opportunity to ask all the questions you can think of about the prospective position and employer. Whether or not you visit, if the prospects for obtaining tenure were not clearly discussed at the campus interview, ask for more detail now. How many tenured and nontenured members does the department have? How many junior faculty members would come up for tenure at the same time you would? How many people have come up for tenure over the last several years? How many were recommended for tenure by the department? How many were granted it? What are the standards the department would expect you to meet in order to recommend it?

Other questions involve the conditions of the offer and the job itself. How many courses are you expected to teach? Will you have an opportunity to teach over the summer for additional compensation? Is there a possibility of released time for research in your first year on the job? What resources will be available to support your research?

If a spouse's or partner's job opportunities will be a major factor in your decision, ideally you have already given some indication of that in an earlier interview. Now, however, is the time to find out exactly what the department meant when you were told that "We should be able to find something attractive for him/her." Possibly you will want to arrange for a visit to the area by your partner, if you can persuade the department to give you that long to reach a decision.

Perhaps you would like to talk to others in the department who were not available on the day that you visited. Perhaps you would like to talk to someone who can knowledgeably discuss local housing and public schools with you. Whatever it is that you feel you need to know, tell the person who makes you the offer so that arrangements can be made for you to obtain the information. Do, however, limit yourself to questions about things that seriously matter to you. If you ask endless questions about what appear to be trivial details, the department may begin to question its judgment in offering you the position.

Negotiating for Time to Consider

Naturally you would like to decide as late as possible, in order to ascertain what other offers you will receive, and the school that offers you a job would like you to accept as early as possible in order to close the search. These competing desires are reconciled through a process of negotiation in which you both agree when you will give the school a binding answer.

Generally this time is measured in weeks. It would be extremely unusual for a school to ask you to decide in less than a week and a two-week limit is more common. Extensions to several weeks are not uncommon, and extensions measured in months are very rare. Before you propose a time to make up your mind, ask the school how long it had planned to give you.

Schools will understand that you may want to see how you have fared in the market. However, if in your interview you have talked enthusiastically about why this school is your first choice, be careful that your behavior now doesn't throw your earlier protestations into doubt. In any case, convey enthusiasm for the offer at the same time as you ask for time to decide. You may take this job and will want to begin it on good terms with your new colleagues.

When Your First Choice Isn't Your First Offer

If you haven't yet had an interview with the school that is your first choice, it's doubtful that you would be able to receive an offer from it before you must accept or reject the job that you have been offered. If you are well into the search process with your first choice, however, it is worthwhile to see whether you can hasten their decision. Furthermore, the information that someone else has offered you a position tends to enhance your chances.

First negotiate with the school that has offered you the position for as long a decision period as it can give you. If you are willing to take a risk, you may be able to buy the most time by saying, "If you need an immediate answer, I'm afraid it's no." Since this answer may put the offer at risk, it's one you should not give lightly; however, if the school is very serious about getting you, this response does offer the greatest incentive for them to give you a longer time to decide. Then immediately contact your first choice to let them know that you have been offered another position and to ask them what their time frame is. This is most effective if you have already interviewed with them.

Negotiating

There will be many terms in your offer, some of which you will be pleased with, others you hope to improve. It is standard practice to negotiate an offer. Institutions will expect you to do so.

It is extremely important to conduct your negotiations verbally, usually over the phone, but occasionally in person, rather than by e-mail. Doing so helps preserve the good feeling with potential colleagues which is your working capital once an offer is extended. E-mail is a good way to confirm changes that have been agreed upon verbally.

You will not want to negotiate every aspect of the offer because you don't want to seem greedy. Focus on those conditions that are of particular importance to you. The following are conditions some of which you might choose to negotiate.

Salary

Whether you will be able to negotiate successfully for a salary higher than you are initially offered depends both upon your discipline and upon the institution with which you're negotiating. Even when the amount you could potentially negotiate is very small, however, it is worthwhile to raise the subject. First, be prepared by knowing appropriate salary ranges for this kind of position at this kind of institution. If possible, try to learn through informal channels how much flexibility the hiring department has to negotiate salary. If, in fact, the salary you are offered seems exceptionally high, you may be less inclined to negotiate than if it is low. If you decide to raise the question of salary or anything else substantive, the right time to do so is after you are offered the position, but well before the deadline for making a decision.

Remember that in the period between the time a department offers you a position and the time you accept it, you are a "buyer," in the strongest position to ask for salary or any other special conditions, such as research support, that may be important to you. Make the most of this opportunity by not rushing into agreements you may later regret. You may well be offered a position by phone. If you do not feel comfortable negotiating on the spot, thank the person making the offer, make sure that you understand its basic dimensions, such as salary, and ask if you can get in touch shortly. In the next conversation you can raise any issues that you would like to negotiate and agree on a time by which you will make a decision.

If you decide that you want to try to negotiate a higher salary, what do you do? Begin by expressing enthusiasm for the job and asking whether the department has any flexibility on salary. Usually someone who is prepared to negotiate will answer, even if negatively, in a way that leaves a tiny opening. Note the difference between: "only in highly exceptional and rare cases," and "I'm sorry, but we follow an institution-wide, union-approved salary pay scale, and there's absolutely nothing we can do about this figure, no matter how interested we are in a candidate."

If you raise the question of salary, be prepared to answer the question, "How much did you have in mind?" Frequently an inquiry on your part will be answered with a response that the person offering you the job will speak with others. This is wonderful, because it gives you both a chance to think further. Take advantage of the opportunity to seek additional advice from faculty members about the figure you have been offered.

As you discuss salary, consider its long-term trajectory. Some well-known institutions pay less at the beginning, but more as faculty become more senior. Some institutions offer relatively small salary increases as faculty are promoted. It's fair to ask the hiring department to tell you the ratio between compensation for new and senior faculty.

Other Things You Might Negotiate

Occasionally someone who cannot offer you more salary may be able to offer you other things (or perhaps there are other things that you want more than salary). These could include a reduced teaching load in your first year, special computer or laboratory facilities, funds for travel and summer research, assistance to a spouse who is looking for a job, extra relocation expenses, or something similar. Here are some things that can be negotiated.

Decision Date

If you are waiting to hear about other searches, particularly, ones for which you haven't yet interviewed, ask if you can postpone the date of your final decision on the offer.

Start-Up Package

This is usually for people in the laboratory-based sciences and related areas. These are the funds you will need to launch and sustain your research program, at least until you get your first grant. With these funds you might buy lab equipment and supplies, hire technicians, fund postdocs or graduate students, or pay overhead costs. Space is also a concern when negotiating start-up packages.

Below is a sample start-up budget for an assistant professor of biology at a private mid-sized Master's institution:

I was given approximately $50,000 starting package for equipment. This is approximately how it was spent:

Tetrad dissection microscope	$7100
Roller drum	$1400
Coulter counter	$13000
Luminometer	$4800
Incubator	$2300
Shaker/incubator	$5000
Micro-centrifuge	$1700
Thermocycler	$8000
Electrophoresis apparatuses	$2000
Waterbath, dual chamber	$950

Whatever left over ($3750) was spent on chemicals, solutions, enzymes, and consumables.

Teaching Load and Teaching Schedule

Sometimes a new assistant professor will want a reduced teaching load first semester in order to get research up and running; others prefer to teach less second semester and concentrate on research once they know their way around the new campus. If you will live a distance from the institution you may want to schedule the courses you teach accordingly.

Research Assistants

If no mention has been made of a research assistant and you're going to need one, ask.

Computer Resources

For many new assistant professors, an exciting part of the job is getting a new computer. If you need special software or access to expensive databases to do your research, now is the time to ask.

Travel Funds and Conference Expenses

Many offers include funding for one conference per year. If you need to attend more than one or need to visit archives, libraries or other types of research sites, negotiate for more travel funds.

Start Date

Candidates can negotiate to defer starting a position for a semester or a year for many reasons, often so that they can complete a dissertation or a research project or give birth and care for a new baby.

Moving Expenses/Housing Help

Many colleges and universities provide this automatically. If your new employer doesn't mention it, find out how much it will cost you to move, and raise the issue.

Job Hunting for a Partner or Spouse

Some institutions may provide help for a spouse. If your spouse or partner is an academic this might come as a chance to meet with a dean or faculty in the appropriate department. If your spouse or partner is not an academic this might come in the form of a referral to resources that might help with getting a job in the region.

Additional Considerations

Sometimes nothing at all will be negotiable. Don't hesitate to raise an issue that interests you, but make sure throughout that you maintain a pleasant relationship with the department so that they will remain glad that they offered you the position.

The terms of the offer may change during negotiation. Be sure to have them put in writing so that there is a very clear understanding, and a record of that understanding, between you and the employer as to what has and has not been promised. This isn't simply a method of trying to pin down the chair. Rather, it is a way to establish a very clear written record and ensure that you and the department have the same understanding when it comes to teaching load, research support, and so forth. Normally all these issues will be put in a letter by the chair. However, it's appropriate, if the chair doesn't do that for you, to say, for example, "I look forward to receiving a summary of all these terms in my offer letter." Or, "My offer letter did not include a summary of all the issues we discussed. Could you please provide that for me?"

Accepting and Rejecting Jobs

At some point you have to decide. Do so with the idea that your decision will be binding for this round of the market. Make your initial acceptance or rejection by phone, then follow up with a letter that confirms what you have said. In a letter of acceptance reaffirm any special conditions that were offered by the department. Once you have made an agreement, you are ethically, and perhaps legally, bound to appear for at least the first year of your appointment.

Once you've sent in your letter of acceptance, immediately get in touch with departments where you've been interviewed, withdraw from the search, and let them know where you'll be working. Begin to think of yourself as a member of your new department and continue to stay in contact with its members until the time you arrive for work.

When you decline a position, do so very politely. Thank the department again for its offer, mention the positive attractions it held for you, and let the committee know where you will be going. Never burn any bridges. You never know when you will interact with the chair or a faculty member from that department again or in what context. You never know when the people you turn down may be able to influence the direction of your career. So always stay on good and polite terms with your colleagues in other departments, including departments that you have decided to reject.

Backing Out on a Job Acceptance

When you accept a job, do so with every intention of taking it. Occasionally situations arise in which a candidate accepts a job substantially inferior to another which he or she is offered shortly thereafter. Is it ever acceptable to renege on a job commitment? Some people would say no, and others would say that occasionally any reasonable person would do so. Ideally, if you find yourself in this predicament, you will be able to sidestep it by getting the second institution to defer your starting date by a year, so that you can keep your first commitment.

If that is not possible, and you feel the second job is by far the most desirable, then you need to examine your own values and anticipate possible reactions of other people and consequences if you back out on the first commitment. By all means discuss the issue with faculty members and administrators whom you respect.

If You Do Not Receive an Acceptable Offer on This Round

Some years the job market is better than others. If you are in a very specialized field and come on the market in a year when there are few openings and many outstanding candidates, it may be difficult to obtain a position. At times a candidate will reject the only academic offer he or she receives in a given year, deciding that it would not be wise to take it, whether for personal or for professional reasons. Many fine candidates obtain positions the second or third time they go on the market. If you know you will face a tight market, begin to formulate a "Plan B" even as you apply for academic positions.

In many cases the best use of your time may be whatever kind of work is most compatible with continuing your research (or finishing your dissertation). The demands of a one-year teaching position are not always conducive to research. On the other hand, if you are interested in a position that stresses teaching and have very little teaching experience, a temporary appointment could be an excellent way to strengthen your credentials.

If you interview for a position for which you think you are particularly well qualified but are not offered the position, consider asking for some constructive feedback. This will work best if you do not seem to be questioning the department's decision. You will need to use your judgment as you listen to any suggestions, realizing that it is unlikely that anyone in the hiring department will share every aspect of the decision with you and that some departments will be reluctant to say anything at all. Try not to take what you hear personally, but, rather, try to incorporate any suggestions in your next interview opportunity. Above all, work closely with your advisor as you evaluate offers, make alternative plans, and learn from the interviewing process.

Of course you will be disappointed by rejections, but try not to let disappointment permeate your outlook. Discouragement can foster a vicious cycle in which you come across in your applications and interviews as cynical and bitter, leading to more rejections and more discouragement. As you are waiting to hear about one option, actively pursue others. If you are particularly hopeful about one job, while you are waiting to hear, plan exactly what you will do if you hear that you have not been selected. It's easy to feel that the application for a position was a waste of time if you are not selected for it. This is rarely true. Preparations for some applications will make other applications easier, the good impressions you've made will last, and the people you've met can become part of a lifelong professional network.

Recognize that job hunting is stressful. Whether or not the immediate outcome is positive, it is also hard work. Whatever the immediate visible results of your efforts, plan to give yourself breaks from the search.

Sample Job Offer by E-mail

Date

Offer for Sofia Smith Applicant to join University of Z GSE Faculty on September 1, ____.

1. An appointment at a starting salary of $_____ (nine month appointment for three years), as an assistant professor. Contractual terms as described in an official letter of offer that I will mail to you if you accept this offer. Under the current faculty contract you will receive an automatic 1.9% increase in salary on January 1, ____.

2. Your responsibilities will include teaching, research and service in the Graduate School of Education. Workload will be assigned by the Chair of the Department of Educational Policy to consist of three courses for the first year; thereafter, the standard GSE workload policy of two courses per semester will be assigned. The Chair of the Department of Educational Policy will also consult with you and assign a faculty mentor to you.

3. You are eligible for the standard benefit package including health, dental, vision, and retirement. Please contact GSE's Business Manager, John Doe (doe@uz.edu) if you have specific questions regarding benefits.

4. One month's summer salary for June ____. You will have opportunities to earn additional salary during the summer for teaching or through external grants or contracts.

5. Within the first two years of your appointment you will be eligible to receive an internal grant from GSE in the amount of $5,000 to $10,000 to support your research. To receive these funds you must submit a research proposal with budget to the Dean.

6. You will be provided with a complete technology set up (hardware and software) for your exclusive use, to be designed by you in consultation with Assistant Dean X (x@uz.edu). Please note that any computer equipment purchased by University of Z will be considered the property of University of Z. You can view our standard technology package for faculty by visiting the GSE home page and clicking on the "faculty" resource link.

7. You will be provided with a private office at the GSE; telephone, internet, hookups; access to postage and duplication necessary to support your professional work.

8. GSE will arrange and pay for moving your professional library, materials, and other items for use in connection with your professional work from your office and home in [neighboring state] to your GSE office. You can contact Mr. Doe to arrange for shipping.

9. Your Department will sponsor you to participate in one national conference per year within the continental US. In addition, the Dean's office will sponsor participation in a second national conference for each of your first two years at University of Z. Conference travel must adhere to University regulations.

10. You will need to inform me, in writing (e-mail), of your decision no later than 12 pm (eastern time) on Wednesday, March 22, ____.

Sample Formal Written Job Offer (on Institutional Letterhead)

date

Jane Candidate
Address
City, State Zip

Dear Ms. Candidate:

I am pleased to inform you that, subject to approval by the Provost, and your ultimate election to the faculty by the Board of Trustees, you are invited to join the academic faculty of the University of X as a tenure-track Acting Assistant Professor in the Department of _____ in the School of Z. Your title would become Assistant Professor upon receipt of the doctor of philosophy degree. The term of this appointment will be three academic years commencing August 30, _____ and is renewable following satisfactory review. The starting nine-month academic year salary will be $_____, paid in nine monthly installments, with the first payment on October 1, _____. In addition, the School of Z is able to offer $____ a year for three years for the purpose of professional development, including conference attendance, to be used at the discretion of you and your departmental chair. We have also confirmed that you will have available parking in lot P-1, adjacent to X Hall. The January _____ letter from current department chair Smith addresses the facilities, equipment, and other provisions applicable to faculty within the School of Z. In addition, we have agreed that your first year you will maintain a reduced teaching load of three courses. Beginning with your second year, you will be expected to resume a normal teaching load.

The terms and conditions regarding your appointment are contained in the Faculty Handbook, and may be found at http://www.x.edu/~provost/policies.htm. Information on faculty benefits may be found at http://www.x.edu/faculty_benefits_handbook.htm. Other policies and procedures relevant to your appointment include those on conflict of interest, ownership of intellectual property (patents, copyrights, royalties, etc.), the disposition of income generated by consulting and other professional activities, and the direct deposit of paychecks. It is your responsibility to be aware of these policies and procedures as well as others that may apply to you. You should be further aware that these policies may be changed from time to time by the governing board or University administration.

Your duties and responsibilities will be determined by Professor Y, incoming Chair of the Department of _____. If you desire further information concerning the University, this position, or any other matter, do not hesitate to call upon Professor Y or me.

Please indicate your acceptance of the terms of this offer by signing below, and returning a copy of this letter to me. Assuming approval by the Provost and verification from the Office of Equal Opportunity Programs that this offer complies with University policies, your acceptance will enable, if warranted, the President of the University to recommend your formal election to the faculty by the Board of Trustees at its next meeting.

We are happy to have you join our faculty and I look forward to our future association in the University community.

Sincerely,

Dean and X Professor

_____
Signature   Date

SSN _____

Date of Birth _____

Part V
After You Take the Job

Chapter 18
Starting the Job

You have received and accepted an offer. Whether it's at a place where you hope to stay or will be only for a year or two, advance preparation can help you make the most of the coming year. If you haven't already done so, complete your dissertation or current research. It's very important to have it behind you so that you can devote your energy to your new research and teaching responsibilities. Set deadlines for yourself and finish before the position begins.

Moving to Your New Job

The most important move you make to your new job is psychological. You are no longer a graduate student whose progress toward a degree is directed by your advisor; you're no longer a postdoc whose research is directed by your mentor. You are now a scholar, about to assume a job which is both demanding and unstructured. You'll have to teach your classes on a schedule, but you will have to devise your own schedule for accomplishing your research and any other professional goals. You will get little feedback unless you ask for it, and your progress will be formally evaluated at infrequent intervals. Therefore, you must serve as your own advisor from now on.

In most cases, you also leave the city where you did graduate or postdoctoral work. Plan to move to your new institution one and a half to two months before your new appointment starts. For most, this means you should start looking for a place to live in April or May. After you accept the job, contact the college or university housing office for information on faculty housing. If you are moving a family and need to consider a partner's job or school or day care for children, have the housing office recommend a realtor or relocation company that can help meet these needs. Get the names of a couple of recently hired people in your department and ask them for housing suggestions. Also ask for help with your partner's job hunt. Most institutions can provide some assistance here. Try to get moved in and settled in July.

Get to know your way around the campus and the town or city. Become familiar with public transportation and driving so you can determine the most efficient way for you to get to your office, your lab, or your classes.

Getting Ready to Teach

While it's summer and things are more relaxed, get to know the staff and learn how the department works. Get your new e-mail account and Web site and find out where to get technical support on campus. Learn now how to get things photocopied; when to place materials on reserve; which departmental meetings you should attend and when they are held. See what your teaching schedule is and start to think about setting up office hours. What are office procedures and deadlines? How are books ordered from the bookstore? Visit and become familiar with the library and computer center. Before classes start and life becomes hectic, get a sense of the timetables. If the institution offers an orientation for new faculty, take advantage of it. It's a good opportunity to meet other new faculty.

The most important thing you can do to assure success in your new job is to establish good working relationships with your new colleagues. Try to get to know them, both senior and junior faculty. Set up some lunch or coffee dates and get advice. Ask them what they wished they had known when they started. Learn as much as you can about both formal structures such as classes and informal structures such as how information is passed on through the department. Discuss students' abilities and expected workloads so you can plan your classes accordingly. If it's likely that you will be teaching large classes, find out how many students must be in a course before it is assigned a teaching assistant.

Every department and school has its own history and its own way of doing things. Listen carefully to everything you are told, but be careful to form your own opinions. If you feel you are hearing only one side of a story, take care to learn the other. While you are still new, try to establish a comfortable basis for communication with everyone in the department. Some of the people who will influence your ability to be productive are not fellow faculty, but the staff people in your department and school. They include secretaries, librarians, business staff, janitors, computing center staff, and the people who staff laboratory facilities. These people can help you greatly or make your life miserable. You should value their contributions and get to know them.

Your Own Research

During the first semester, you will probably have very little time to accomplish your research goals. Try to keep thinking about your research even when you can't really work on it. Do you want to continue with your prior research plans, or do you feel you're in a dead-end area of research and need to use publication as your opportunity to redefine your work? Try to have one day or a half day a week of uninterrupted time for your own work. Some junior faculty find it helpful to dedicate this time to research only and avoid checking e-mail, chatting with colleagues, or doing other busy work.

If you are used to working closely with your mentor, you may miss the stimulus of that interaction, as well as the structure imposed when you work with someone else. Of course, you will want to keep in touch with your advisor, but start thinking about others with whom you wish to collaborate or with whom you wish to discuss your ideas. Giving a talk on campus can give you useful feedback and help you make yourself known to people with similar research interests. You can use deadlines for calls for papers as a way of giving yourself a realistic schedule for your work. If no one but you knows or cares about your research and you face no deadlines, you risk putting day-to-day demands ahead of the more major goals you wish to accomplish.

If you are a scientist or engineer, your major initial task will be setting up your lab. You may need not only to order and assemble equipment, but also to recruit the people who will work for you on your research project. Your institution may or may not be proactive in helping with this project. Avoid future problems by taking the initiative to learn all the regulations with which you'll need to comply. Meet the people responsible for administering your grant. If you're doing something for the first time and know someone, at your new institution or anywhere else, who has already been through the process, save yourself time by consulting with that person. If this is the first time you've supervised people, spend time learning how to do that effectively, as well.

Teaching

You will have to make policies for your students and stick to them. Before questions arise, think about how you are going to keep order. Are you going to grant extensions and under what circumstances? How will you grade work? What are guidelines for grading in the department? Talk with other faculty and get suggestions.

If you're teaching a semester-long course for the first time, don't try to make it perfect. Instead set guidelines for the amount of time you'll dedicate to your classes and stick to those guidelines. For example, if you give yourself two hours to prepare a class you might do it in the two hours before it starts so that you will have a deadline that will force you to work efficiently. Try to choose a textbook that you already know. If you're developing a new course, do an Internet search and see if someone has already taught the course. Contact them for permission to use some of their materials.

Be as organized a teacher as possible. Do your lecture notes in whatever style best suits you. Keep your notes from year to year. Write them on a computer so you can both easily change them and keep them. Some people avoid teaching new courses in the spring and offer new subjects in the fall when they have had the summer to prepare.

You may be given a big class that no one else wants, such as a survey or introductory course. Try to put your personal stamp on it and make it your own, yet, at the same time, don't feel you have to know everything. If you haven't had much experience preparing lectures, talk with some of your new colleagues or some of your former professors from your graduate institution. Find out if your institution provides any help to new professors such as videotaping of teaching and feedback and seminars to improve pedagogy. Such services are often offered by university teaching centers.

Students

In addition to developing your teaching style, think about your students. In many institutions they are seventeen to twenty-two years old and come with problems that go with that age. They are involved in themselves: trying to figure out who they are, academically, socially, politically, and personally. Academic matters are not their only concern. You may also have older students in your class whose lives and goals are quite different from those of the younger, traditional students. Develop an approach that will reach these students.

In addition to setting office hours you should decide how you will manage e-mail communication with students. Will you meet with students more than once per project? Will you accept papers and other work electronically? What kinds of exceptions will you make for students who miss deadlines or are absent? Talk with your new colleagues and find out what they do and then develop your own plan.

Some students want to connect with professors because they are really interested in the subject; others are more interested in monitoring their grade. Some students might want to engage with you on a personal level. However, it is probably the best policy to be friendly with your students but not friends with them. Sometimes junior faculty members use their title to indicate this boundary to students and request to be called Dr. X or Professor Y.

Self-Evaluation

You might consider asking your students for a mid-semester evaluation to get a sense of how your classes are going and how your teaching is perceived. You can use these comments to improve your course during the second half of the semester. At the end of each semester you will most likely be asked to evaluate your teaching in a more systematic way. Then you can decide what you want to do differently and incorporate those changes as you begin planning for the second year. It can be helpful to get an informal discussion group going with other junior faculty and share ideas on successful teaching.

Keeping Lines of Communication Open

It is important that you get involved in the life of your department and take on some responsibilities that feel important, such as directing honors students, supervising independent study, freshman advising, or running the colloquium series. Choose carefully a few responsibilities and do them well. Then you can say no to other things including university service. Try not to get involved in university committees during your first few years so you can concentrate on teaching and research. You'll have a better idea of where you want to concentrate your energy once you've had a chance to settle in.

You can strongly influence your new department's view of you. Establish an interesting, positive, and comfortable way of discussing your own work and teaching, speak up about the kinds of achievements you wish people to associate with you, and take an informed interest in what other people are doing. Try to develop a relationship with a senior professor who can help you out as you feel your way through the first year. Ask him or her to visit one of your classes and then give you feedback. Also find out how your colleagues perceive you. Are you seen as fitting into the department? Are you seen as carrying your load? Are you seen as productive? As an assistant professor you are entitled to regular discussions with the chair and senior people as to how you are doing. Such regular feedback will help you keep on track in the process of obtaining tenure.

It's also important to continue to maintain networks beyond your new department. Get to know other parts of your school or university and stay deeply involved with national and international networks in your own discipline. This involvement will help you stay aware of trends and keep you flexible in developing your own work. Since you'll never have enough time to do everything that it might be desirable to do in your new job, frequently take a break to review your priorities. We hope these include "having a life," taking care of yourself, staying involved with family and friends, and other personal interests.

Special Considerations for Non-Tenure-Track Positions

If the position you have taken is on a nonrenewable contract and you will go on the job market again soon, it's especially important to stay in touch with everyone in your network. You need to plan your time extremely carefully, to balance your teaching and research with the demands of your job search. Do everything you can to protect your time, limiting your office hours and turning down all but unavoidable committee assignments. You will be tempted to focus on your teaching and your job search and to do no research. However, research may be what helps you get another job, so build in regular time to work on it.

Chapter 19
Knowing About and Getting Tenure

Most institutions have some form of tenure. When you interviewed for your job or during the acceptance discussion, you probably asked some questions about tenure at your new institution. As you start your position and think ahead to the future, you should have a sense of how many junior faculty, both in your department and institution-wide, were granted tenure in the last ten years and how they were evaluated. Institutions often include a basic description of their tenure system on the faculty section of their website. Reading it and talking with your new colleagues should provide you with a reasonable understanding of the situation at your institution.

The movement for the tenure system began in the early 1900s and became very strong after World War I. It was developed to provide faculty with freedom of expression. Proponents of tenure believe it is healthy for the nation to have a body of individuals who can say what they want and be protected. Opponents of tenure believe it protects the incompetent and reduces institutional flexibility.

The tenure system allows the new assistant professor a chance to grow comfortable with the institution, with teaching, and with research. It allows the institution an opportunity to evaluate his or her work. The usual span of time before making the tenure decision is six years, with tenure granted or denied by the seventh. Some places, however, go eight or nine years before making the decision.

Criteria used to determine tenure also vary from place to place. At a major research institution, research publications are most important. Quality, not quantity, is the issue. Usually at least one book and some articles in refereed publications are necessary in the humanities and social sciences, while several journal articles are crucial in the sciences. The department may count only certain journals, so be sure to know which are considered important. Often, particularly in the sciences and engineering, much of your success will be determined by your effectiveness in obtaining funds to support your research. Concentrate on research, publication, and teaching—in that order.

At small liberal arts colleges, while teaching is the most significant crite-rion, research has increased in significance. At such a school you should refine your teaching skills and develop your own personal teaching style that is well received by students and ensures that they learn.

At a community college, once one has taken a permanent position, ten-ure usually takes on more the quality of a natural step. While there is usu-ally some review process, it is less demanding than at most four-year institutions and the default presumption is that candidates will be awarded tenure. However, it's important to learn the process and requirements at the time you accept a community college position.

Example of the Tenure Process at One Large Research Institution

The tenure process is different in each institution, and it is important that you learn early what the process is for you. The following illustrates the process at one large research institution.

Appointments

Appointments for assistant professors are made for three or four years, to be renewed for three years. Review for promotion usually comes up after six years and is quite lengthy and complicated. Less common is a ten-year tenure track, in which case the decision is made in the ninth year.

The Review Process

At the beginning of the sixth year, the review process begins in the depart-ment with the appointment of a three- to four-person subcommittee (all tenured faculty). The committee collects publications and teaching records from the candidate as well as oral and written recommendations from inside and outside the university. After these items are reviewed, the department has a meeting to take a formal vote.

Letters of support from outside the institution are very important. The department puts together a list of outside reviewers who are prominent in the field. You may be asked to suggest additional reviewers. This list is vet-ted at the dean's level and later at the provost's.

If the departmental vote is favorable, the chair writes a letter that includes the majority and minority opinions, adds his or her own opinion, and sends the letter with the review materials to the dean.

The dean refers the packet of material to a personnel committee com-posed of tenured faculty. This committee has three subcommittees: humanities, social sciences, and natural sciences. The subcommittee reads everything and makes recommendations to the committee as a whole. If this committee includes a member of the candidate's department, he or she will not participate in the discussion and will not vote but will answer questions. The chief job of this committee is to look at outside letters to see if the research is judged important. When the committee has voted, the dean writes a letter and sends the results on to the provost.

The provost gives the materials to a committee consisting of deans and other senior administrators. This group reads the outside letters and examines the financial base for the position, since most tenure decisions involve millions of dollars over a period of time. After a vote is taken, the materials go to the president.

The president reviews the files and usually accepts the provost's decision. The president takes the decision to the trustees, who act formally and legally on the case. A letter from the trustees comes to the successful candidate a few months after the decision.

The process can take months because it takes a long time to get the outside letters. At some large institutions the provost asks each school to bring up all its cases at once. Therefore the slowest department controls the process.

Example of the Tenure Process at One Small Teaching College

At one small private college where the emphasis is on excellent teaching, the tenure process is somewhat different.

There are two evaluations before tenure. The first is held in the fourth year and is becoming less pro forma. The second is for making the tenure decision and is held at the beginning of the sixth year.

The three criteria for all evaluations, including those for full professors, are teaching, professional development, and collegiate citizenship. Teaching is the most important. Professional development, which includes publications, has become increasingly important, whereas it used to be equal in importance to collegiate citizenship. Collegiate citizenship is mainly committee work but also includes recruiting students, alumni activities, and advising some student organizations.

The candidate, often in consultation with the department chair, comes up with a list of persons from whom letters are requested. Two or three faculty members from other departments are invited to visit the candidate's classes and write letters of recommendation, but recommendations from the candidate's departmental colleagues usually matter the most, with those of tenured faculty carrying the most weight. In addition to those from colleagues, letters from students and recent alumni as well as from scholars at other institutions play a significant role in the evaluation process at this and many other small colleges. The dossier of letters is sent to the provost, who makes a recommendation to the president by a certain date. The formal power for granting tenure then lies with the board of trustees who meet near the end of the academic year. The candidate learns the result immediately.

Advice

The years until tenure consideration will be the toughest in your academic life. Concentrate on research and teaching. Try to avoid being department chair or serving on many committees until you have tenure, unless you know for sure that your institution weighs such service heavily in tenure decisions. If you are the only woman or minority person in your department, your presence on all kinds of committees will be sought. Learn to say no to most requests. Know the tenure criteria well before you have to provide documentation that you have fulfilled them. At many institutions, teaching records are important. Letters are requested from students and recent graduates. Save teaching recommendations and start building that file early.

Seek regular feedback about your progress from senior faculty members whose judgment you trust. Listen seriously to this feedback. Make an effort to talk with faculty in the department to let them know what you are doing. Talk with colleagues about your teaching and about good classes so that they perceive you as a strong teacher. Remain in touch with those in the field at other institutions in case you need external referees. Send them drafts of papers, solicit their advice, meet them at conferences.

Usually the candidate knows at what stage of the review process he or she is. How strongly does your department support you? If it begins to look increasingly unlikely that you will be awarded tenure, you may want to start looking at other jobs before the formal evaluation process begins. Also consider the likelihood of tenure from an institutional perspective. How stable is the institution's financial condition? How is your department regarded?

Try to keep the whole process in perspective. Tenure decisions ultimately involve many variables, some of which, such as an institution's financial situation, have nothing to do with a candidate's abilities. Hiring committees at other institutions are fully aware of that. So if you do not obtain tenure, you will do what many other highly competent people in that situation have done. You will obtain another position and continue with a productive career.

Meanwhile, the whole tenure process typically occurs when you are building in other areas of your life as well. You may be raising a family, buying your first house, meeting obligations to other family members, building a strong network of friendships that are deeply meaningful to you. You will not have unlimited time for these other areas of life, but don't neglect them either. Not only are they important in and of themselves, but the perspective that comes from realizing there's more to life than the next paper frequently makes the time you spend working more creative and productive.

Chapter 20
Changing Jobs

At some point you may decide or need to change jobs. There can be many reasons for changing jobs besides not being granted tenure, and each will require slightly different job seeking strategies.

Perhaps you originally wanted to work at a different type of institution but were unable to find such a position during your original job hunt. Or, for one reason or another, you planned to stay for only a few years. Maybe you feel that the institution hasn't lived up to its original commitment to you in terms of lab space, research assistance, library funding, or something else that was negotiated during the offer. Perhaps you have been approached by another institution. Possibly your partner or another family member is unhappy with the location or institution and the situation cannot be improved for him or her. If you have been conducting a long-distance marriage or relationship for several years, you may have decided that being together is more important than your job.

Be Ready for Opportunities

Continue to stay in touch with people at other institutions, even if you are very happy where you are. These contacts are a vital means of engaging in your profession. In addition, knowing faculty at other institutions gives you greater access to information about positions that may be opening up and a group of people who can comment favorably on your work.

If you got your degree from an institution that has a credentials file service, continue to build it even if you don't expect to change institutions. It's a form of insurance you can draw on if you decide you must or want to change positions and it will be difficult to get letters from past references.

Keep your vita current. For a few years you will probably continue to keep your education as one of the first sections. If previously you gave a lot of detail about your graduate work, you may now begin to omit it. For at least several years after obtaining your doctorate, however, retain your dissertation topic and advisor's name. Add recent experiences and condense earlier ones. For example, if you earlier included detail about what you did as a teaching assistant, you may now merely retain the notation that you held the position. In general, it is a good idea to condense items, even if drastically, rather than drop them altogether. Do not drop early publications and presentations.

If You Want to Make a Move

Keep in mind that academia is a small world, and that if you put out feelers, chances are your department will hear about it. Mention in cover letters that you don't want your institution contacted unless you are considered a very serious contender. You will need someone to recommend you. While it is true that you can send out letters in a credentials file without the knowledge of the letters' authors, there is no guarantee that at least one of these people will not get a phone call about you. Therefore it is a better idea to speak with your recommenders, let them know what you are interested in, and ask them to keep your search confidential. Your advisor, of course, is an ideal person to play this role. It would be helpful to have a recommendation from someone in your current department. You will have to use your best judgment about the advisability of letting someone there know your plans. While your current chair may be sorry to learn that you wish to leave, you may be surprised to find that that person is willing to provide you with a good recommendation.

If you begin interviewing extensively, it is almost inevitable that your department will learn that you are looking elsewhere. It will depend very much upon the individuals involved whether they view this as a perfectly reasonable activity or a lack of commitment. In any case, it is preferable that the chair hear from you, rather than from someone else, that you are looking. You may want to defer this communication until you are almost certain that the person is about to have the information anyway. Never use the threat that you will look elsewhere as a negotiating point. If you do not find another position quickly after making such a threat, your bluff will have been called forever.

To make such a move responsibly, minimize new commitments, such as agreeing to supervise a doctoral thesis, in which your departure at year's end would seriously compromise someone else's plans.

If You Have to Move

A very common reason for changing jobs in academia is that of not getting tenure or of being very certain that it will not be awarded. Or it may be that you have accepted a short-term, nonrenewable position. In either case you will not need to keep your search quiet within the department, and you may find some very active allies there as you conduct your search.

If you felt it was likely that you would be awarded tenure and you were not, it is almost inevitable that you will feel intensely disappointed. You may also feel very angry or depressed or experience a sense of personal failure. These feelings are natural and will run their course. Try to make every effort, however, to minimize their effect on your professional behavior. If you can deal with department members and interview as if you are confident and happy about your future prospects, you will receive more positive feedback and results which, in turn, will make you genuinely feel better. Meanwhile, outside of work, take up a new activity, spend time with friends and family, seek help from a counselor, become involved in community service, or do whatever else your experience has shown you is restorative for you.

Don't lose any time in applying for jobs as soon as you find you will need to look. While you may have some impulse to avoid other department members after receiving a negative tenure decision, now is precisely the time you should be talking to them. Ask your strongest supporters if they will be willing to recommend you. Let everyone know the kinds of jobs you will be looking for, and ask people to let you know of openings they hear about. Give strongly interested and supportive people copies of your vita.

Let all your professional contacts know that you are on the market. It is most comfortable for all concerned if you take the responsibility for obtaining information. For example, rather than asking people to "keep you in mind," ask whether they can suggest whom you might call at a specific institution, what they have heard lately about a particular department, if they know someone that they might be willing to call on your behalf at an institution where you have applied, and so forth. Keep in touch about your search with those who seem enthusiastically supportive of it. If you sense that others are lukewarm, continue to keep in touch on a professional basis, but don't pursue the topic of your search with them.

When Someone Else Wants You to Move

A different kind of reason for changing jobs is that of an unsolicited advance by another institution. It's attractive to be sought out, so, if you decide to move, take your time and negotiate a good offer from the institution that is pursuing you. If you don't want to move, this is a great opportunity to give your institution a chance to keep you, through increased salary, an early, favorable tenure decision, or whatever else you might choose to negotiate for. Be aware, however, that, unless your work is truly world-class, this is an exercise you will not be able to repeat very frequently. Whenever you say, "I will take this offer unless you do X," there is a possibility that your employer will say, "We'll be sorry to lose you, but it looks as if you had best take the offer, because we certainly can't do that." As when you negotiated for your first salary, begin with open-ended questions, and don't give ultimatums unless you are willing to stand behind them.

The Graceful Exit

As soon as you have accepted an offer at another institution, let your department know. Do everything you can to tie up loose ends in terms of responsibilities to other people. If there are those in the department to whom you are genuinely grateful, be sure to express your appreciation. If you can't wait to leave every person there behind you, at a minimum, be courteous. Satisfying as you might fantasize it would be to tell everyone exactly what you think before you leave, doing so would almost certainly be something you would later regret.

After you leave, keep in touch with people with whom you have enjoyed working. The opportunity to build a rich network of contacts, to have a group of people who live all over the country, and possibly the world, whom you know you will always enjoy seeing at an annual meeting, with whom you can correspond and exchange ideas, is one of the rewards of the academic career you have chosen.

Part VI
Additional Considerations

Chapter 21
Dual Career Couples, Pregnant on the Job Market, and Related Concerns

Many of the conventions of academic job hunting developed when most candidates were American men whose spouses, if they had them, did not have careers. Today, both male and female candidates in the American academic job market are increasingly part of two-career couples and many intend to have families. Some institutions are well aware of this and have policies in place to assist couples on the job market and to support faculty members as they start their families; others may deal with these situations on a case-to-case basis. As has been discussed throughout, as a job candidate, it is best for you to stress the common professional interests and identity that you share with those who may hire you before raising more personal concerns. Although every situation is unique, included here are some examples of job candidates who are part of dual-career couples or were pregnant job seekers whose stories might help you make decisions about how to handle your own situation.

Dual-Career Couples

If you are part of a dual-career couple, before you go on the job market you and your partner need to articulate your goals so that you will be able to devise a search strategy that supports your personal and professional goals and answers potential employers' questions honestly and clearly. Colleges and universities, like other employers, realize that a candidate may be part of a dual-career couple. Very often if a department is serious about you, they will do what they can to assist your partner.

It's a good idea to talk to other couples and find out what has worked for them. Consider the following questions in terms of what is right for the two of you, not what you think an employer wants to hear.

- If one of you has fewer possibilities, perhaps because of being in a very small, specialized field, will that person find a job first, before the other one starts looking?

- Will you both go on the job market at the same time?
- Will you go only to the same geographic location as your partner?
- What will you do if you both get great job offers but they are on opposite sides of the country?

If you agree that you are willing to apply for and accept positions that are not in the same location, consider the following:

- Can you afford two residences, travel expenses, duplicate household furnishings, and large phone bills?
- Who will do the most commuting? How difficult is travel? A nonstop 2000-mile plane trip may be easier than a 300-mile drive, especially in the snowbelt.
- How will frequent travel affect you?
- How good are you at getting along alone? Consider that it will be necessary to be both single and part of a couple at the same time.
- Will your department allow you to concentrate your teaching into two quarters and be away the third? Can you teach only two or three days per week so as to have long weekends? (Don't ask for these privileges until after you have received an offer.)

It is usually a good idea to reach a joint decision about where both of you will search and within which geographic areas you are each free to act independently. Waiting to discuss these issues until you each have a wonderful job offer in locations thousands of miles apart sets you up for deciding who will "sacrifice" an offer. If the relationship is your priority, it may work out better to decide in advance on geographic locations in which you believe you can both find satisfying employment, whoever gets the first offer, and to concentrate your search on those areas.

If you are considering tenure-track positions, look beyond the first job for your partner to other opportunities. For example, if you are offered a tenure-track position by a university that arranges an attractive postdoctoral position for your partner, consider what you both will want to do after the postdoc has run its course. In general, dual-career couples will find greater opportunities in metropolitan areas, where it may be possible to change jobs without changing locations.

The fact remains that, given the national nature of the academic job market, it can be quite difficult for two academics to make career development their top priority while remaining married to each other. It is particularly difficult if both are in highly specialized areas with very few openings. Accepting at least short periods of geographic separation may help to make it possible, but separation in itself often puts a strain on a relationship. On the other hand, if one member of the couple is miserable because he or she doesn't have a job, and the other is miserable because he or she does, commuting may begin to look more attractive. Most people find they need to make a series of choices over the course of a career. The decision you make now will reflect your current priorities and may well be reevaluated as time goes on.

Once you have made your decisions, be very clear with your advisors about how you would prefer that they explain the situation. Be aware that a department wondering whether you will accept a job offer may well make a phone call to someone in your department to ask how your personal situation is likely to affect your acceptance. For example, your advisor might be asked if your husband would really be willing to move. While discrimination based on couple status or parenthood is not legal, unfortunately we can't say it never occurs. Employers may be as likely to call the person they know best in your department as they are to call your advisor, so it is generally to your advantage to have as many people as possible know that you are willing to commute, are committed to a particular geographic location, or whatever else is the case.

Decide at what stage to tell employers that there are two of you: before the interview, during the interview, or after the interview, well before any offer is made. If you will accept or reject an offer totally independently of opportunities for a partner, there is no particular need to discuss your partner's plans at any point of the negotiation. More commonly, however, your partner's reaction to the location of the position or success in finding a job for himself or herself in that location will be a factor in your decision.

In that case, it's difficult to decide when to ask about opportunities for a partner. If you ask too early, you may lead the employer to wonder whether you will be willing to accept the position and, hence, perhaps to give less weight to your candidacy. If you ask too late, particularly if you make it clear that you will not take the job unless your partner finds a suitable opportunity, you may lead the hiring department to feel as if you've suppressed important information. In addition, if your recommenders feel that they've gone out on a limb for you unnecessarily, they may be less willing to do so again, especially if you've turned down an extremely desirable position. You'll need to use your own judgment, which will be improved if you seek advice from advisors and colleagues whom you respect.

Your strategy will be affected by your partner's situation. Each couple will have a unique configuration of degrees and career goals, some of which are articulated here. Also included are several narratives generously volunteered by individuals who faced the job market with their partner.

Ph.D. and Ph.D. in Similar Fields

Job sharing may be an option if you are willing to consider it. Hiring institutions, however, may be skeptical about the arrangement unless they have had previous successful experience with it. Before you pursue this option, make every effort to identify and talk to some people who have done it successfully, so that you can get some firsthand advice.

More commonly, you each want your own job. If there is any likelihood that you will actually be competing for the same positions, how you will handle the competition is something to consider. If you and your partner are applying to the same department, you may hope that no one will notice that you are attached to each other. Even if you have different last names, however, that is unlikely, given the small-world nature of most academic disciplines. Thus it is also important to let those who are recommending you know how you plan to handle your searches so that they can help you reinforce that impression. A department that feels it would be "pitting husband and wife against each other" might end up interviewing neither.

Couple: Two Ph.D.s in the humanities

Because we began dating in college and married in graduate school, we starting discussing our career plans very early in our relationship. We both felt that we wanted to be as close to each other as possible, but neither of us wanted to deny the other the chance of studying at a premier graduate school or accepting a great job.

As she was completing her dissertation, my wife applied to and was offered a tenure-track position at a large research institution. I went on the job market the following year and won a postdoctoral two-year fellowship at another research institution in the region, about 100 miles away. In my second year there I accepted a position as director of a new MA program in Communications. This was not a tenure-track position, however, and after two years, we both decided to apply for positions that would allow us to live together (we had a new baby).

To this end, my wife applied to and was offered a tenured position at a large state university. The English department there was aware of her spousal situation (although she didn't mention it to the hiring committee until an offer had been made) and began negotiations with the Film School to find a position for me. I was invited to give a job talk and in the end was offered a tenure-track position at this institution. This was clearly a terrific opportunity for both of us. Her current institution, however, had just hired a senior person in Cinema Studies, was in the process of hiring another assistant professor in the field, and was looking to build to strength. Ultimately, this English department offered me a tenure-track position, which I accepted. It was difficult for us to decide between the two schools, but I think we made the right choice.

It's difficult to give advice as we were unusually fortunate in our search. We did find that spousal hires at one institution were easier to negotiate than offers at two different institutions. Even if you can't negotiate this for your first tenure-track job, you might find that as you both grow professionally, opportunities open up.

Ph.D. and Ph.D. in Different Fields

At some point in the search process you will probably want to tell the search committee that your partner is also looking for a job and see if they will put in a word for him or her with the appropriate department at the institution. This practice is becoming increasingly common. Keep in mind that the second position offered may be less desirable in terms of rank or salary. This can cause a sense of resentment to develop in the partner who accepts the less desirable position.

Couple: Ph.D. in the social sciences and MFA* in the visual arts
(*The MFA is the terminal degree for many areas of the arts.)

Ph.D.: When I conducted a faculty job search my husband was in a tenure track faculty position that he had held for three years. The institutions near us were not right for me; his institution didn't have graduate programs, and I teach graduate students only. Because my husband is an artist, I could only apply in urban areas with an art scene, which was hard because my field is higher education and most of the top programs are in the Midwest. I applied in Atlanta and worked there for three years and then moved to my current institution in the Northeast. We tried to look for institutions that had opportunities for both of us, but the timing of this was hard.

Currently, my husband teaches as a lecturer, works as a writer and artist, and started a nonprofit related to studio space for artists. Many times it happened that we had offers in different places—we went with his offer the first time because it was so important for him to have a tenure track job. The second time, we went with mine—it was my first tenure track job—we took a huge pay cut because I had been working in administration for years. But we made it—with a new baby—my husband got a job part-time and then a full-time faculty position after about a year. This was the hardest time of our life together thus far—we didn't have any money and we were really stressed out. We would never live in separate places.

Our ability to negotiate job hunting help for each other has increased as we've grown professionally so that when I came to my current institution and had a lot of publications and a lot more bargaining power, the dean helped my husband with some connections. The flexibility of our jobs has helped with the raising of our daughter. We get to spend a lot of time with her.

MFA: We began discussing our career plans when we first met. It was always understood that each of us had independent career goals, and that each would support the other in the job search. We tried to limit ourselves to geographic areas that were acceptable to both, although not necessarily to institutions that had opportunities for both. When both of us had offers in different places, we thought carefully about our choices. Often our decision had to do with who was at a critical point in their career—who could benefit most by taking a job in a particular place at a particular time. Additionally, we were often able to find job-hunting help for the other partner.

Advice: All of our decisions were made together and we tried to think about each other's needs. Every job we applied for we discussed in depth, measuring the pros and cons. Be very candid with one another about what you want—not just in a job, but a place to live and a lifestyle. How you spend each day can be as important as which institution you work for.

Ph.D. and Non-Ph.D.

When it appears to you that a search committee is seriously considering you for the job, you may wish to tell them about your partner and ask if they can offer any kind of placement assistance, such as names of people to contact. Certainly, if you want help for your partner, ask for assurances about it between the time you are offered a job and the time you accept it.

Couple: Ph.D. in the life sciences and MBA who works in public relations for an international agency

We discussed our career plans with each other well before either of us submitted any applications. We applied all over the country even though there were definitely areas of the country we were less enthusiastic about living in. However, it was extremely helpful to interview at several places. Doing so is useful for several reasons: it gives you a great perspective on the various opportunities available, a chance to practice interviewing skills, and, if you get a couple of offers, bargaining power. Really, you never know where you might end up liking it. In our case the institution where we are now wasn't our first choice until we visited. In my case, my husband decided to go back to school, so I did not need to negotiate for job search help for him.

Advice: Make sure the non-scientist partner understands what a science career is about and how grants are very important. It needs to be very clear. Though we didn't take advantage of job search assistance, I've now been involved in dual career couple hires. If the university really wants one of you, they'll do a whole lot to find a fitting job for the spouse. Absolutely take advantage of that! Don't limit yourself by only applying in certain geographic areas.

Unmarried and Same-Sex Couples

If you are part of an unmarried or same-sex couple, the same personal considerations will apply. You will also, however, have to consider employers' attitudes toward your relationship. In general, they will probably be willing to do somewhat less for an unmarried partner than for a married one. Whether to put on the table immediately the existence of a personal relationship of which some employers may not approve is a highly personal decision. If you decide it's something you wish to keep private, make sure that everyone who will recommend you understands that. On the other hand, some couples decide that, since they don't want jobs in which they must conceal their private lives, they will be as open about their relationship as they would choose to be if they were married. It may be helpful to talk with other couples in the same situation to find out what their experience has been and what they recommend.

Partners in same-sex academic couples stress the importance of asking questions at interviews to try to assess how partner-friendly an institution is. Junior faculty are particularly good sources of information regarding an institution's attitudes and practices. It is more and more common for both members of a couple to be seeking faculty positions together. While many universities are used to handling this situation, others haven't worked this issue out for either straight couples or same-sex couples. In addition, benefits for same-sex partners are available at many institutions but not all. Some state institutions may not be able to provide partner benefits, regardless of how welcoming the institutions may be to same-sex couples, because their state legislatures do not allow for this. Faculty members often suggest not bringing up the existence of a spouse or partner until you have an offer. This is particularly true in the case of same-sex couples who want to make sure their instincts are correct about the institution before revealing aspects of their personal lives to which some others might respond negatively.

Pregnancy on the Job Market

The time frame for an academic job search coincides with the prime childbearing years for many women candidates. Being pregnant while conducting a job search has its own special challenges. It's important to think about how to present the pregnancy.

If you are not visibly pregnant when you go on interviews, you don't have to say anything about it. However, when you go to campus interviews and are obviously pregnant, you should probably bring up the subject yourself; otherwise it could become the issue everyone tiptoes around but no one talks about, since legally interviewers should not bring it up. (For discussion of illegal interview questions, see Chapter 14.)

You can put everyone at ease by saying that, as they can see, you're starting a family (or having a child) and that you want to let them know that you'll be ready to begin a job in the fall. It's very likely that there have been other pregnant women on the faculty and the department is familiar with this situation. You may find them offering suggestions and describing colleagues who have had babies in the summer, taken maternity leaves, shared course loads, and so on. Participate in this discussion politely and attentively but eventually move the conversation back to the interview itself.

As the interview proceeds, there may be a time where you can bring up your organizational skills, your ability to plan for courses, or whatever else will emphasize your ability and willingness to begin the fall in full gear. If you already have child care arrangements (e.g., family in the area, spouse/partner who works from home) and want to mention that, you can, but don't feel required to do so.

You want the search committee and all the people you meet to remember you primarily as an outstanding candidate for the position, not as the pregnant candidate. You want to assure them that you will be fulfilling your responsibilities as a professor after you have had the baby.

Here follow the stories of two pregnant job candidates.

Candidate 1

I didn't plan to be pregnant on the job market, but I knew it was going to be a real possibility. I found out that I was pregnant in April 2005 and had my daughter in

December 2005. The knowledge of being pregnant did not stop me from aggressively pursuing a job. Additionally, I specifically did not take a maternity leave in spring 2006 because I needed to be a fully enrolled student in order to defend my dissertation and complete my degree (and I wanted to be able to outline this plan in my cover letter which I wrote up in the fall).

I had a male advisor who was very understanding concerning my pregnancy and made no fuss about it at all. There was no conversation about the job market or anyone who questioned my ability to finish or go on the job market. I can't speak for these folks, but maybe the fact that I already had one child and was successful in moving along with my degree didn't bring up any doubt in their minds?

I had given birth to my daughter by the time of my first conference interviews (indeed, I got a phone call to schedule my first campus interview while I was in the hospital in the early stages of labor—that's a funny story). I went to the [name of professional association] conference less than two weeks after delivery, so I was leaking milk and feeling pudgy. But I did do a mock interview with a career counselor in November when I was very pregnant. I remember asking her about what I should do if I got called for an interview and was still pregnant. She said to always use the fact that I was a mother to my own advantage, that is, talk about how raising children while getting my degree and publishing had made me a master at time management. And this is what I did when the issue came up.

When I asked members of the faculty in my department what I should do, one member suggested that I try to "hide" my pregnancy: wear bulky, flowing clothing. I did not do this, nor would I have done this.

The issue of pregnancy, marriage, kids, etc. did not come up during conference interviews at the [name of professional association]. The issue did come up at my campus interviews—partly because I was uncomfortable NOT talking about this part of my life. I used the advice I had been given and I talked about having children during graduate school as evidence that I could multi-task. I focused on my accomplishments—finishing my Ph.D. in six years, publishing two peer-review articles and one book chapter, AND having two children.

The most difficult part of my job search was coordinating travel to on-campus interviews. My husband and mother helped a great deal during the spring semester of 2006 when I was in the thick of the conference season and campus interviews. My husband worked from home, so he had a flexible schedule. During that spring semester, my husband was the primary caregiver. I was teaching, but was done with writing my dissertation for the most part. My mother came to stay with us during the [name of professional association] conference, and also during the subsequent three campus interviews that took place in February and March.

I would not have done anything differently—I landed a tenure-track job at a prestigious institution in a department where 40% are women (4 out of 10) and 3 of the 4 women are tenured full professors! If I had waited to go on the job market until the fall of 2007, I would have missed the opportunity to get this job.

Candidate 2

My pregnancy was unplanned. Fortunately I had a great relationship of the utmost confidence with my advisor who, moreover and even more fortunately, has a positive view toward child-bearing and parenting.

I was almost forty-one weeks pregnant when I had my [name of professional association] interviews. If the [name of professional association] hadn't happened to be in the city where I was living, or if my daughter had been born on time, I wouldn't have gotten a job that year. Because she had to be induced, I was able to choose my inducement date. I chose the last day of the conference, which meant that I could go to my five interviews and my panel talk. Afterward, my husband picked me up in the evening from the conference center and drove me to the hospital. I had my daughter the next day after quite a long labor.

As for the interviews themselves, it was very hard to know how to handle their acceptance and scheduling. In the end, I only told one school that I was pregnant and that my due date was a little over a week before the conference. I didn't say a word to the other four, simply accepted and scheduled the [name of professional association] interview.

In the interviews themselves, I only discussed my pregnancy with three committees (one being the committee I had forewarned). In the first of the other two situations, I had to break the ice and say what was incredibly obvious, which was that I was expecting any day. I went into the interviews knowing that people would most likely be reticent about discussing my unmistakable condition because of legal implications, but that on the other hand it is a topic of natural human and practical professional interest and that I might be doing everyone (and myself) a favor by initiating and thereby permitting discussion about it. I didn't bring it up in the fourth and fifth interviews because I knew from the outset that it wasn't a good match, so maybe that in and of itself is telling—that is, that the desire to share pregnancy information is reflective of one's general interest and comfort level in an interview.

Traveling to campus interviews just after my daughter's birth was incredibly painful! I have never ever in my life done something so difficult as to write a job talk from scratch when my daughter was only four weeks old. And eventually, after about three weeks of torturously fragmented work (something that now seems totally normal!), it was done.

My first interview was with an institution on the west coast, so I had to leave my by then eight-week-old who was nursing and co-sleeping with me for three days and two nights. At that institution everyone was very understanding about my need to pump and allowed me to use a private office to do so. In the introduction to my talk itself, the chair told everyone with an admiring tone that the last time they had seen me, I had been fairly ready to pop and that I had a newborn at home. Even though I ultimately didn't get the offer, I think it had much more to do with the complicated internal department politics than anything related to my pregnancy.

My second campus visit took place quite a bit later when my daughter was a little over three months old. The chair again included in his pre-talk introduction to the department how extremely pregnant I had been when they had seen me last, and it was in a positive light that did not overshadow his emphasis on the intellectual dimension of the talk I was about to give. It was hard as always to be separated from my daughter for two nights, but the trip was overall much easier than the first. I was offered and accepted a job at this institution.

Advice: I guess my general advice to pregnant/post-birth job seekers would be to regard themselves as extraordinary and to assume that others will follow suit. There has been a great deal of talk and study of the so-called "pipeline effect" of women falling out of the Ph.D. career path from grad studies to tenure, and this has been highly correlated with child-bearing and care-taking. Any woman who beats these odds is fighting against all kinds of tremendous pressures to perform as though she had no such parenting obligations or concerns. In our current academic cultural climate, institutionalized expectations are in no way adjusted to counterbalance or otherwise allow for the "life" demands in the work-life balance that are particular to maternity or primary infant childcare. To function academically and intellectually at one's own baseline standards of excellence and rigor is nothing less than

herculean, even if it is seen by the institutional community as simply fulfilling minimum expectations for performance. This can be very discouraging, but it can also
be a source of confidence if one can manage to project instead the determined will
to triumph in one's intellectual endeavors.

It also sometimes happens that a pregnancy is discovered after accepting
an offer. It is important to tell your new chair right away. The main question the chair will have is whether you are planning to take a leave. If you're
hoping to miss only a few weeks of classes, you'll need to discuss with the
chair how coverage will be managed. Offer to take care of this as much as
you can. For example, there may be someone else some of whose classes
you could take in the fall in exchange for coverage for yours while you're
out. If you want to be out an extended period of time and you haven't yet
accepted the offer you could negotiate a start date of January. If you've
already accepted, see if the job—and the tenure clock—can start in at the
beginning of the next semester.

Parenting and Early Career Faculty Members

Combining children and tenure-track decisions is a concern for many academics. When is the most advantageous time to have children? Of course,
this is a question that can have many answers. Two qualitative social scientists decided that as soon as one of them had a tenure-track position they
would adopt their first child. One partner, whose career involves funded
research positions and replacement faculty jobs, does much of the child
care. As this person's pipeline of work became steady, the couple decided
to adopt a second child.

One scientist shared her observations on having a young family during
the early stages of her research career:

You might want to think about having a baby before you go up for tenure. For those
disciplines that do not require a lengthy postdoc, this might not necessarily be true.
There is a biological clock and for me waiting until I got tenure to have kids would
have meant waiting until I was 40 (and that is assuming that everything would go
smoothly, receiving tenure and conceiving right away).

My husband took off work when the first baby was born. I wrote one grant when
I was three months pregnant and had to renew another when I had an infant. I got
the first one right away, the second one only after the third try. I knew I would have
to reply for the renewal in the two years after I got the grant. These two years
included nine months of pregnancy and six months with an infant. While this
might sound bleak, the good thing is that the University of X, and most other similar institutions, provides an extra year toward tenure for each baby, allowing you to
catch up.

You may find your child extraordinary and parenthood one of your life's
most rewarding experiences, but, as much as possible put that same energy
into discussing topics of professional interest with your new colleagues. If

you can prove that you are intellectually engaged and committed to the mission of your department, people will be more willing to help you down the line when you need to have a class covered because you're staying with a sick child or making one of the other adaptations that parenthood requires. Be sure to develop a network of supporters with whom you can discuss your situation. Because many people outside academe don't fully understand the demands and expectations of an academic career, make sure you talk with other faculty parents. You'll learn a lot from those at the same stage of life as you, as well as from those who are further along.

Chapter 22
International Scholars, Older Candidates, and Gaps in Your Vita

In recent years candidates in the American academic job market have become increasingly diverse in cultural and international backgrounds. In addition, some job candidates are pursing academe as a second career and thus are older than many other candidates. Continue to emphasize the professional background that is your link to the department's mission. Additionally you should also be able to discuss what makes you a strong, if atypical, candidate.

International Scholars Seeking U.S. Employment

First, think realistically about your long-term goals. If you want to work in the United States only for the duration of your practical training period, don't apply for tenure-track positions. Instead, concentrate on short-term appointments, which frequently will carry titles such as "Visiting Assistant Professor" or "Lecturer." They are less likely than are tenure-track positions to be nationally advertised, so it may be worthwhile to make direct inquiries of departments you would like to join. Be aware that if you accept a visiting position you may be subject to travel restrictions.

Work Permission

If you would like to work in the United States indefinitely, you and the department that hires you will need to deal with the question of work permission. Generally this is not a great problem in academic hiring, since academic positions are likely to have very specialized qualifications; this will make it easier for a hiring department to demonstrate to the U.S. government that it needs you. In addition, most colleges and universities are familiar enough with the process of hiring foreign nationals that questions of work permission should not in and of themselves complicate your search.

However, a great deal of paperwork is involved. Work with the office that advises international students and scholars at your current university. If your goal is eventual permanent residency or U.S. citizenship, it is particularly important to see that each step of the process is handled correctly. You may wish to obtain your own legal counsel. If so, choose the lawyer carefully. The university office may have suggestions.

Cultural Differences in the Job Search

You have doubtless become aware of American ways of conducting a job search during your stay in the United States. However, when you begin to search for a permanent job you may need to behave in ways that still do not feel entirely appropriate to you. Remember that, however supportive your advisor may be, you, rather than your mentor, are expected to make the most effort on your own behalf. You are expected to show initiative during interviews and in meeting new people at conferences or all-day visits to campuses. In interviews, Americans expect that you will speak confidently about yourself and your successes. Making eye contact with even the most senior people will be seen as a sign of confidence rather than of disrespect.

Some of these differences may present challenges to you in preparing for interviews, but console yourself that many Americans do not find the process of job hunting easy either. If you come from a culture in which the assertiveness required in an American job search would appear rude, it is important for you to make a particular effort to talk confidently to others and to initiate conversation. You can do so with confidence that you will almost certainly appear polite.

English

Any institution, whether it emphasizes teaching or research, will probably pay considerable attention to your ability to both speak and write in English. Writing and speaking are just as important to research as they are to teaching. As hiring institutions increasingly demand excellent teaching, a strong command of spoken English is absolutely crucial. Your campus undoubtedly has resources for strengthening your English. If you have any doubt about your ability to be understood, take full advantage of these services.

If your written English is correct but not colloquial, have a native speaker read drafts of your cover letters. Hiring departments will assume that your written English is at least as good as, if not better than, your spoken English, so be sure cover letters are both correct and colloquial. Pay particular attention to the section on cover letter writing in this guide. American-style cover letters may be less formal than those you would write at home.

Also be aware that phone interviews are often used to assess one's ability to speak English clearly and correctly.

Older Candidates

In any search, there will be applicants who have gone from undergraduate to graduate work at breakneck speed, others for whom graduate study is a second or third career, and others whose graduate careers were interrupted for any number of reasons. As a result, the ages of applicants can vary widely. Those at the older end of the scale are often concerned about age discrimination.

Unfortunately, this is a realistic concern. However, some hiring departments may welcome the additional experience older candidates have accrued. Anyone who feels "too old" has to take care not to turn a realistic concern into a self-fulfilling prophecy. Since age discrimination is, in fact, illegal, it's helpful to be aware of your rights and of the possibility of seeking redress when you have evidence that they have been violated. However, at least initially, it's best to approach everyone in your search as if they will assess your candidacy fairly.

If you are trying to assume a faculty position after considerable related professional experience, try to publish in an appropriate scholarly venue and to get some recent teaching experience, even if you have to do the latter for next to no pay. It's important to realize that, in many fields, your previous nonacademic experience will not be a main factor in hiring. Present it on your vita in drastically condensed form.

As you interview, it's best to address an employer's potential concerns without saying you're doing so. If assuming a faculty position would require you to take a salary cut, you will need to convince hiring committees you're willing to do this. It's probably best to do so indirectly, by stressing your enthusiasm for the job. Make sure you're above average for your field in technological literacy, because the older you are, the more some departments may assume you're resistant to technology and reluctant to learn new things. To avoid seeming like a "threat" to younger, less-experienced potential colleagues, stress that you're eager to learn from them.

Significant Gaps in Your Vita

It is possible that due to serious health problems, such as cancer or another disease, injuries related to an accident, mental health-related issues, or other life-changing events that affected you or a family member, you were unable to work or continue with graduate school for a significant period of time. Though this experience may have made you feel isolated and different from other candidates, it is more common than many people realize. It is important that you figure out how to talk about this gap in a way that acknowledges it, yet doesn't draw unnecessary attention to it. You want search committees to know that your gap was legitimate and you dealt with it responsibly but that what defines you is your scholarship.

You might find you want to mention the gap in the cover letter. If you feel this is necessary, make the mention of the gap secondary and subordinate to your scholarly qualifications, and put it near the end of the letter. Depending on the situation, your letter writers might refer briefly to it in the most positive way possible, for example, "Despite Jane's need to care for a terminally ill parent for most of 2006, she continued to act as assistant editor of the *Journal of X* which is published by our department." Also be prepared to explain a gap to an interview committee, for example, "I was out of the lab for almost a year due to health problems, but have since gotten back on track and have submitted two articles."

Additional Concerns

Anything that makes you not a "typical" job candidate in your field could be a factor in your job search. Candidates sometimes worry about gender, race or ethnicity, disability, and sexual orientation, but there may be others. For instance, if you've come from a working class family and obtain a Ph.D. in a field in which many of your colleagues come from upper middle class backgrounds, you may have a sense of "difference" at times. In general, it's easier to be a "standard" candidate than a "nontraditional" one, because you may appear to have less in common with the people who interview you. The implications of various "differences" are beyond the scope of this book. Here are a few suggestions which have general applicability.

- Talk as frankly as you can with your advisor about factors which may be of concern (legally or not) to potential employers. What does this person think might concern a hiring department, and what information can you volunteer to alleviate the concern?
- See whether your scholarly/professional association has a caucus, subcommittee, or task force which addresses these concerns and provides the opportunity for networking among those who share a common situation. Many specialized discussion forums and electronic lists serve the same function. If you make these connections, you'll have plenty of people to ask, "How did you handle this situation?"
- Make an even greater effort to find out what you may have in common with the people who will interview you. Stress those points of commonality. Make an effort to learn ahead of time about topics unfamiliar to you which may be used as icebreakers.
- These issues and others are frequently discussed in *The Chronicle of Higher Education*, another good reason to read it. There is a vast literature of advice for candidates who are minorities in just about any sense.

Read other people's advice and experiences, avoiding the material which is merely enraging or depressing and seeking out that which you find helpful.

- In some cases there are laws which offer protection from discrimination in employment. Your campus affirmative action officer should be a good source of information. It's useful to know when you are protected by the law. However, it offers total protection only after a successful lawsuit, a major undertaking which can derail a career and should be undertaken only after great deliberation and extensive consultation. What you really need to be successful in your field are allies, rather than adversaries. Concentrate on building alliances.

Some candidates feel that a discussion of their background might help an institution understand their scholarship as well as their accomplishments. If this is the case for you, you might consider including it near the end of your letter. For example, one candidate's life experience very much informed and explained her research direction. This candidate, who studies Mexican migration, wrote in the penultimate paragraph of her letter, "I believe that my personal background would be an asset to your institution given that I am a first generation immigrant from Mexico, a teenage mother, and a returning student who has climbed from the bottom of the ladder, from cleaning houses to an inspiring future academic career. I am very proud of my experiences, and my personal background has helped me to enrich my teaching, my research, and my interactions with those who surround me."

Chapter 23
Thinking About the Expanded Job Market

Higher education is changing drastically as it becomes more market-driven. As a result, it's difficult to map out an academic career far into the future, because the rules keep changing. In almost every field in which one can obtain a Ph.D., studies show that a substantial number of people with that degree work at something other than faculty positions. Despite your best efforts, sometimes you find that events do not unfold according to plan. Perhaps your advisor is denied tenure and becomes disheartened and preoccupied halfway through your research. Perhaps you fall in love with someone rooted to a particular geographic location and you no longer are willing to move anywhere in the country. Perhaps you look at the stress your advisor is under and decide that kind of life is not for you. Perhaps the topic you were promised would be "hot" has lost its allure and you have not gotten a tenure-track job after three cycles of the job market. Whatever the specific circumstances, in many cases people who had planned to spend their careers as faculty members start to ask themselves whether that goal is attainable, or, even if it is attainable, whether it any longer seems desirable to them.

When you are considering changing fields because of limited opportunities, it becomes a very individual decision as to when you've tried "enough." In most fields there's a point of diminishing returns in the pursuit of tenure-track positions and you need to be realistic about when you've reached it. At first, the additional postdoc or short-term teaching position enhances your credentials. At some point it stops contributing anything. How long is "too long" is not the same for all fields. Find out the norm for yours so that you have some yardstick against which to measure your own perseverance. For example, many candidates in the humanities obtain a tenure-track position after a year or two of one-year appointments, but after five to ten years of one-year appointments the odds no longer favor success in finding such a job.

Even when you feel you have no options, the fact remains that people with Ph.D.s have some of the lowest unemployment rates in the country and the economy always has many places for people smart and persevering enough to earn a doctoral degree. Depending on how applied your background is, you may be able to move instantly and easily into another kind of work or it may take you a few years to make a successful transition. Everybody is marketable; the only question is how quickly so.

Learn how things work in your own field. Seeing the world in terms of tenure-track positions at four-year colleges and universities versus everything else obscures some natural connections. Some changes are more drastic than others. Nonacademic jobs are almost standard in some fields. For example, chemists frequently work in industrial research and economists frequently work at the Federal Reserve Bank. Some academics stay in academia in administrative positions. On the other hand, some people go into fields completely unpredictable from their graduate training, as when an English professor opens a restaurant or becomes a systems consultant. Some Ph.D.s consider teaching at a community college or a secondary school a career change; others don't. In some professional fields career paths may move naturally between universities and professional practice. In other fields, leaving the university is likely to be a one-way street.

Whether you are leaving the academic market because you're strongly drawn to an alternative or because you feel you have little choice, think of identifying your next career move as a major research project. Just as in your scholarly field you can't immediately write a journal article without having first framed the question and done the research, it's unlikely that you'll immediately write a successful job application without having first laid some groundwork.

Assessing Your Skills

For anyone who has spent the time required to earn a Ph.D., how much of the specialized training to use in a new career is a big decision. Some people decide they want no more to do with academic pursuits and are happy to do whatever else meets their needs, even if it has no obvious connection with their prior academic training. Others are concerned with more explicitly using their graduate education. If you find you don't want to leave your field entirely, think about what aspect of an academic career continues to appeal to you. If it's the teaching you really love, you may be inclined to look at a wider range of teaching opportunities than you had initially targeted. Or you may decide to pursue another line of work for your "main" job but continue to teach on a part-time basis. If you are most interested in research, it will depend on your field as to how many opportunities to pursue the subject are available in nonacademic settings. If you love simply being in a university, you may look at non-teaching administrative roles, such as advising, development, or administration.

If you are willing to leave the specific content of your graduate education behind you, then you can consider a wide array of options. Look back at your interests before you decided to pursue a Ph.D. Were there other interests you seriously considered which you want to investigate? While you were a graduate student or postdoc, did you develop other expertise that you found as compelling as your research? What really matters to you, and what are you really good at?

Whatever your field of study, you have much to offer that the economy rewards. What you can offer an employer includes the things you know, drawn from the content area of your field of study, specific technical and methodological skills you have mastered, more general skills, such as the ability to analyze complex data, and character traits. Content areas can be framed to meet the interests of employers. For example, research on Native American health practices could be construed as knowing something about Native Americans, about public health, or about American history. Research methods can be generalized. For example, one historian who studied the powerful individuals who governed Paris in the sixteenth century parlayed her expertise in researching individuals into a position in development research.

Count among your assets the qualities you needed to complete your degree, such as perseverance, focus, and the ability to meet deadlines. Then think about some of the skills you developed as a graduate student or a postdoc. Some may be specific to your field of research such as conducting ethnographic interviews; others may be skills acquired in the task of pursuing the Ph.D. such as sorting through a wide array of information to find a creative and manageable project. In order to complete your research you may have had to develop strong people-management skills, negotiating relationships with various stakeholders be they your committee members, governmental or nongovernmental organizations with which you work, personnel that you supervise in your lab, or students who look to you for intellectual connection.

Some of the skills you've gained will have a direct connection to nonacademic careers; others you'll have to translate for employers so they can see their relevance. Examples of the former could include computer programs, foreign languages, quantitative or statistical skills, proven grant writing success, or event organization; examples of the latter could include presentation skills honed through teaching, ability to work independently and/or in teams, trouble shooting problems and solving them, ability to write clearly about complex ideas, and ability to deal with setbacks and move on from them. A list of former graduate students and postdocs by field, position, and employer type follows to provide examples of the myriad possibilities open to Ph.D.s.

Field	Degree	Title/employer type
Anthropology	Ph.D.	Public information officer for a national historic site
Biochemistry	Ph.D.	Analyst for an intellectual property consulting firm
Bioengineering	Ph.D.	Clinical intelligence consultant for a health care research and consulting firm
Computer Science	Ph.D.	Director of bioinformatics in a biotech start-up
English	ABD	Assistant director of grants at a major science museum
Folklore	Ph.D.	Executive director of a small regional historical society
French Literature	Ph.D.	Career advisor to Ph.D. students and postdocs at a large research university
History of Art	Ph.D.	Director of pre-med/health advising at a small liberal arts college
Linguistics	Ph.D.	Test specialist for a professional testing board
Materials Science	Ph.D.	Analyst in firm-wide risk at a major investment bank
Molecular Biology	Ph.D.	Consultant in an international management consulting firm
Neuroscience	Ph.D.	Medical writer for a medical/scientific communications company
Physics	Ph.D.	Real estate manager for a large university
Political Science	Ph.D.	Consultant for an organizational consulting company

Identifying Alternatives and Researching Them

Many faculty members are most familiar with faculty career paths. Even if you're in a situation where you can comfortably discuss your plans with your advisor, that person may or may not be very knowledgeable about alternatives. Fortunately, there are some sources of information available.

Some books written specifically for academics who want to change careers are noted in Appendix 2. In addition, many professional associations have developed materials on their Web sites about a wide array of career alternatives. You'll find information at your university career center and probably a good collection of links on its Web site. Your own department surely has produced some Ph.D.s who have taken nonacademic positions. Even if no formal record is kept about the whereabouts of graduates, by asking faculty and departmental administrative staff and recent graduates, you can probably identify them.

If you're fortunate, all this investigation will lead you to a clear first-choice focus for your job search in an area where you've ascertained that, with persistence, you will surely find a good job. However, it's more likely to be the case that research both uncovers interesting possibilities and, at least temporarily, further confuses you. Since you have a limited amount of time, you may need to be fairly arbitrary in deciding how you'll direct your job search time and energy. Many people develop fairly complex decision schemes. For example, "If I can get X kind of job on the West Coast in a location my partner considers suitable for work, then I'll do that. Otherwise, if nothing comes through by February, then I'll look for Y kind of job in the Chicago area, where I'm now based."

Networking and informational interviewing are crucial parts of researching new career possibilities. Remember that networking is both a noun and a verb. You have a network of people with whom you can discuss your career concerns and ideas. They may include family, friends, fellow graduate students or postdocs, former colleagues, and the official alumni networks of your graduate and undergraduate institutions. Networking—both with people you know and by meeting people recommended through your network who work in positions or fields that possibly interest you—can provide advice to inform your decision-making process. Taking the initiative and being open with others when discussing your career goals is one of the best ways to learn about new opportunities even if it might feel uncomfortable at first, even if it takes effort, and even if it not your normal mode of operation.

Searching

In the academic job search you follow a fairly predictable sequence in identifying and applying for jobs. Once you think about a broader range of options, you find that there are many right ways to apply for a position, most of them highly unstructured.

Conducting academic and nonacademic job searches at the same time is difficult. Depending upon how different the nonacademic alternative is, you may need to have two sets of interview clothes and use two different vocabularies, two different sets of people to recommend you, and two different sets of job hunting documents. Often, you will need to develop both a resume and a vita. We've included five examples of resumes at the end of this chapter, and books listed in Appendix 2 will give you more examples as well as ideas and guidance. In many cases, if you're looking for both kinds of jobs, it makes sense to concentrate on academic applications in the fall when many jobs arc announced and to turn your attention to other options later in the academic year. However, if you're looking at major corporate recruiting, be aware that the corporate recruiting cycle often begins as early as the academic one.

One of the best ways to job hunt is to tell everyone what you're looking for. However, you may be in a situation in which you feel a need to keep your plans somewhat confidential. Whether you're afraid your department will be reluctant to award your degree on time if you pursue a nonacademic career or that your teaching contract won't be renewed if you're seen as lacking commitment, there are some real, in addition to imagined, risks to announcing plans that are different from those that key people expect you to have. How you resolve this dilemma is a judgment call; however, it will definitely take you longer to make a career change if you can't discuss your plans and immediate goals with someone. In many cases, this person will be outside your department, or even outside academe.

There are several potential sources of good career consultation, although you may need to try more than one until you find a source that seems credible. If you're finishing a degree, a good place to start is with your university career center. However, it may or may not be very familiar with the situations of doctoral students. Since many career centers provide alumni services, your undergraduate institution is another option, as is the career center at an institution where you may be teaching. Career centers which don't provide service to doctoral candidates can sometimes provide referrals to private counselors who have worked with Ph.D.s.

Also check with your scholarly or professional association. Nearly all associations provide at least some career services for their members. While it's the exception rather than the rule, some have staff members who can advise members on applying their skills in new fields. Others have provided Web sites with an interactive mentor feature.

You may consider working with career counselors and career counseling services operating on a for-profit basis. A related service being widely offered is professional coaching. The quality of such services varies wildly. Avoid those who charge a large up-front fee and look for those who have had experience working not just with career changers in general, but with academics in particular.

While there are several steps you must take to make a successful career transition, they aren't necessarily sequential. You may find, for example, that you originally identify a career goal which proves impossible to achieve. Then you may need to return to your self-assessment and research. Or you may have an interview for a job for which you are turned down, but where the interviewer suggests that you interview the next day for something related. In that case, you may need to jump ahead to the application and catch up on research later. It's important both to develop goals and to remain flexible as you pursue them. Even if you end up doing something you never imagined when you began your doctoral study, it's likely that the result of your nontraditional search will be work that is rewarding and that uses the skills you've developed over the years you pursued an academic career.

A Note About the Sample Resumes That Follow

The following examples, generously volunteered by real candidates, are provided to give you an idea of what such materials look like. Other than changing the names of the job candidates, their most recent institutions, and some dates, we have tried to alter them as little as possible. In order to save space, some sections may have been truncated. If a section has been shortened there will be a note in brackets, such as "[Two additional talks follow.]".

You will see that these resumes of Ph.D.s are shorter than vitas and targeted to the position or field to which the individual applied. When academic experience is included, the functions performed and skills developed are stressed over the knowledge base gained in a course of study. Employers expect a succinct document that enables candidates to show how they fit the specific job or field requirements. To have an effective resume it is necessary to omit information that isn't relevant. In some areas of business a one-page resume is standard. In other sectors a longer resume is acceptable. As you transition out of academia to a new field you should try to get field-specific advice that is beyond the scope of this book.

These examples should be regarded as excellent, but not necessarily perfect. They are not all in the same format, and they do not all subscribe to the same stylistic conventions, so you can see there are many ways for a Ph.D. to construct a good resume. Don't attempt to copy any single example. Rather, look at all of them to see which forms of presentation might suit your own taste or situation.

Sample Resume of a Humanities Ph.D.
Accepted position as the executive director of non-profit organization

CHARLOTTE A. PRESERVATIONIST

SUMMARY	CONTACT
• Project management	Address
• Program development and implementation	City, State, Zip code
• Grant-writing and review experience	Telephone
• Expertise in culturally relevant preservation	Email

PROFESSIONAL PRESERVATION EXPERIENCE
Independent Preservation Consultant, City, State   **1997 – 2000; 2006**
Preservation Consultant for Planning, Interpretation and Research
Clients include:
• Site interpretation and planning: State Organization for Museums and Interpretation consultant for non-profit grantee (Mini Historic Site, City, State)
• Archive management projects: NPS Site, City, State
• Archives database design: Awbury Arboretum Association, City, State
• Staff training and supervision: Awbury Arboretum Associaton, City, State
• Architectural research: Lower Merion Conservancy, City, State
• Site research: History Now!, City, State
• Tri-national project participant, International Non-Profit, NY, NY, and Country

Awbury Arboretum Association Intern, Philadelphia, PA   **May – August 1997**
Cultural Landscape Researcher / Fels Intern in Community Service
• Researched and prepared Cultural Landscape Report, Part I, for Awbury Arboretum Association.
• Proposed recommendations that the Board of Directors adopted for Master Plan.

PROGRAMMING, GRANTING, AND ORGANIZATIONAL EXPERIENCE
Famous Foundation, Localtown, NY
Temporary Assistant in Finance Department   **January – March 2006**
• Helped streamline financial payments system and introduced improved electronic filing system.
• Trained administrative staff in these payment and filing systems.

Navigating the Dissertation Program, University of X, City, State   **2004 – 2005**
Grant Advisor
• Designed School-wide presentations on successful grant-writing for 30+ students.
• Assisted individual students with applications for national grants.

Important Pediatric Hospital, Localtown, NY   **2004 – 2005**
Grant Writer and Editor
• Assisted medical researchers with proposals, including a successful $1million NIH R01 grant.

Small National Niche Society, City, State   **2004 – present**
Program Officer, Executive Board (invited position)
• Handle paperwork for 300+ membership for annual conference and foster collaborations.

University of X, City, State   **2002 – 2005**
Independently-funded Researcher / Ph.D. Candidate
• Thesis focus: the contested development of a historic neighborhood in ex-Yugoslavia, 1895-1989.
• Won Fulbright and IREX IARO (public policy) national competitive grants, 2001– 2002.
• 8 academic publications and several popular ones in preservation and anthropology.

Charlotte A. Preservationist, p. 2

Committee for International Affairs, Medium-sized National Society, USA   2002 – present
Committee Member (invited position)
- Annually select recipients for Committee's travel grants and develop granting strategies.
- Expanded Society membership to include one new country through targeted recruitment (2003).
- Co-planned, organized, and chaired forum with participants from five continents (2004).

U.S. Fulbright Selection Committee, US Embassy, Country   **Winter 2002**
Fulbright Selection Committee Member (invited position)

The Niche Colloquium, University of X, City, State   **1999 – 2005**
Co-Founder and Co-Head
- Developed, fund-raised for, and administered two long-term programs for members (1999 – 2005).
- Managed fellow members in program implementation (1999 – 2005).

Graduate Student Section, Medium-sized National Society, USA   **1998 – 2000**
Co-Convener (elected position)
- Revitalized Section in collaboration with Society leadership.

EDUCATION
2005   Ph.D., M.A., Graduate Program in Folklore and Folklife, University of X
- Focus: heritage, preservation, and urban planning

1997   M.S., Historic Preservation Program, School of Fine Arts, University of X
1990   B.A. Russian, Soviet and East European Studies, Williams College

COMPUTER SKILLS
- Excellent skills in word processing, databases, presentation software and internet research. Very experienced with Microsoft Word, Access, Excel, PowerPoint, Outlook, Netscape, and Explorer.

PUBLICATIONS AND TALKS
- Eight academic publications in peer-reviewed journals (1999 – 2005), sixteen academic talks (1998 – 2004), and several professional reports (1996 – 2000) available for review, upon request.

Sample Resume of a Humanities Ph.D.
Accepted position in academic advising in a large research university

Stuart Scholar, Ph.D.

Address • City, State, Zip code • phone
Email

OBJECTIVE

To find a position that takes full advantage of my experience as an educator committed to the ideals of the study of the liberal arts and allows me to continue to grow as an administrator, teacher and scholar.

EDUCATION

- *University of X* Ph.D. History of Art. Dissertation: *Expanding Antiquity: Andrea Navagero and Villa Culture in the Cinquecento Veneto.* 2003.
- *University of X* M.A. History of Art. Master's Thesis: *Carlo Maderno and the Engineered Landscape of the Palazzo Barberini* 1995.
- *Princeton University.* A.B. Art History. Senior Thesis: *The Sketchbook of Villard de Honnecourt: Gothic Architect or Twelfth-century Observer?* 1988.

EXPERIENCE WITH STUDENTS

- Lecturer. Department of the History of Art, University of X, City, State. *Italian Renaissance Art, The High Renaissance: Leonardo, Raphael and Michelangelo, Early Italian Renaissance Art* and *European Art and Civilization 1400-Present.*
- Adjunct Professor. Department of Fine Arts, Y University, City, State. *Italian Renaissance Art and Architecture.*
- Adjunct Professor. Department of Architecture, Z University, City, State. Courses Include: *Improving Nature? The History of Landscape and Garden Architecture; Architecture and Society; Baroque and Rococo Architectural Theory* and *The History of the Villa.*

ADMINISTRATIVE EXPERIENCE

- Coordinator, Visual Studies Program. The University of X. Responsible for the Senior Seminar and Senior Thesis Project. Duties include students advising, support for faculty advisors and director of the program, management of seminar calendar, and preparations and installation of Senior Thesis Exhibition.
- Zigrosser Fellow. Department of Prints, Drawings, and Photographs, *Museum of Art*, City, State. American Drawings Cataloguing Project.
- Research Assistant. *Provost's Interdisciplinary Seminar on the Power of Sight.* Involved with the administration of a faculty seminar on the History of Vision and Optics aimed at offering a variety of new courses in the University. Responsible for the selection of texts and multi-media sources for courses in the 'History of Vision from Classical Antiquity to the Renaissance' and the 'Power of Vision in Islamic Art and Architecture'.
- Administrative Assistant. Graduate Program in Historic Preservation, University of X. Primarily responsible for managing the departmental budget, and providing faculty support, I also coordinated and directed the review of new student applications and assisted student searches for internships.
- Research Assistant. Department of the History of Art, University of X. Director of project to integrate art historical teaching and the internet. Developed prototype for Internet delivery of classroom materials to undergraduates in the History of Art Survey. Participated in planning sessions that ultimately resulted in the selection and installation of digital equipment suitable for art history classrooms.

Stuart Scholar

- Research Assistant. *Kalenderhane, Volume II*. University of X. Directed preparation of excavation reports for final publication, including copy editing, layout of text and illustrations, design of the volume and correspondence with the contributing authors.
- Trench supervisor for the University of X's Promontory Palace excavations at Caesarea, Israel. Primarily responsible for the investigation of suspected gardens or plantings.
- Assistant Gallery Director, The Works Gallery, City, State. Managed daily operations of leading American Contemporary Craft Art gallery. Curated exhibitions of fiber and ceramic art, installed exhibitions of art jewelry and photography.

PROFESSIONAL EXPERIENCE

- Presented public lectures and conference papers at numerous cultural institutions including the Philadelphia Museum of Art, Loyola College of Baltimore, Bryn Mawr College, the Sixteenth Century Studies Conference and the Renaissance Society of America Annual Meeting.
- Published articles include: "Dancing Turks: Ferdinando I de'Medici and the East," to appear in *The Turk & Islam in the Western Eye*, James Harper Ed. (forthcoming: Spring 2007); "Sacred Villeggiatura: Cardinal Agostino Valier, Domenico Brusasorzi, and the Ideology of an Episcopal Villa," *Oculus: Journal for the History of Art*, Vol. VI, 2003; "Expanding Antiquity: Andrea Navagero, Renaissance Gardens and the Islamic Landscape," *Rutgers Art Review*, Volume 19, 2001.
- Reviewed monographs, collected essays and exhibition catalogues for professional journals including the Sixteenth Century Society Journal.
- Awards and Fellowhips include: Getty Foundation Non-Residential Post-Doctorate Fellowship (2004); Keck Fellowship (2000), Delmas Award for Venetian Studies (1999); Fulbright Fellowship (1998), Samuel Kress Travel Fellowship (1998)
- Language skills: Spoken and written Italian, Reading knowledge of French, Spanish, German and Latin, basic conversational Spanish.

REFERENCES

[The names of five references follow.]

Sample Resume of an Education Ph.D.
Accepted position as assistant dean for students in a large research
university

LILY ANNA CANDIDATE

Address •City, State, Zip code •phone number •e-mail address

EDUCATION	**University of X Graduate School of Education**, City, State May 2006
	Doctor of Philosophy (Ph.D.) in Policy, Management, and Evaluation. Higher Education focus. Dissertation examines organizational leadership and change at Swarthmore, circa 1921-1940.

Harvard University Graduate School of Education, Cambridge, MA   June 2002
Master of Education in Administration, Planning and Social Policy. Higher Education focus.

Swarthmore College, Swarthmore, PA   June 2001
Bachelor of Arts with High Honors in English and Education. Course major in German.
Honors Thesis: "Using Literature to Teach the Holocaust in America's Schools."

University of Regensburg, Regensburg, Germany.   January-July 1999
Gained German proficiency. Independent Research: "Holocaust Education in German Schools."

PROFESSIONAL **ABC & Associates**, New York, NY
EXPERIENCE   *Higher Education Consultant*   February 2006-Present
• Assist higher education and nonprofit institutions in solving complex strategic challenges including institutional positioning and strategic transformation.
• Perform interview-based research and site visits to collect data for benchmarking studies.
• Facilitate meetings, retreats, focus groups, and brainstorming sessions.
• Write and present documents detailing findings.
• Clients include Princeton University, Queens College, Jewish Board of Family and Children's Services, NYC Center for Charter School Excellence, among others.

University of X Graduate School of Education, City, State
Lecturer   June 2006-Present
• Teach graduate courses "The College Presidency," "Administration of Student Life," "The Small Liberal Arts College in America," and "Practicum in University Administration."

University of X Office of Career Services, City, State
Senior Career Counselor, College of Arts and Sciences   July 2002 – June 2005
• Advised students and alumni in all aspects of career development.
• Developed, marketed, and taught career-related workshops and panels.
• Oversaw university-wide private school teacher recruitment.
• Served as liaison to Greek organizations, providing specialized outreach and programming.
• Collaborated with Counseling and Psychological Services to facilitate workshops.
• Spearheaded new office undertaking of offering Myers-Briggs interpretation to alumni.
• Managed large-scale Penn-in-Washington summer speaker series and associated budget.
• Collected and maintained employment trend data.
• Supervised administrative assistants and student workers and served on hiring committees.

Isaacson Miller Executive Search Management and Consulting, Boston, MA
Higher Education Research Associate   September 2001-June 2002
• Supported consultants in searches for colleges, universities and mission-driven organizations.
• Identified and interviewed prospective candidates.
• Assisted research department with project to identify minority leaders in Higher Education.

ADDITIONAL   **Stevens Institute of Technology**, Hoboken, NJ
TEACHING &   *Adjunct Professor/Professional Tutor*   January-December 2006
ADVISING   • Coached students in writing and presentation skills as part of pilot program. Delivered
EXPERIENCE   lectures, met with students individually and in groups, collaborated in grading.

City University of New York, College of Staten Island, Staten Island, NY
Adjunct Professor   January-May 2006
• Taught undergraduate course "Career Development." Developed syllabus, delivered lectures, facilitated group Myers-Briggs and Strong Interest interpretation, graded papers.
City University of New York, College of Staten Island, Career Office, Staten Island, NY

LILY ANNA CANDIDATE Page two

Part-time Career Counselor January-May 2006
• Advised students and alumni in all aspects of career development.

Chaitanya Counseling and Stress Management Center, Hoboken, NJ
Part-time Career Counselor September 2005-May 2006
• Administered Myers Briggs and other assessment tools to assist clients with career planning.

University of X, Philadelphia, PA
Teaching Assistant May-August 2004
• Assisted with advising, lectures, and grading for graduate course "Career Development."

CAMPUS COMMITTEE EXPERIENCE

Swarthmore College, Office of Admissions, Swarthmore, PA
Admissions Reader January March 2005, 2006, 2007
• Read approximately 150 applications per cycle and prepared evaluative summary reports.

University of X, Graduate School of Education, City, State
Committee on Degrees September 2004-September 2005
• Evaluated and ruled on appeals from students requesting exemptions from academic policy.

Student Organizations Council September 2004-September 2005
• Worked with committee to determine semi-annual budget allocations to all student groups.

Resource Group Leader September-December 2004
• Conducted information sessions and informal course advising for incoming doctoral students.

Swarthmore College, Dean's Advisory Council, Swarthmore, PA
Focus Group Leader/Independent Consultant January-April 2004
• Moderated four student focus groups aimed at assessing student satisfaction on campus.
• Presented findings and provided written research report to Dean's Advisory Council.
• Collaborated with deans, Director of Institutional Research, and Director of Human Resources.

Swarthmore College Search Committees, Swarthmore, PA
Career Services Search Committee Member September-November 2002
• Appointed as alumni representative on committee to select Director of Career Services Office.

Dean Search Committee Member October 2000-March 2001
• Elected as student member on committee to select new Dean of Admissions and Financial Aid.

Faculty Search Committee Member, English and German Departments April 2000-April 2001
• Elected by fellow majors to represent student opinion in selection of three new professors.

Harvard University, Graduate School of Education, Cambridge, MA
Higher Education Student Association Speaker Chairperson September 2001-May 2002
• Assisted 30+ graduate students in arranging meetings with Higher Education professionals.

Undergraduate positions include Admissions Fellow, Resident Advisor, Annual Fund Intern, Student Affairs Council, Foreign Study Committee, and College Planning Committees.

PUBLICATIONS

"Teaching the Holocaust in America's Schools." *Intercultural Education, Special Edition on the Holocaust.* Vol. 14.2. June 2003.

"The Abolition of Women's Fraternities at Swarthmore College." *Swarthmore College Bulletin (online edition).* Summer 2003.

"The Criminalization of Hate Speech in the Netherlands." *Humanity in Action.* 2001.

SKILLS & ACTIVITIES

Computers: Advanced Internet and journal research. Microsoft Office.
Swarthmore Class Agent, Alumni Interviewer, Reunion Committee, Externship Coordinator.
Humanity in Action Human Rights Senior Fellow.

Sample Resume of a Science Ph.D.
Accepted position as a medical writer in a scientific communications firm

LEON T. NEUROSCIENTIST
Address, City, State, Zip code
Phone number, email

WRITING AND EDITING EXPERIENCE
Author of five publications in peer-reviewed biomedical journals, including three as primary author, and one invited publication (2002-2006)
Author and successful recipient of a Ruth L. Kirschstein National Research Service Award from the National Institutes of Health (2006)
Author of the doctoral thesis: The dystrophin-glycoprotein complex associates with and localizes the inwardly rectifying potassium channel, Kir4.1, in glia.(2005)
Coeditor on the Graduate Program in Neuroscience Website & Brochure Design Committee at the University of State (2003-2004)
Coeditor on numerous manuscripts published in high impact, peer-reviewed biomedical journals (1998-present)
Author and presenter of myriad scientific abstracts, posters, and speaking engagements ranging from in-house colloquia to national conferences (1996-present)

RESEARCH EXPERIENCE
University of X, Department of Neuroscience, 2005-present
- Directing laboratory research investigating the function and modulation of ion channels involved in heart disease and neurological function

University of State, Department of Neuroscience, 1999-2005
- Investigated the role muscular dystrophy proteins play in visual function

Y University, Department of Neuroscience, 1998-1999
- Studied the mechanisms of neuronal degeneration in Huntington's Disease

University of Massachusetts, Department of Psychology, 1996-1998
- Examined the effect of maternal stimulation on the reproductive development of rat pups

TEACHING AND ORGANIZATIONAL EXPERIENCE
Teaching Assistant for the electrophysiology and molecular biology modules for neuroscience PhD students at the Lake Itasca Biological Station, University of State, 2001-2003

Teaching Assistant for the neuroanatomy lab for first-year medical students, University of State, 2001

Member of numerous committees at the University of State, including:
- Annual Neuroscience Student Retreat Organizational Committee, 2001-2002
- Department of Neuroscience Admissions Committee, 2002-2004
- Graduate Program in Neuroscience Colloquium Committee, 2003
- Graduate Program in Neuroscience Self Study Committee, 2002
- Graduate Program in Neuroscience Website & Brochure Design Committee, 2003-2004

HONORS AND AWARDS
National Institutes of Health postdoctoral National Research Service Award (2007)
Stark Fellowship/Travel Award, University of State (2003)
Student Leadership Award, University of Massachusetts (1998)
Psychology Honors Program Member, University of Massachusetts (1997-1998)

EDUCATION
University of State, PhD in Neuroscience, January 2005
University of Massachusetts, B.S. in Psychology, Summa Cum Laude, June 1998

References and writing samples are available upon request.

Sample Resume of a Science Ph.D.
Accepted position as a consultant at a management consulting firm

Joseph A. Candidate
Email
Address, City, State, Zip code
Lab Phone, Home Phone

Objective: Seeking an Associate Consulting position at a top management consulting firm, where I can produce maximum impact on the development of client businesses using the analytical, creative, quantitative, and communicative skills I developed as a scientist and organizational leader.

Education

University of X, City, State	**PhD,** 5/05

Cell and Molecular Biology, Biomedical Graduate Studies
   Thesis: Patterns of transcriptional regulation during long-term memory formation   GPA: A-
   Advisor: Name
MD/PhD program, Medical Scientist Training Program, School of Medicine   transferred 6/99

University of City, Country   **MSc,** 9/01
History and Philosophy of Science (supported by the Prestigious Award foreign exchange scholarship)
   Thesis: Inter-theoretical constraints in the debate between classical and connectionist cognitive
       architectures

Bucknell University, Lewisburg PA   **BS,** 5/98
Cell Biology and Biochemistry, with honors   GPA: 3.9

Leadership Experience
University of X
   Biotechnology Club, co-president: consulting and programming   5/04-5/05
      Lead over 500 members from Business, Biomedical, Medical, Law, Engineering and elsewhere.
      Organized volunteer consulting firm, cross-disciplinary education program, and job-talks.
   Graduate Student Association, Vice Chair: administrative affairs (two terms)   9/03-present
      Co-founded the first student government to represent over 600 biomedical graduate students.
      Drafted the constitution, organized elections, and raised funding.
   University Council, first ever Medical School Representative   9/03-5/04
   Professional and Graduate Students Association, first ever Biomedical Representative   9/03-5/04
   PAGSA finance committee   9/03-5/04
      Created an automated system for processing event funding requests
   Cell and Molecular Biology executive committee, student representative   9/03-9/04
   Undergraduate Residence, Graduate Assistant   8/01-6/03
      Advised and mentored undergraduates as a residential staff member.
   Supervised the research of three undergraduate students: Name, Name, Name

Bucknell University
   Men's club volleyball   8/94-6/98
   Lambda Chi Alpha Fraternity vice president   1/97-12/97

Test Scores

GMAT: 750 (99th percentile) 49 quantitative, 42 verbal; (2004)
MCAT: 35: Verbal: 10, Physical Science:13, Biological Science:12; (1997)
SAT: Math 800, Verbal 590. (1993)
CBAT: 780 chemistry, 800 math II, 710 writing (1993)

page 1/2

Joseph A. Candidate

Honors and Awards

University of X
Prestigious Award foreign exchange scholarship   8/00-8/01
    Full scholarship plus stipend to attend any Overseas Master's degree program (see above).
Medical Scientist Training Program: full scholarship plus stipend for MD/PhD   8/98-6/99

Bucknell University
President's Award for academic achievement, Honors in Cell Biology, *Summa cum laude*   5/98

Publications

[Citations for two papers in preparation, one book review and one abstract follow.]

Research Experience

University of X   8/01-present
    Used microarrays to detect patterns of gene regulation in the brain during long-term memory storage
    Developed a novel bigenic reporter system to detect transcription factor activation during long-term
        memory formation in transgenic mice using imaging and enzymatic reporter gene assays
    Co-author with advisor on a research proposal that was successfully funded for $625,000

Y Research Institute, City, State   6/97-8/97
    Pediatric Aids Foundation student intern award, included salary support
    Used phage display to identify epitope mimics of HIV, advisor: Name

Children's Hospital, City, State   6/96-8/96
    Detected proviral HIV in Biohazard 3 tissue culture, advisor: Name

Additional Information

Affiliations: Regional Bioinformatics Alliance, Society for Neuroscience, AAAS, ACS
Enrichment:
    Capoeira martial arts performance group   11/01-9/03
    Foreign language classes Portuguese I, II (audited)   8/02-5/03
    Bucknell Dance Company   1/97-6/98
    Adventure travel: 14 foreign countries and 40 states, backcountry, hostelling, sailing, and more

Appendices

Appendix 1: National Job Listing Sources and Scholarly and Professional Associations

Websites That Include Job Listings of Interest to Scholars in All Fields

The Chronicle of Higher Education/Chronicle Careers
www.chronicle.com/jobs
Print copy published weekly (49 issues per year)
202-466-1000; 202-296-2691 (fax)
The *Chronicle* has been the newspaper of higher education for more than forty years. Articles cover all aspects of teaching, research, administration, and student life. The focus is on American higher education with additional coverage on the rest of the world. Grant deadlines, upcoming scholarly conferences, and book reviews are included. The *Chronicle* also publishes an annual report on faculty salaries.

"Chronicle Careers" has extensive listings for faculty and administrative position announcements from institutions worldwide, although primarily from those in the United States. In addition there are several Career Forums that focus on such topics as interviewing, balancing work and life, the tenure track, and leaving academe, and allow readers to share experience and advice. See "Career Talk" for a monthly column by Julia Miller Vick and Jennifer S. Furlong.

Diverse Issues in Higher Education (formerly *Black Issues in Higher Education*)
www.diverseeducation.com/
Print copy published every two weeks (26 issues per year)
800-783-3199, 703-385-2981; 703-385-1839 (fax)
This resource covers a wide range of issues in higher education and how they affect African Americans and minorities. An annual special report covers careers in higher education, including salaries. Many pages of each issue are devoted to faculty and administrative position announcements from institutions across the United States and abroad.

Science*Careers* (formerly *Science's Next Wave*)
www.sciencecareers.org
Produced by the American Association for the Advancement of Science, this resource includes job listings (life sciences, physical sciences, engineering, and

related areas), career discussion boards, articles on all aspects of the job search and on being a career scientist as well as on leaving bench science.

Selected Scholarly and Professional Associations

Many associations include job listings in association newsletters that once were printed but now are, for the most part, Web-based. These can also include grant deadlines, information on conferences, news of members, and short news articles. Some associations have a separate job listing available to members and nonmembers for an additional charge. Sometimes job announcements are password-secured for association members.

For each association listed here you will find the association name, URL, contact e-mail address when available, discipline(s) it serves, information about job listings, time of the annual convention, convention placement services, and title of its discipline-specific handout on job hunting if there is one. If the organizations relevant to your discipline are not listed here, consult the annual *National Trade and Professional Associations of the United States* (there is an online version available for a fee), the *Scholarly Societies Project*, www.scholarly-societies.org, or your advisor.

Academy of Management
www.aomonline.org ; placement@aom.pace.edu
Management
Placement services are available on the Web. If you do not have a membership, enter as a guest. With membership, you can post your resume and teaching preferences. The convention is held in August. In order to attend, membership is required. Placement services (interviewing space) are made available during the convention.

African Studies Association
www.africanstudies.org ; asaed@rci.rutgers.edu
African Studies
ASA News is issued three times a year. The annual conference is held in November.

American Academy of Religion
www.aarweb.org ; aar@aarweb.org
Religious Studies, Theology
Openings: Employment Opportunities for Scholars of Religion is issued 12 times a year to members of the American Academy of Religion and the Society of Biblical Literature and made available online. The annual meeting is held in November (weekend before Thanksgiving). Employment Information Services Center provides interview space. Interviews are set up by employers and candidates.

American Anthropological Association
www.aaanet.org ; placement@aaanet.org
Anthropology
Anthropology News is issued 9 times a year to members. *Placement Service Notes*, 10 issues per year, includes job listings. Jobs are also listed online. The convention is usually held in November. Job listings (free for members) are posted and candidates can apply at the convention. Space is provided for convention interviewing.

American Association of Anatomists
www.anatomy.org ; exec@anatomy.org
Anatomy

The online Career Center lists faculty positions and several other career opportunities. Members receive the *AAA Newsletter*, which is published quarterly and also contains career opportunities. The annual meeting is held in the spring.

American Association of Immunologists
www.aai.org ; infoaai@aai.org
Immunology
AAI maintains several Training and Job Opportunity Lists, including faculty positions, posted on the Web site. The *AAI Newsletter*, published 5 times a year, also lists job opportunities. The print version is free for members; the archive is available online free of charge. The annual AAI Meeting is held in May.

American Astronomical Society
www.aas.org
Astronomy, Astrophysics
Jobs are listed in the *American Astronomical Society Job Register* (electronically or in hard copy), issued monthly to members and also posted on the association's Web site. Meetings are usually held in winter and summer. A Job Center, set up to connect applicants and employers, is available for members and nonmembers.

American Chemical Society
www.chemistry.org ; service@acs.org
Chemistry, Engineering
ChemJobs, an online database of job listings, is free to members, with no access to nonmembers. The weekly *Chemical & Engineering News* (*C&EN*) carries the same ads. National meetings are held twice a year, usually in March and August, and include the Career Resource Center.

American College of Sports Medicine
www.acsm.org
Sports Medicine
ACSM Career Services offers many career resources to students and professionals, including resume posting, and a searchable database of jobs, internships, and assistantships. Some faculty positions are listed. The ACSM annual meeting is in May or June.

American Economic Association
www.vanderbilt.edu/AEA/index.htm ; aeainfo@vanderbilt.edu
Economics
Job Openings for Economists, published 10 times a year, is available to members and nonmembers by subscription. The convention is held in January each year and includes a placement service.

American Educational Research Association
www.aera.net
Education
Educational Researcher is published 9 times a year for members and accessible online, at AERA's Web site. Job openings are listed in its classified section. The convention is held in the spring. Interview facilities are made available.

American Folklore Society
www.afsnet.org
Folklore and Folklife

AFSNews is issued bimonthly to members. The annual convention is held in October.

American Historical Association
www.historians.org
History
Perspectives is issued monthly during the academic year to members. The convention is held in January. The Job Register enables departments to register for interviewing space at the annual meeting. The AHA publishes *Careers for Students of History.*

American Institute of Biological Sciences
www.aibs.org
Biology
BioScience, a monthly publication, includes job listings. Jobs are also posted to the association's Web site. The annual meeting is held in March. The AIBS publishes *Careers in Biology.*

American Institute of Chemical Engineers
www.aiche.org
Chemical Engineering
The Institute offers an electronic job-posting service. The convention is held twice a year.

American Institute of Physics
www.aip.org ; aipinfo@aip.org
Astronomy, Physics
The AIP serves a federation of physical science departments. *Physics Today Career Network* is an online searchable jobs database and lists hundreds of job openings.

American Mathematical Society
www.ams.org ; ams@ams.org
Mathematics
Notices of the American Mathematical Society is issued monthly to all members. *Employment Information in the Mathematical Sciences* is issued 7 times a year, extra charge for members and nonmembers. Ads can be browsed for free on Web site. The convention is held in January. The Employment Register organizes formal interviewing. The AMS publishes *The Academic Job Search in Mathematics.*

American Musicological Society
www.ams-net.org ; ams@ams-net.org
Music
AMS Newsletter is published semi-annually. The convention is held in October or November.

American Philological Association
www.apaclassics.org
Greek and Latin languages, literatures, and civilizations
Positions for Classicists and Archaeologists is provided monthly and online. The convention is usually held in early January. Interviews are scheduled by the association. The APA publishes *Careers for Classicists.*

American Philosophical Association
www.udel.edu/apa ; apaOnline@udel.edu
Philosophy

The *APA JobSeeker Database* is available to members only. Three conventions a year are held: Eastern Division in December (largest), Pacific Division in March, Central Division in May. A placement service is held at each one.

American Physical Society
www.aps.org
Engineering, Physics
The Career Center lists many employment opportunities.

American Physiological Society
www.the-aps.org
Physiology
The online Careers Overview offers many resources for students, postdoctoral fellows, and investigators. A large number of faculty positions are listed. The conference is held between August and November.

American Planning Association
www.planning.org ; CareerInfo@planning.org
City and Regional Planning
The job database, *JobsOnline,* includes some faculty positions. The annual convention is held in March or April.

American Political Science Association
www.apsanet.org ; apsa@apsanet.org
Government, International Relations, Political Science
eJobs is a comprehensive online political science job database available for members. The convention begins the Thursday before Labor Day. Interviewing space is available.

American Psychological Association
www.apa.org ; convention@apa.org
Psychology
PsycCareers, APA's Online Career Center, offers an online searchable database, as well as many other career resources, and is available at http://psyccareers.apa.org. The convention is held in August and includes interviewing opportunities.

American Society of Criminology
www.asc41.com
Criminology
The Employment Exchange offers both position listings and a candidate listing form, which candidates can use to post information about their qualifications and about the type of position they are seeking. The annual meeting takes place in November.

American Society for Biochemistry and Molecular Biology
www.asbmb.org ; asbmb@asbmb.org
Biochemistry, Molecular Biology
The website lists career opportunities online, primarily faculty positions. Members receive a free subscription to the *ASBMB Today,* published monthly, which also lists career opportunities. The archive is available online free of charge. They also publish a career brochure, which offers advice for those pursuing an academic career. The ASBMB annual meeting is held in the spring.

American Society for Cell Biology
www.ascb.org ; careers@ascb.org
Cell Biology
The Career Development site offers the ASCB Job Board, an online service for job seekers and employers, as well as several downloadable career books. Many faculty positions are listed online. The *ASCB Newsletter*, published monthly to members, contains career strategy articles that are also available for download. The ASCB annual meeting takes place in December.

American Society for Microbiology
www.asm.org
Microbiology
ASM hosts two career information sites: www.healthecareers.com, which features some faculty jobs listings, and www.microbiologycareers.org, which includes information about their conference placement service.

American Society for Nutrition
www.nutrition.org ; sec@nutrition.org
Nutrition
ASN lists many job positions online, primarily faculty positions. Job advertisements are also listed in *Nutrition Notes*, a newsletter published and distributed to the membership. It is also available by subscription to nonmembers. Current issues are posted online. The ASN meets annually at the Experimental Biology Meeting, which is held in April.

American Society for Pharmacology and Experimental Therapeutics
www.aspet.org ; info@aspet.org
Pharmacology
ASPET lists professional opportunities on the Web site, as well as in *Molecular Interventions*, which is published 6 times per year and distributed to members in print or online. Most of the positions listed are faculty positions. ASPET members attend the annual Experimental Biology Meeting in April.

American Society for Public Administration
www.aspanet.org ; info.aspanet.org
Public Administration
PublicServiceCareers.org lists professional opportunities including faculty positions. The conference is held in March and includes a job fair.

American Society of Civil Engineers
www.asce.org
Civil Engineering
ASCE Career Connections on the Web site provides job listings. The convention is held in October.

American Sociological Association
www.asanet.org ; executive.office@asanet.org
Sociology
The ASA Job Bank is available online to members only. The convention is held in August. Employers submit job descriptions and set up interviews.

American Statistical Association
www.amstat.org ; asainfo@amstat.org
Statistics

AMSTAT News is available monthly to members and available to nonmembers for an additional charge. The convention is held in August. Employers and applicants preregister for placement service.

American Studies Association
www.georgetown.edu/crossroads/asainfo.html ; asastaff@theasa.net
American Studies
ASA *Newsletter* is available monthly online. The convention is held in the fall.

Archaeological Institute of America
www.archaeological.org ; aia@aia.bu.cdu
Archaeology, Classical Studies
The *American Journal of Archaeology* (*AJA*) is published quarterly in both print and electronic (PDF) form. The APA/AIA Placement Service offers a monthly listing of jobs, CV posting in the annual Placement Book, and interviewing facilities at the annual meeting held in January.

Association for Asian Studies
www.aasianst.org ; postmaster@aasianst.org
China and Inner Asia Studies, Northeast Asia Studies, South Asia Studies, Southeast Asia Studies
"Personnel Registry" provided in *Asian Studies Newsletter,* is issued 4 times a year to members. New listings are posted online on the first and third Monday of each month at www.aasianst.org/employment. The convention is held in the spring; candidates and employers can register and set up interviews.

Association for Education in Journalism and Mass Communication
www.aejmc.org
Communication, Journalism
The online Employment Center lists job openings. The convention is held in August and a placement service is available.

Association for Theatre in Higher Education
www.athe.org ; info@athe.org
Theatre
Jobs are posted on the website in the ATHE Job Bank The annual convention is held in July or August.

Association of Collegiate Schools of Architecture
www.acsa-arch.org ; info@acsa-arch.org
Architecture
ACSA News is issued monthly during the academic year. The annual meeting is usually held in March.

Association of Writers and Writing Programs
www.awpwriter.org ; joblist@awpwriter.org
English, Writing
AWP Job List is issued 7 times a year to members. Job listings are also posted on a password-protected Web site for members. A dossier mailing service is available to members only. The annual conference is held in the spring.

Biomedical Engineering Society
www.bmes.org ; info@bmes.org
Bioengineering

The *BMES Bulletin* is issued quarterly to members and is available online free of charge. In it are listed employment opportunities. Jobseekers are directed to BMEnet, www.bmenet.org, to search for job listings. The BMES annual meeting is held in the fall.

Biophysical Society
www.biophysics.org ; society@biophysics.org
Biophysics
The online Career Center offers several resources, including academic career listings, educational resources, mentoring, and a placement service. Many postdoctoral and some faculty positions are listed. The Biophysical Society also publishes *Careers in Biophysics* which is available online. The Biophysical Society annual meeting is held in February or March.

College Art Association
www.collegeart.org ; nyoffice@collegeart.org
Art History, Fine Arts (Studio)
The Careers section of the website includes job listings, a place for posting resumes, and sample job hunting materials. The convention is normally held in late February. Interviewing space is made available for members.

Council on Social Work Education
www.cswe.org ; info@cswe.org
Social Work
Job listings and other career services can be found on the Career Center Web site, careers.cswe.org. The convention is held in March.

Endocrine Society
www.endo-society.org ; placement@endo-society.org
Endocrinology
There is a searchable Employment Opportunities database available on the Web site, which includes academic research and faculty positions. The ENDO annual meeting is held in June.

Federation of American Societies for Experimental Biology (FASEB)
http://faseb.careers.org ; career@faseb.org
Biomedical Sciences
FASEB advances biological science through collaborative advocacy for research policies that promote scientific progress and education and lead to improvements in human health. It currently has 21 associated societies, several of which are included in this list of associations. *FASEB Career Center* offers resume posting, and job postings online.

Geological Society of America
www.geosociety.org ; gsaservice@geosociety.org
Geology
GSA's Employment Service Center maintains a Web-based database for job seeking members to post career profiles. Participating employers have access to applicants' profiles customized according to the employers' specific search criteria. The convention is normally held in the fall. Space for interviewing is provided.

Gerontological Society of America
www.geron.org ; geron@geron.org
Gerontology

The Career Center offers job listings, resume posting, and personal career management accounts, www.agework.com. The convention is held in November.

History of Science Society
www.hssonline.org ; infor@hssoline.org
History of Science
The Newsletter is issued quarterly to members. Employment opportunity listings are on its Web site. The convention is held in the fall, usually early November.

Institute of Electrical and Electronics Engineers, Inc. (IEEE)
www.ieee.org ; ieeeusa@ieee.org
Electrical/Electronics Engineering
IEEE Web site offers a searchable job database for members, http://careers.ieee.org. The IEEE hosts more than 300 conferences and meetings each year.

International Communication Association
www.icahdq.org ; icahdq@icahdq.org
Communication
ICA Newsletter is issued bimonthly to members. The convention is held in late spring to midsummer.

International Society for Computational Biology
www.iscb.org
Bioinformatics, Computational Biology
The Web site has a searchable database of job listings, many of which are postdoctoral and faculty positions. The annual meeting is cosponsored by the International Conference on Intelligent Systems for Molecular Biology (ISMB) and the European Conference on Computational Biology (ECCB), and is held in July.

Latin American Studies Association
lasa.international.pitt.cdu ; lasa@pitt.edu
Latin American Studies
Employment opportunities are posted to the Web site.

Linguistic Society of America
www.lsadc.org ; lsa@lsadc.org
Linguistics
Job listings on the Web site are available to members only. Convention is held in January. Announcements and vitas are collected and space is made available for interviewing.

Materials Research Society
www.mrs.org ; info@mrs.org
Engineering, Materials Science
MRS Bulletin includes job listings and is available to members only on the Web site. Two conventions are held: West Coast in spring, East Coast in fall. Members' benefits include the Job Placement Center at MRS meetings.

Modern Language Association of America
www.mla.org ; joblist@mla.org
English, Comparative Literature, Modern Languages and Literatures
The *JIL* is a searchable electronic database of academic job openings in depart-

ments of English and foreign languages and can be accessed by members only. The site also offers career and job market information and guidelines for job seekers and hiring departments. Graduate students and faculty in member departments of the Association of Departments of English and Association of Departments of Foreign Languages have free access to the online *JIL* through the ADE, www.ade .org, and ADFL, www.adfl.org, Web sites. The convention is held in December. Interviewing space is made available for members.

National League for Nursing
www.nln.org ; generalinfo@nln.org
Nursing
NLN Online offers current information on meetings and career and educational opportunities. The NLN Career Center offers a searchable job database and a career management account free of charge. The annual Education Summit is usually held in September or early October.

National Women's Studies Association
www.nwsa.org ; nwsaoffice@nwsa.org
Women's Studies
Members have free access to employment listings online. The annual conference is held in June. A Job Fair area is available for posting information about jobs as well as for interviewing.

Population Association of America
www.popassoc.org ; info@popassoc.org
Demography
Job announcements are available for free on the Web site. The convention is held in the spring and includes an Employment Exchange.

Radiation Research Society
www.radres.org ; info@radres.org
Radiology
Faculty and postdoctoral positions, and information regarding funding and fellowships, are posted on the Web site. The annual meeting is held in the fall.

Society for Industrial and Applied Mathematics
www.siam.org
Mathematics
Job opportunities are posted on the Web site. The annual conference is held in July.

Discipline Index to Major Scholarly Associations

Scholarly associations exist for other disciplines not listed here, and disciplines listed here may additionally be served by associations not listed above.

American Studies: American Studies Association
Anatomy: American Association of Anatomists
Ancient History: American Philological Association
Anthropology: American Anthropological Association
Archaeology: Archaeological Institute of America
Architecture: Association of Collegiate Schools of Architecture

Area Studies: African Studies Association, Association for Asian Studies, Latin American Studies Association

Art History: College Art Association

Astronomy: American Astronomical Society, American Institute of Physics

Astrophysics: American Astronomical Society

Biochemistry: American Society for Biochemistry and Molecular Biology

Bioinformatics: International Society for Computational Biology

Biology: American Institute of Biological Sciences

Biomedical Sciences: Federation of American Societies for Experimental Biology (FASEB)

Biophysics: Biophysical Society

Cell Biology: American Society for Cell Biology

Chemistry: American Chemical Society

City Planning: American Planning Association

Classical Languages and Literatures: American Philological Association

Communication: Association for Education in Journalism and Mass Communication, International Communication Association

Comparative Literature: Modern Language Association of America

Computational Biology: International Society for Computational Biology

Criminology: American Society of Criminology

Demography: Population Association of America

Economics: American Economic Association

Education: American Educational Research Association

Endocrinology: Endocrine Society

Engineering: American Chemical Society, American Institute of Chemical Engineers, American Physical Society, American Society of Civil Engineers, Biomedical Engineering Society, Institute of Electrical and Electronics Engineers, Materials Research Society

English: Association of Writers and Writing Programs, Modern Language Association of America

Fine Arts: College Art Association

Folklore and Folklife: American Folklore Society

Geology: Geological Society of America

Gerontology: Gerontological Society of America

Government: American Political Science Association

Greek: American Philological Association

History: American Historical Association

History of Science: History of Science Society

Immunology: American Association of Immunologists

International Relations: American Political Science Association

Journalism: Association for Education in Journalism and Mass Communication

Latin: American Philological Association

Linguistics: Linguistics Society of America

Management: Academy of Management

Materials Science: Materials Research Society

Mathematics: American Mathematical Society, Society for Industrial and Applied Mathematics

Microbiology: American Society for Microbiology

Modern Languages and Literature: Modern Language Association of America

Molecular Biology: American Society for Biochemistry and Molecular Biology

Music: American Musicological Society

Nutrition: American Society for Nutrition

Nursing: National League for Nursing
Pharmacology: American Society for Pharmacology and Experimental Therapeutics
Philosophy: American Philosophical Association
Physics: American Institute of Physics, American Physical Society
Physiology: American Physiological Society
Political Science: American Political Science Association
Public Administration: American Society for Public Administration
Psychology: American Psychological Association
Radiology: Radiation Research Society
Regional Planning: American Planning Association
Religious Studies: American Academy of Religion
Social Work: Council on Social Work Education
Sociology: American Sociological Association
Sports Medicine: American College of Sports Medicine
Statistics: American Statistical Association
Theatre: Association for Theatre in Higher Education
Theology: American Academy of Religion
Women's Studies: National Women's Studies Association
Writing: Association of Writers and Writing Programs

Appendix 2: Additional Reading

This selective listing is provided to give you ideas about the type of additional reading that may help you in your job search. It is not intended to be a comprehensive bibliography. For current articles on topics such as the job market in your field, trends in higher education, and academic life, consult your professional association and library and online resources, including *The Chronicle of Higher Education.*

General

Boufis, Christina and Victoria C. Olsen, eds. *On the Market: Surviving the Academic Job Search.* New York: Riverhead Books, 1997.

> This collection of first-person accounts gives a realistic perspective on what to expect in an academic job search.

Caplan, Paula J. *Lifting a Ton of Feathers: A Woman's Guide to Surviving in the Academic World.* Toronto: University of Toronto Press, 1993.

> After outlining myths and catch-22s, the author discusses general and specific suggestions for women from the time they enter graduate school through retirement from academia.

DeNeef, A. Leigh and Craufurd D. Goodwin, eds. *The Academic's Handbook.* 3rd ed. Durham, N.C.: Duke University Press, 2006.

> Chapters written by several professors describe the structure of the academic career and the life of an academic. Sections cover academic employment, teaching, getting funding, and publishing.

Dews, C. L. Barney and Carolyn Leste Law, eds. *This Fine Place So Far from Home: Voices of Academics from the Working Class.* Philadelphia: Temple University Press, 1995.

> This collection of first-person essays by successful academics for whom entering the professoriate meant moving between social classes includes many essays by scholars from minority groups which are underrepresented in higher education.

Ferber, Marianne A. and Jane W. Loeb, eds. *Academic Couples: Problems and Promises.* Champaign-Urbana: University of Illinois Press, 1997.

> Sixteen experts examine the special challenges faced and presented by academic couples, both from the perspective of the individuals involved and from that of educational institutions.

Jones, Lee, ed., foreword by Na'im Akbar. *Brothers of the Academy: Up and Coming Black Scholars Earning Our Way in Higher Education.* Sterling, Va.: Stylus, 2000.

Twenty-seven essays by black male scholars present first-person and historical and sociological perspectives.

McNaron, Toni A. H. *Poisoned Ivy: Lesbian and Gay Academics Confronting Homophobia.* Philadelphia: Temple University Press, 1997.
This volume is based on both the author's first-hand experience and on a survey of 300 lesbian and gay academics with at least 15 years in their profession.

Phillips, Gerald M., Dennis S. Gouran, Scott A. Kuehn, and Julia T. Wood. *Survival in the Academy: A Guide for Beginning Academics.* Cresskill, N.J.: Hampton, 1994.
Written by four professors for the Speech Communication Association, this book is on life as an academic, including teaching, research, and criticism. Of special interest to job seekers are chapters on securing a position, starting out, and professionalism.

Toth, Emily. *Ms. Mentor's Impeccable Advice for Women in Academia.* Philadelphia: University of Pennsylvania Press, 1997.
The author offers witty and on-target practical advice about resolving a variety of dilemmas. A great deal of the commonsense information is actually quite relevant to men, as well as to women.

Humanities/Arts

Gustafson, Melanie S., ed. *Becoming a Historian: A Survival Manual for Women and Men.* Washington, D.C.: American Historical Association, 2003.
This guide focuses on the job search. It has an interesting chapter on "The Professional Couple" and an extensive discussion on "Getting Published."

Showalter, English, Howard Figler, Lori G. Kletzer, Jack H. Schuster, and Seth R. Katz. *The MLA Guide to the Job Search: A Handbook for Departments and Ph.D.s and Ph.D. Candidates in English and Foreign Languages.* New York: Modern Language Association, 1996.
This is a comprehensive guide for language and literature Ph.D.s. The chapter on "The Academic Job Search" is extensive. One section addresses experienced candidates. The *Guide* also includes chapters on community and junior colleges and advice to departments.

Science/Engineering

Boss, Jeremy M. and Susan H. Eckert. *Academic Studies at Work: Navigating the Biomedical Research Career.* New York: Kluwer Academic/Plenum, 2003.
This book is an excellent resource for early career scientists. It guides readers not only through the job search process, but also through many career issues academic scientists will face, such as getting funding, managing a lab, negotiating relationships with colleagues, and teaching and mentoring students and postdocs.

Feibelman, Peter J. *A Ph.D. Is Not Enough: A Guide to Survival in Science.* Reading, Mass.: Addison-Wesley, 1993.
The author suggests science survival skills useful from the beginning of graduate school on through one's career. Chapter 5 covers academic and industrial career choices and chapter 6 deals with job interviews, including responding to offers.

Fiske, Peter S. and Aaron Louis (illustrator). *Put Your Science to Work: The Take-Charge Career Guide for Scientists.* Washington, D.C.: American Geophysical Union, 2000.
This book is a complete revision of Fiske's earlier work *To Boldly Go: A Practical Career Guide for Scientists.* It includes practical advice for finding traditional jobs in science as well as other options. In providing sample resumes and cover letters and stories of scientists who have moved into a variety of careers it informs the reader of many career possibilities.

Reis, Richard M. *Tomorrow's Professor: Preparing for Academic Careers in Science and Engineering.* New York: Wiley-IEEE Press, 1997.
This volume includes both general strategies and individual vignettes and stories. Reis also maintains a very active Web site and listserv at http:// ctl.stanford.edu/ Tomprof/index.shtml.

Rosen, Stephen and Celia Paul. *Career Renewal: Tools for Scientists and Technical Professionals.* San Diego, Calif.: Academic Press, 1997.
Useful to anyone seeking to change career direction, the book includes both success stories and do-it-yourself exercises.

Social Sciences

Boice, Robert. *Advice for New Faculty Members: Nihil Nimus.* Needham Heights, Mass.: Allyn and Bacon, 2000.
This book includes suggestions, not only on getting started in teaching, but also about establishing the writing schedule and human relationships which will increase the chances of achieving tenure.

Diamond, Robert M. *Preparing for Promotion and Tenure Review: A Faculty Guide.* 2nd ed. Bolton, Mass.: Anker Publishing Co., 2007.
This volume is on the American Sociological Association's publication list.

Frost, Peter J. and M. Susan Taylor, eds. *Rhythms of Academic Life: Personal Accounts of Careers in Academia.* Thousand Oaks, Calif.: Sage Publications, 1996.
A large compendium of essays by scholars, the book examines both traditional and nontraditional career paths and the role and future of business schools in higher education.

Menges, Robert J. *Faculty in New Jobs: A Guide to Settling In, Becoming Established, and Building Institutional Support.* San Francisco: Jossey-Bass Higher and Adult Education Series, 1999.
This collection of essays by a variety of scholars draws on a study conducted by the National Center on Postsecondary Teaching, Learning, and Assessment.

Rheingold, Harriet L. *The Psychologist's Guide to an Academic Career.* Washington, D.C.: American Psychological Association, 1994.
This very comprehensive guide offers advice about graduate study, the job search, and getting established in and developing an academic career. Much of the advice is relevant to scholars in related disciplines.

The Expanded Market

Debelius, Maggie and Susan Elizabeth Basalla. *So What Are You Going to Do with That? Finding Careers Outside Academia.* Rev. ed. Chicago: University of Chicago Press, 2007.

This volume is aimed at the graduate student who is questioning whether to finish the graduate program and seek an academic career. People who have left the academy for a variety of options are profiled. Also included are self-assessment tools, interviewing tips, and suggestions for repackaging one's academic experience.

Kreeger, Karen Young. *Guide to Nontraditional Careers in Science.* Philadelphia: Taylor and Francis, 1998.
This very comprehensive guide both describes a variety of career options for scientists and provides detailed resource information for learning more about them.

Newhouse, Margaret. *Outside the Ivory Tower: A Guide for Academics Considering Alternative Careers.* Cambridge, Mass.: Office of Career Services, Harvard University, 1993.
This book suggests how Ph.D.s may assess their skills and explore the wide variety of nonacademic careers. Two particularly useful features are a lengthy list of skills graduate students may have developed and a chart relating them to career fields. Though out of print, this is an excellent resource.

Robbins-Roth, Cynthia, ed. *Alternative Careers in Science: Leaving the Ivory Tower.* 2nd ed. San Diego, Calif.: Academic Press, 2005.
A series of first-person accounts profiles a variety of alternatives for Ph.D. scientists.

Sindermann, Carl J. and Thomas K. Sawyer. *The Scientist as Consultant: Building New Career Opportunities.* New York: Plenum Press, 1997.
For scientists at all career levels, this book describes the many issues to be attended to by a scientist who hopes to establish an independent consulting practice.

*Science*Careers, www.sciencecareers.org
This online career section of the esteemed journal, *Science,* is published by the American Association for the Advancement of Science. Current articles and the archival collection cover a range of topics on both traditional and nontraditional careers for scientists.

WRK4US, www.jhfc.duke.edu/fhi/index.php
This international email discussion list on nonacademic careers for people with graduate education in Humanities, Education, and Social Science disciplines was founded in 1999 by Paula Foster Chambers, who continues to manage the list today with the support and collaboration of Duke University's John Hope Franklin Humanities Institute, Career Center, and Graduate School in partnership with the Graduate School at the University of North Carolina at Chapel Hill.

Index